From the Bicycle to the Bullet

The story of the company
and the people who made it great: 1851-1969

Anne Bradford
edited by Ray Knight

BREWIN BOOKS

*Cover: Royal Enfield employees leaving work in the early 1900s.
Inset: John Brittain on the Devil's Staircase in the
Scottish Six Days Trial, watched by his parents.
Back cover inset: 1914/18 gun-mounted military bike.*

Cover design: John Bradford

Contents

Acknowledgments — 5
Introduction — 7
Cycle history — 9
Royal Enfield; from the archives — 11

Chapter One	Hard times in the twenties	30
Chapter Two	Almost a life sentence	40
Chapter Three	Into the thirties	53
Chapter Four	Enfield at war	60
Chapter Five	Of diesels, atoms, rockets, gun mountings and radar predictors, with compulsory sun tan	74
Chapter Six	The new designs	84
Chapter Seven	The competitive Enfields	92
Chapter Eight	Testing – testing	110
Chapter Nine	Learning for a living	123
Chapter Ten	Enfield India	134
Chapter Eleven	The lull before the storm: American Indian, an early scooter and the Britax Hurricane	138
Chapter Twelve	The end in sight	146
Chapter Thirteen	Requiem	159

The Royal Enfield Owners Club — 166
Conclusion — 167

First published in Great Britain
by Amulree Publications in 2006.

This edition published by Brewin Books Ltd, 56 Alcester Road,
Studley, Warwickshire B80 7LG in 2015
www.brewinbooks.com

© Anne Bradford 1996 & 2015

All rights reserved. No part of this
publication may be reproduced by any means
without the prior consent of the publisher.

ISBN: 978-1-85858-532-1

The moral right of the author has been asserted.

A Cataloguing in Publication Record
for this title is available from the British Library.

Typeset in Adobe Garamond Pro
Printed in Great Britain.

Acknowledgments

Ivor Mutton, the undoubted expert on Royal Enfield history is, unfortunately, no longer with us but in 1982, Mike Johnson made a twenty-minute video of Ivor telling and demonstrating with bikes, the history of Royal Enfield. Our thanks to Mike for allowing us to quote from this video. Copies of the video are available from Mike on (01527) 892228.

Ivor's memorabilia was very kindly donated to Redditch Library by his family and has proved an invaluable source of information and photographs. Many interesting facts have also been obtained from two unpublished books by W J Solloway, *Motor Cars in Needleland* (1961) and *Early Redditch Motor Cars* (1970), both in Redditch Library. The local history librarian, Philip Davis, gave his customary enthusiastic assistance to the project.

We are also grateful to the following for providing information and material:

Doug Young (archivist, Royal Enfield Owners Club), Malcolm Barrett (expert on Enfield cycle history), Philip Coventry (chairman of Redditch Pictorial Society), Chris Eadie-Hughes (descendent of Albert Eadie), Ralph Richardson, Maurice Clarke, Mr and Mrs Ian Hayes, Mike Wojczynski, Ruby Fisher, Wilf and Edna Kinchin, Diane Long, Phylis Gibbs, Christine Deaner, Gladys Hodgetts.

Bibliography

Hartley, Peter
The Story of Royal Enfield Motor Cycles
Patrick Stephens, 1981

Bacon, Roy
Royal Enfield, The Postwar Models
Niton Publishing, 1992

Hundreds of old records and magazines have been consulted. Where particularly relevant, references have been listed in the text, but some of the newspaper cuttings in the Mutton collection are unsourced.

All interviews have been checked with the contributors. Many of them asked us to emphasise that all this happened a long time ago and so they may not be 100% accurate on names and dates.

In order to produce a book at reasonable cost, Ray Knight has had to carry out some vigorous editing. A copy of all interviews in their entirety have been lodged at Redditch Library and in the archives of the Royal Enfield Owners Club.

Introduction
Ray Knight

Motorcycle Development

The story of Royal Enfield motorcycles began in the early 1850s when George Townsend built a needle-making factory. Thirty years later his son began manufacturing bicycles. There is little doubt that the members of the Townsend family were very inventive, clever engineers, with many patents recorded in their names.

The story is essentially a family story, a family of workers, and this has been exhaustively researched and chronicled by Anne Bradford in interviewing many of the surviving members of the workforce. Their stories bring to life the birth and death of one of the great names of the British motorcycle industry and their slogan, 'Built like a Gun' is one that lives in the annals of the sport.

Some of the mechanical landmarks in the history of the company begin very briefly, with the first mechanical vehicle advertised by what became the Enfield Cycle Company. This was in 1899 and was available in both tricycle and quadricycle form. Motive power, like many at that time, was provided by a De Dion 1½hp engine, mounted on the back axel. A 1901 model was a replica of the French Ader and used an 8hp engine.

Two years later came the first motor bicycle, little more than a heavyweight bicycle, with the engine clamped to the front down tube. There were three models shown at the 1902 Stanley Cycle Show; one had a 2hp Minerva engine fitted behind the front wheel and in front of the bottom bracket of the frame.

A model powered by a 2¼hp V-twin Motosacoche engine in 1909 was followed by a move in 1911 to bigger V-twin engines from J A Prestwich; 770ccs and rated at 6 hp. These were to earn themselves a name as haulers of combinations and also featured an innovation that was to live on throughout the range, the cush drive hub.

In 1912 the 3hp 425cc V-twin was the first to employ an engine entirely built at Enfield. It was another model that led its contemporaries with forced oil feed by mechanical pump to the big ends. This was a feature that preceded its general introduction onto the market of this system, by something like eighteen years.

There was a sidecar model on which was mounted a Vickers machine gun for war department use in the 1914-18 war and for Red Cross work there was a model with a stretcher instead of the sidecar. Not content with producing 500 machines a week for the war office, Enfield were also engaged in producing shells for the artillery.

For 1924, the company entered the sporting market with single cylinder 346cc, or 2¼hp models, using the JAP engine in overhead and side valve form. The following year the company had real sporting pretensions and entered Stanley Woods in the TT. However, a broken handlebar put paid to their first racing venture.

Another design feature that was to become a permanent feature of Enfield models was introduced in 1930, and was the incorporation of the oil tank into the front of the crankcase. This was continued right through until they ceased production and certainly cleaned up the exterior appearance of the machines, with the lack of exterior oil piping.

There's nothing new about four-valve cylinder heads, and while Ricardo naturally has much of the credit for their general introduction, Enfield were early in the field with their own design in 1931 with the model JS, the forerunner of the later and very popular Bullet range.

The first of these was the 250, in 1933, then followed the 350 and 500, which were the bread-and-butter of the pre-war range. With the introduction of the big V-twins, the 976cc model K and the 1140cc KX, Enfield intended to compete with the likes of Harley Davidson.

After the war of 1939-45 there were economical designs like the 250 and 350 Clippers, there was a model powered by the Villiers twin two-stroke, the continuing 125, trials, scrambles and racing versions of the Bullet, even a dally with a purpose-built clubmans' road racing machine, the GP5.

However, the first parallel twin appeared in 1949, the 500 twin, to be followed in 1952 by what was virtually two 350 Bullets on a common crankcase, the 692cc Meteor. This machine was to be developed and refined in the battle to stay competitive with models from Triumph, BSA, Norton and AJS/Matchless.

It progressed through Super Meteor and Constellation versions and culminated in the 736cc Interceptor as the company ran into increasingly troubled financial times, with the rest of the British motorcycle industry. As the company was taken into the Norton Villiers Group, Norton forks were fitted to the Interceptor.

The final throw of a machine bearing the Enfield name was the Rickman, as the name implied, it was the Rickman brothers chassis housing the Interceptor Series II engine. This carried with it, disc brakes and the sporting heritage that Rickman had built up with their race developed frames. But the biggest British twin of its day was no more able to stem the tide of Japanese technology than the rest of the industry.

The real story of Royal Enfield is best told by the people who lived and worked at Enfield. Their recollections have been captured by Anne Bradford in the personal insights, recollections and anecdotes in these pages.

Personally, I first became involved in this book as a contributor to the chapter on 'The Competitive Royal Enfields', having cut my road racing teeth on a Super Meteor. My contact with Anne Bradford and interest in the marque soon led to a greater involvement, as my 25 years as a magazine editor seemed to lead me into being invited to edit this book.

However, the book became like 'Topsy', it just 'growed and growed'. Anne Bradford is something of a local historian around her native town of Redditch, where the Royal Enfield name has its roots. Indeed, she actually lives on Enfield Road.

Anne has several books of local interest to her credit, including a most successful one on ghosts around the area. It was Anne's contact with the Royal Enfield Owners Club which set this work in motion. They suggested that the story of the past employees who had worked at 'The Enfield' would not only make a fascinating local history, but would prevent the history of a great marque slipping away. Subsequently, a short piece in *Motor Cycle News* requesting ex-employees to get in touch with Anne, produced not only that desired result but brought about my own involvement.

Having met with people like Jack Booker and Charlie Rogers while racing Enfields, and even interviewed for the position of draughtsman, I had developed an affection for Royal Enfield motorcycles, which I would always hold were at least the equal of the rest of the British motorcycle industry.

As Anne recorded more and more of the ex-Enfield employees personal stories, the work began to assume the proportions of an encyclopedia and I had to perform much heavy editing to bring this book within commercial budgets; inevitably therefore, some anecdotes have been shortened and even deleted as accounts have overlapped in recording common experience.

This book is not a detailed story of Royal Enfield motorcycles, though they are not neglected, nor is it just about the workforce who made the company that became the very heart of the town of Redditch. In current books on the British motorcycle industry, it is unique in the personal insights into the people who ran the company and, in their views, the reasons for the eventual failure of it.

Cycle History

MALCOLM BARRETT: *Royal Enfield Owners Club No 4001, S Midlands Branch. RE Marque Enthusiast for Veteran Cycle Club*

The late 1890s proved busy years for the Eadie/Smith duo as they developed and improved their cycles at Hunt End. Gone were the high wheels, solid tyres, block chains and heavy cross frames. The Eadie company were concentrating on the newer types of cycles and components with the Diamond frames, the Hyde Freewheel, Enfield 2 speed hub and the well-known Eadie Coaster.

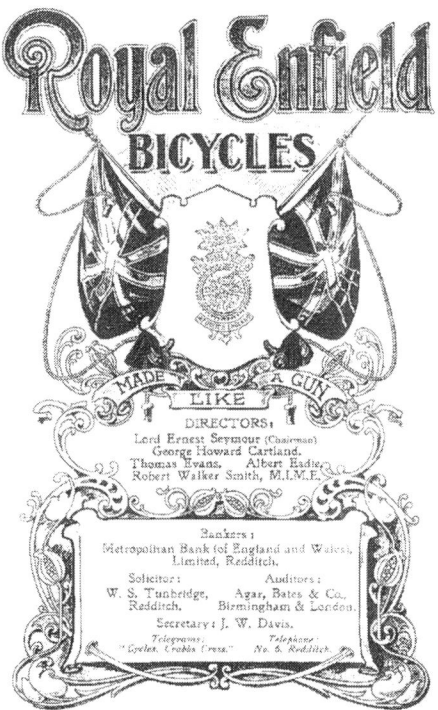

As a challenge to the now competitive market of 1901, the new Enfield Cycle Company Limited marketed a new cycle called the Flexible Bicycle, the frame comprising a large coil spring inset in both rear forks with laminated steel strips in the lower end of the front forks and rearward chain stays. This model was obviously short-lived as it did not appear in the 1903 catalogue.

Also for 1901 RE produced the Royal Enfield Duplex Girder Frame bicycle, the 'posh' version being the 'Riche Model', having more refined fittings. These frames, when tested at Lloyds proving house, withstood a riding strain of two tons compared with the conventional diamond frame which collapsed under a strain of eighteen cwt. These were last illustrated in the 1927 catalogue.

In 1907 the cycle industry continued at the new Hewell Road works in Redditch, producing run-of-the-mill conventional cycles of the Roadster, Sports and Racing range. There was a major change in 1950 when a new exciting frame was developed called the 'Royal Enfield Unitized Frame and Fork'. Used on the Royal Enfield 'Bullet-3' bicycle it comprised a special welding technique eliminating the use of frame lugs.

Finally, in 1960, through until the company closed in 1967, another cycle was developed as Enfield's answer to the 'Moulton', the innovation of small-wheel cycles. This was the 'Revelation' using a completely new design of frame and twenty inch wheels, and was the brain child of a long standing engineer and designer at the Enfield, Vic Bott.

When the Company closed down in 1967 the cycle division was taken over by Kirk and Merifield, a well-known cycle manufacturer from Bradford Street, Birmingham, who used the trade mark 'Royal Enfield – Made like a Gun'.

So the cannon kept on turning after a hundred years of wonderful cycle history.

Royal Enfield; from the archives

Givry Needle Works, Hunt End, Redditch, circa 1865.

It is difficult to believe that the two great Royal Enfield factories at Hunt End and Redditch have now almost completely disappeared. Only the name of Enfield remains. The two acre site of the first factory at Hunt End is now a trading estate off Enfield Road. The enormous thirty-five acre site in the heart of Redditch is now the Enfield Industrial Estate, a collection of assorted industrial units.

The story of Royal Enfield goes way back to the first half of the last century when George Townsend, born in 1815, the son of an Alcester needle-making manufacturer, settled in Hunt End. This village already supported several small mills manufacturing the needles and fish-hooks for which Redditch and its satellite villages were famous.

The *Illustrated Midland News* of September 4th 1869 tells us that by 1851, George Townsend had saved enough money to build his own needle-making mill, which he named Givry Works. It was a red-bricked, three storey factory with a little cottage attached, and although the original building has

The Reducing Room, Givry Needle Works, Hunt End, Redditch, circa 1865.

disappeared a replica, built about the same time, still stands at the other end of Enfield Road, numbers 62, 64 and 66. The census of that year shows that the factory was sufficiently established to employ sixteen men and two boys.

Over the next few years, the factory flourished. By 1871 Givry Works was described as the 'only engineering shop of any importance for miles around' and was employing 170 workers. For a description of the Townsend's products, specialities and awards, we have only to look at the advertisement in the 1873 Littlebury's Directory for Worcester, which reads:

Townsend George & Co. Inventors of stamping sewing machine needles in 1851, patentees of the treble grooved needles; makers to the British Government, manufacturers of needles, shuttles, reels, springs &c., for sewing machines, also every description of hand sewing needles of superior quality made from the best refined cast steel, prize medals.

London, 1862; Paris, 1867; and Havre, 1868.

The advertisement then lists the addresses of offices in London, Paris and Canada. A tradition of excellence was established and the foundations of a healthy export trade were in place. Townsend also manufactured the machinery with which needles were made.

George Townsend passed away in 1879 at the age of 64 and his son George and his half-brother (known as Foster Townsend) took over the running of the works. George now seems to have become the predominant partner as 1881 finds him living in Givry Works' House, the cottage attached to the factory, with his wife and two small children.

Foster then fades from the scene but before he does so, he inadvertently changes the whole direction of Givry Works. He took into the factory one of the first 'boneshakers'. It had a backbone of iron, with wooden wheels, iron tyres and pedals of triangular pieces of wood. The bike was the source of some amusement and no doubt George and his team felt that they could easily improve on it.

The earliest types of the modern safety bicycle with two wheels of equal size had appeared in about 1880. The bicycle boom had begun and most manufacturers with adequate facilities were trying their hand at this new venture. No doubt George Townsend was toying with the idea of entering this new market, when, in 1885, he had a stroke of luck. William Cook, working in his little wooden hut at Headless Cross nearby, invented a saddle which only used one length of wire in the two springs and in the framework. This was adopted by Townsend, patented and marketed as the Townsend Cyclists Saddle and Spring. The bicycle parts trade was entered into and the services of several skilled craftsmen obtained.

By 1888, Townsend was producing bicycles himself and supplying a wide range of parts to other manufacturers. He was described as being one of the very few manufacturers who made everything on his own premises, thereby establishing a tradition of self-sufficiency.

Givry Works was growing rapidly, it had extended along half of one side of Enfield Road and the stamp shop had even been built on the other side of the Wharrage Brook.

Over the next three years he developed his own range of over two dozen machines which were exhibited in 1891 in London's prestigious Crystal Palace with such names as 'The Scorcher', 'The Business Rider' and the 'Ecossais'. The Townsend cycle was well-known for its sturdy frame (the 'Diamond' frame), a reputation which all Enfield bikes were to follow.

The tradition of enhancing their reputation by entering and winning competitive racing began as early as 1889, when a member of the Irish Champion Cycling Club, du Cros, rode a Townsend safety bike for the first time in an Irish sporting event and won five bicycle and two tricycle championships plus four challenge cups.

These successes were continued by Fred Shelton who joined the company straight from school to work in the tool room and proved himself to be such an excellent cyclist that whenever a potential customer came to inspect the cycles, Fred would be called to jump on and ride up nearby Littlewoods Hill. He came third in the one mile handicap at Cheltenham in 1890, but his greatest triumph was the winning of the George's Challenge Cup at Oakengates, near Telford in 1895.

In 1890, the firm was made into a limited liability company but, to quote the late Ivor Mutton:

They got into a little bit of financial trouble in about 1890 and called in some financiers from Birmingham. They didn't quite see eye to eye with the financiers and so they left the company and the financiers brought in Albert Eadie and Mr R W Smith.

The Rags to Riches Story

In the words of the *Kings Highway* of August 1918, R W Smith 'became intimately acquainted' with Albert Eadie during the 1880s. Robert Walker Smith (usually known as 'R W' or 'The Guv'nor') was assistant works manager to D Rudge & Co in Coventry. The company supplied bicycle parts to Perry & Co Ltd in Birmingham where the young Albert Eadie had rapidly risen to become sales manager. No doubt Smith and Eadie recognised in themselves an ideal partnership. Albert Eadie was a great front man, said to be 'the most successful cycle salesman this country has ever known'. Robert Walker Smith was the creator, the brain, working energetically behind the scenes.

Townsends financial difficulties provided an ideal opportunity for a joint venture and Smith and Eadie decided to take the enormous risk of leaving their comfortable, well-paid jobs to throw in their lot with the impoverished George Townsend & Company Limited.

Both Smith and Eadie came from quite conventional backgrounds. Albert Eadie was born in the jewellery quarter of Birmingham in 1863, his father was an engraver-jeweller and although Albert had eight brothers and sisters he seems to have been the only member of the family to have had an interest in engineering. He left school at thirteen to become an office clerk in Harborne, then a traveller for Perry and Co Ltd of Lancaster Street, Birmingham. Perry's manufactured small items such as pen-nibs and pencil cases and Eadie was responsible for persuading them to enter the bicycle parts trade. He soon became sales manager.

The nearest town was Redditch, three miles away from Hunt End, with a sprinkling of dark, satanic mills but

Robert Walker Smith.

principally a quiet country town of some 15,000, known world-wide for its needles and fishing tackle. Its inhabitants had never before met anyone quite like Albert Eadie. He took them by storm. Known as the Emperor, his telegraphic address was 'Emperor, Redditch'. Eadie was a tall, well-built man, towering over his colleagues; round-faced but said to be very handsome. His flamboyant clothes made him even more noticeable and his day-to-day dress usually comprised a brightly-coloured waistcoat, a bow tie and a stetson. His coachman was equally ostentatious wearing a buff-coloured livery with light blue cuffs and a cockade.

He was a great extrovert, articulate, good-humoured, generous and extremely popular. Cycling events clamoured for his support and he was very much in demand as a judge. He held various prestigious offices over the years, among them Chairman of the Midland Cycle Records Association and Vice-President of Liverpool and District Cycle Trades Association. When the older folks talk about Givry Works they tend to call it, 'The Eadie factory'.

Robert Walker Smith was Eadie's assistant to manage the production side. In years to come it was not the flamboyant Eadie who took over the reins of the factory but R W Smith. He was born in Stamford in Lincolnshire and the family moved to Wolverhampton when he was a child as his father had obtained a post as an engineer in the Great Western Railway workshops. R W Smith served his apprenticeship in these same workshops, obtaining additional technical education at the Wolverhampton School of Art. A brilliant engineering student, he won the Queen's prize for machine construction. He developed an interest in cycle racing while at Wolverhampton. When he was in his late twenties he went to work at D Rudge & Co Ltd, not far from the workshops, but in 1880, Dan Rudge died and the company was sold to George Woodcock of Coventry so R W Smith had to move to Coventry with the firm, eventually becoming assistant manager.

Albert Eadie and R W Smith took control of Townsend's in November 1891. Albert Eadie was a mere 28 years old, R W Smith was seven years older and the departing Townsend was 36. Townsend moved away from Redditch and established another cycle manufacturing factory in Aston Cantlow, between Redditch and Stratford. In the spring of the following year, April 1892, Eadie took over as managing director. In the August of that same year the firm was re-christened 'The Eadie Manufacturing Company Limited'.

Their first priority was to get the company on a sound financial footing. Eadie persuaded a number of businessmen to invest in the company. Their chief benefactor was George Cartland, the third son of a wealthy Birmingham brass-founder, better known as one of the men responsible for the foundation of the Edgbaston cricket ground.

The new venture teetered on the edge of bankruptcy and despite selling the needle-making interests to Alfred Shrimpton & Sons Ltd, George Cartland was asked for more and more financial backing. The turning point came when Albert Eadie managed to obtain a lucrative contract to supply

precision rifle parts to the Royal Small Arms factory in Enfield, Middlesex, where the Enfield rifles were made.

To celebrate the contract, Smith and Eadie decided to call their first new design of bicycle, the 'Enfield'. Eadie had been keeping this one up his sleeve for some time, ready to be launched at his new factory. One innovation was pneumatic tyres instead of the old rubber ones, which gave a much more comfortable ride. A new company was created to market the cycles, The Enfield Manufacturing Company Ltd and showrooms were opened at 166 Edmund Street, Birmingham. By October 1892, only a matter of weeks after Albert Eadie took up his post as managing director, the Enfield bikes were announced to the public. The following year Smith and Eadie had the brilliant idea of adding the word Royal (from the Royal Small Arms company) and thus Royal Enfield began. Also in 1893, the Royal Enfield trademark 'made like a gun' appeared. Britain was caught up in a patriotic fervour and the slogan caught the spirit of the time.

By 1896, their initial financial problems were over. The bicycle boom had arrived. For many they were the sole means of transport, for some they were a means of recreation as nearly every village and town had its cycling club. It was now decided to raise more capital by going public and launching £125,000 shares at £1 each. They were fully subscribed. Those departments which involved complete bikes were brought together and called the New Enfield Cycle Co Ltd, leaving the parent company, the Eadie Manufacturing Company Limited, to deal with the parts.

By 1897 Givry Works was employing 600 workers and producing between 300 and 400 cycles weekly as well as providing spare parts for other manufacturers. The factory was bursting at its seams. It was decided that Eadie would have his own factory in Redditch to supply 'fittings and components to the Continent of Europe and other parts of the globe'. One of these parts was the world-famous Eadie Cycling Hub, the first drum brake ever to be fitted to a cycle although why it bore his name is a mystery as the hub was not invented by him and was patented in France. To give the Eadie Manufacturing Company a fresh image, the word 'new' was added but it never seems to have been in common use and was officially dropped a year later.

In 1899 there came a slump in the cycle market, brought about by rising unemployment and over-production. However, the Eadie Manufacturing Company and its subsidiary companies managed to survive. A ceremony took place at the White Hart, Headless Cross, in November 1901 to celebrate the tenth anniversary of Eadie and Smith taking over Townsend's. The two men were the heroes of the hour. Congratulatory addresses were read and they were officially thanked for making the venture such a financial success.

At the ninth Annual General Meeting of the Enfield Cycle Company Limited in 1905, shareholders were told that, despite a loss on the motor department, profits on cycles had been higher than any other since the boom. By now, Givry Works had trebled in size. The Board had therefore decided to build another factory in Redditch and between five and six acres of land had been purchased from Lord Windsor for this purpose. The land was near to the railway line in the centre of Redditch and fronted on to Hewell Road. The following year, directors put forward proposals to transfer the whole of cycle manufacture to the Redditch factory. The move would enable plant and machinery to be laid out for large scale cycle manufacture.

The Enfield Cycle Company did not completely vacate Givry Works until 1907. That same year, Albert Eadie sold out to the Birmingham Small Arms Group. He resigned from Enfield's and was appointed manager, then managing director, of BSA.

Four wheels and three

No doubt many of the Victorian engineers who pedalled their bicycles up hills dreamed of some kind of power unit which they could attach to their machines to do the hard work for them. When the value of the petrol-drive engine was recognised in about 1886, many of them tried fitting an engine in front of the handlebars, only to find the machine too unstable to ride. The first ventures of the Enfield Cycle Company into motorised vehicles was therefore with three and four wheeled vehicles, rather than two.

In Great Britain, the development of the motorcar was lagging behind that on the Continent because, in 1865, an absurd act of Parliament required that every 'road locomotive' should be preceded at a distance of 100 yards by a man carrying a red flag and its speed should not exceed four miles per hour. This law at one blow crippled a great and promising industry and was not repealed until 1896, then the speed limit was raised to twelve miles per hour. In 1900, Harry Lancaster, who later became managing director of Enfield Autocar, was fined for driving at 23 mph.

Within a year from the repeal of the act, R W Smith was building himself a motorised vehicle, aptly known as a quadricycle. It was simply a bike with four wheels and a French (De Dion) engine placed under the saddle between the rear wheels. A passenger could be carried on a padded seat fixed between the front wheels – from where he or she would be first to hit any obstruction! It is said that the quadricycle created so much interest that R W Smith decided to start building them under licence from De Dion Bouton, but Smith and Eadie had probably been watching the market for some time.

During the next two years a variety of experiments were carried out which included using more powerful engines, stronger frames, and having three wheels instead of four. Although quadricycles looked more like wheelchairs than cars, they seem to have been surprisingly robust. An Enfield quadricycle completed the 1,000-miles road trial of 1900, organised by the Automobile Club of Great Britain and Ireland to demonstrate to the public that a motorised vehicle could travel long distances with very little trouble. The Enfield vehicle was awarded a silver medal, although it had its share of troubles and breakdowns.

Two speed gear

By the turn of the century Royal Enfield had three main models which they exhibited at the Stanley Cycle Show in London, all using a 2¾hp De Dion engine. A motorised cycle was on display, despite its instability, and there were two motor quadricycles, one of these incorporated a brilliant, patented design by R W Smith – a two-speed gear. By operating a hand lever the gear could slide either into the left or right hand gear box or could remain in the central position

Mr Myers, who later became a Royal Enfield dealer, takes his father for a spin on his quadricycle.

(neutral) for starting. Early motorized vehicle development tended to be a battle of patents, each new development would be hastily registered then competitors would study it and try to produce a similar result without infringing the patent.

Smith and Eadie decided to extend the range of quadricycles and tricycles to include motor cars. During the next twelve months a series of bizarre shapes emerged from the factory gates. A team of experts were engaged, in addition to the manager, Walter Grew, there was Walter Gobiet, a Belgian engineer who had previously been in charge of cycle building at Henri Guillaume's business in the Midlands, and the foreman, Samuel Gallimore from Wolseley. Additional designers were David Doyle and, of course, R W Smith. Louis Hadley was in charge of the experimental shop, a small building to the rear of the factory, where he worked with one assistant. Mr Hadley had been recruited from Coventry and remained with the Enfield Cycle Company for the rest of his working life. His daughter was secretary to R W Smith in the l950s and has contributed some of her memories later in this book.

Until Enfield's motor department was able to produce its own vehicles, it was necessary for them to buy in from other manufacturers. In January 1901, therefore, a deputation visited a motor exhibition in the Grand Palais, Champs Elysees, to make their choice. They ordered 50 of the Ader car made by the Society Industrielle des Telephones.

The Ader carriage was decorated with broad vertical stripes and the small, box-shaped engine had a series of grill slits at the front and sides. The steering wheel rose vertically from the floor and a park-bench type passenger seat was attached to the rear. The car was open-topped but a white canvas canopy with scalloped edges was available.

Walter Grew went to Paris with two drivers and collected three cars. Advertising for the new four seater as a car, at £350, began at the end of August, without any mention of 'Ader', implying that it was Enfield-built. Retribution came in the form of the Glasgow Exhibition Motor Trials in September.

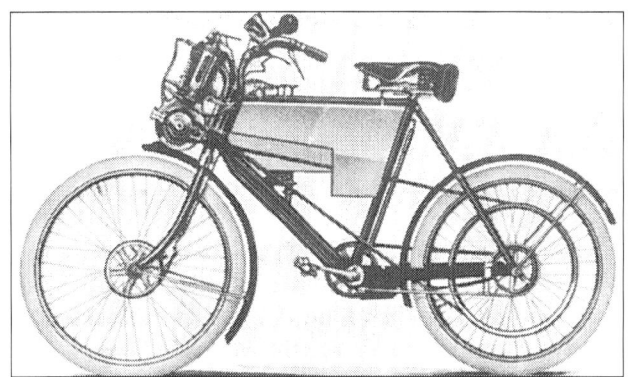

The 1901 172cc motorcycle.

A piston blew and the vehicle had to be withdrawn from the event. Evidently, problems with pistons had occurred before, so the Enfield Cycle Company immediately cancelled their order for the remaining 47 cars.

The first Royal Enfield car was built in 1901 and was running on the road in 1902. It was a replica of the French-built vehicle and was an 8hp, using a De Dion engine which was single cylinder, water cooled and positioned at the rear to drive the rear axle. The body was made in Leicester and painted yellow so that the car was known as 'The Yellow Car'. They evidently experienced many difficulties as these were not shown at the 1902 Stanley Cycle Show.

However, three motorcycles were on show, the results of experiments with two-wheeled vehicles. At first, engines had been placed between and just below the front handlebars and had driven the front wheel. Monsieur Gobiet reasoned that if the engine drove the back wheel, the motor cycle would be more stable. In 1901, therefore, a machine was produced with a long belt running from the engine to the rear wheel, and although the stability did not seem to be improved, it was put on the market.

The engine obviously needed to be in the centre of the bike, the problem was that this had already been done and patented by Werners. R W Smith and Monsieur Gobiet discovered that it was possible to get round the patent by looping the bottom tube of the frame under the crankcase, the engine could then be located at the bottom of the front sloping tube of the frame. Two of the machines at the show had engines so-positioned, the third had a 2hp Minerva engine fitted behind the front wheel in front of the bottom bracket of the frame. The motorised bikes at the Show were covered by two other patents, one referred to the new design of transmission system and the other to the fact that one chain only was required to transmit the drive from the engine to the rear wheel.

Walter Gobiet left in 1903 to go to the Premier Cycle Co Ltd and Walter Grew joined a publishing company, later becoming editor of *The Motor Cycle*. Trevor Rapson now arrived as manager, a Cornishman who had studied and worked in the USA, 'a good and clever engineer, Rapson really made things move and brought out a car in his own right'.

It was due to Rapson's hard work that three cars were available for the 1903 Stanley Cycle Show. One was a 6hp Voiturette which was entirely bought in but the name of the manufacturer was not disclosed, and the other two were 10hp cars which were Enfield's own. Both had twin vertical cylinder engines which were water cooled, one had a rear entrance and the other had a Tonneau body. The new Enfield twin cylinder engine was not quite ready, so the stand had a mounted display model of the new engine in the hope that buyers would assume this was to be used, but in actual fact, De Dion engines were to be installed. Louis Hadley manned the stand with another employee to answer queries but no orders were received. Nevertheless, cars were beginning to be sold through a network of sixteen agents sited throughout the British Isles.

The first two Enfield cars had been made at Hunt End but the motor department was taking up valuable room needed for cycles and so premises had been rented at British Mills in the centre of Redditch and car production moved there. Some twenty or thirty vehicles were produced at British Mills.

Albert Eadie, now used his charm to persuade the directors and shareholders to allow him to purchase a small piece of land at Hunt End between Givry Works and the Red Lion beerhouse, in order to build a factory specifically for the manufacture of cars and motorcycles. By the spring of 1904 the new factory had been built and the Enfield motor department moved back to Hunt End again, into new, purpose-built premises.

Two Enfield cars were exhibited at Leeds in 1904. The 6hp retailed at £175 and the 10hp for £300. The 6hp was a strange-looking vehicle, the driver's seat rose from a rectangular platform, so tall that the driver was looking down upon the engine.

In the same year, the Reliability Trials for small cars was organised by the Automobile Club of Great Britain and Ireland, based at Hereford. The Enfield motor department entered an 8hp with the following result:

Monday morning – seven stops which included a broken water pipe and ignition. Monday afternoon – one stop for a puncture.

The 1904 10hp, four seater, with honeycombed radiator.

Tuesday morning – one stop for a broken wire. Tuesday afternoon – no stops. Wednesday morning – three stops, one to repair the clutch, one to fill with water and to repair the ignition. Wednesday afternoon – broken oil pipe used for cylinder lubrication. Car retired.

Trevor Rapson departed shortly afterwards to work at the Premier Cycle Company.

Although performance of the motorcars were giving problems, the motorised bikes had one of their first major racing successes. At the New Brighton track, before a crowd of three or four thousand spectators, Louis Hadley rode his 2hp Royal Enfield Minerva (of the type shown at the Stanley Cycle Show in 1902) to victory.

The directors now imported Mr W M Jenkins, of American origin, to take charge of the motor department. He had previously been general manager of the Galick Motor and Cycle Company in Cape Town and he arrived in September 1904. Mr Jenkins was able to make a number of improvements to the 10hp car, including a perfectly circular, honeycombed radiator which was made on site in the tinsmith's department. By the December, he was marketing vans, apparently by fitting a van body to a 10hp and 20hp car chassis. The 10hp van carried a load of l5cwt and cost 300 guineas (£3l5). These were exhibited at Olympia in February, 1905.

Also employed was a French engineer and designer from the Farique Nationale in Belgium, William Guillon. He set to work designing two new chassis which were manufactured and assembled in time to be on view at the Olympia Motor Show in November 1905. Model X was 15-20hp with a double-phaeton body, Model Y was 24-30hp chassis, with a body from outside suppliers. Three patents had been applied to the Enfield cars by Monsieur Guillon which covered the control of the ignition and throttle, the differential gears and the rear axle.

These were beautiful-looking cars, long and low with padded leather upholstery and a larger than normal radiator. Monsieur Guillon worked very hard on the sales aspect, taking the car to exhibitions and giving demonstrations to prove its capabilities, assisted by Louis Hadley. Despite finding the English language a struggle, he managed to interest a number of dealers.

A new managing director was appointed, Harry Lancaster. He was born in Italy in 1876, educated in London, apprenticed at Rugby, employed in Paris then moved to London as the managing director of the Clement Motor Company. Eadie said of him, 'This youth appeared to me… as a worthy object of capture… and he was bagged accordingly'.

In 1906, the motor department took a further, and very significant, step into the unknown. From that year onwards, they would cease to be supported by the sales of bicycles. Over £20,000 had been spent on motorised vehicles and the directors decided that the time had come for the motor department to be independent. A new company was therefore floated, the Enfield Autocar Company Limited, to handle the manufacture, marketing and sales of motorized vehicles. Furthermore, Enfield Autocar was to have the whole of the Hunt End factory. Bicycle manufacture was to move away from Hunt End and into the new factory in the centre of Redditch.

The first ten cars had been produced by May 1906, and advertising began. Five variations of the 30hp car was put on the market, together with a 30hp 4-cylinder motor lorry, called a one tonner. Also in May, a 10hp twin-cylinder Royal Enfield entered the non-stop run from Swansea to Tenby and back organised by the Welsh Automobile Club and obtained a non-stop certificate.

It was unfortunate that from 1906 to 1907 the company was hit by a slump in car and motor bike sales, too many manufacturers were chasing a market which became smaller with rising unemployment. Enfield Autocar had two basic lines of motorcycles, both were single cylinder models with Enfield engines and frames, one was belt driven and the other chain driven. Both lines had been over-produced and so it was decided not to manufacture any more motorcycles for the time being.

In October 1906, came the annual Motor Show at Olympia and for the first time, Royal Enfield had its own stand instead of exhibiting under the name of an agent.

Harry Lancaster, assisted by William Guillon, had designed two new cars, a 15hp four-cylinder with coil ignition and a 25hp, which was a redesigned 30hp. The 15hp was the most popular. With its long bonnet, heavily-padded double seats and six-sided radiator it revealed, as the catalogue described, 'an elegance and smartness', and it sold for only 350 guineas (£367.50). A journalist from *Autocar* drove the 15hp for 60 miles and praised its performance highly. In the first few days of the show, 150 cars were ordered and the London agents, Keele & Co, doubled their original contract.

Unfortunately, these orders did not begin to be supplied until the following February. There were problems in recruiting sufficient skilled craftsmen and, when they were found, no accommodation was available. The management could not get hold of the necessary tools and machinery, and aluminium was in short supply.

By July, the production problems had been overcome and a night-shift was put on to cope with the demand for the 15hp model. At last, the company seemed to be flourishing. Then the bomb fell. At the Second Ordinary Meeting of Enfield Autocar in September 1907, a loss of £19,264 was revealed. The reasons given were that the first model, the 30hp, had been too expensive to manufacture and that there had been delays on the production of the 15hp.

The 15hp models were exhibited in Paris in December, 1906. Three days before the Show closed, the Enfield representatives found their stand swarming with half-a-dozen French officials including the Commissionaire of Police. The French claimed that the lever, which was not of Enfield manufacture, infringed their copyrights. The cars were impounded and the gate and change speed levers were forcibly removed from the chassis. 'After long delay and payment of the costs, some fifty francs and a certain amount of diplomacy, the cars were released'. They were needed for a January show in Ballsbridge, Ireland. The cars were exhibited but without the gate and change speed levers, a cruel blow for a company struggling to survive.

Two days before Christmas 1907 the major shareholders met the directors. Thomas Evans, the new chairman, presided. He said that, as he had only held the position of Chairman for a limited period, they could not expect him to give a detailed history of the company. Albert Eadie offered to invest £8,000 in the company if the shareholders would contribute the remainder of the working capital required but it was decided to opt for voluntary liquidation. The suggested price was £18,000.

On 6th April, 1908, company plant and stock were put up for auction in one lot at the Grand Hotel, Birmingham. The reserve price was not reached and so the lot was withdrawn but was sold the following Friday to the Directors of Alldays and Onions Pneumatic Engineering Company Limited, of Small Heath, Birmingham.

1907-1914 – Two wheels to the fore

In the first years of the twentieth century no-one ever dreamed that a motorcycling craze would ever sweep through Great Britain. Motorcycling was thought to be a temporary enthusiasm which would soon die out. A brief spin on a motor bike could take several hours of preparation; the tiny water-cooled engine had to be carefully tuned, the tyres pumped, the gears (either countershaft or variable) oiled – if there were any gears at all – and a supply of spare parts packed. It is not surprising, therefore, especially after the disaster of Enfield cars, that for the first eighteen months the new factory at Redditch produced bicycles only.

Although it is the Royal Enfield motorcycles which have captured the imagination and given Royal Enfield its glamour, it has, except for a few years, been the bicycles on which the fortunes of Royal Enfield depended. Then, in 1909, Royal Enfield surprised the biking world. To quote Ivor Mutton:

In the motorcycle show of 1909 they showed a small 2¼hp V twin engine machine with direct valve drive from the engine to the back wheel and this had a Motosacoche engine which was, of course, of Swiss manufacture. A very nice little machine because it was built in the Swiss tradition, reliable like a watch, and it ran very well.

For the following season, 1911, they did field another model which was a 2¾hp, in other words, a slightly larger capacity, and this had got all-chain drive and also incorporated the well-known Enfield two-speed gear. This was composed of two twin chains from the engine to the gear box which you alternatively engaged according to whatever gear you wanted, high or low, and the final drive was by chain. It was rather a nice little machine and it remained up until about 1914 and then it was phased out.

There is no doubt that R W Smith was heavily involved in these designs. Tributes to his engineering ability are on record from the workforce and the trade journals. In *The Motor Cycle and Cycle Trader* of 17th March 1916, Mr Paskell said that there had hardly been an instance where a cycle firm had introduced a bike which had not been modelled on the Triumph, and added:

Almost the only notable exception which did not join the rank of the 3½ single is the Enfield, due perhaps to the independent 'never follow anyone' style of man, that mechanical genius, R W Smith.

The 1914 catalogue for the 2¾hp gives the price as £45 and proudly announces:

The first Indian Tourist Trophy Race – A terrible ride over rough, boulder strewn roads, far worse than anything imaginable in this country – was won on a Standard 2¾hp Royal Enfield Motor Cycle....

The 2¾hp also won the Bloemfontein Hill Climb in South Africa and the Svenska MK Reliability Trial in Sweden as well as a number of races and trials at home.

Then came two of Royal Enfield's most famous bikes which made the name a household word. First was the 6hp Combination Motor Cycle and Sidecar which appeared at the November 1911 Olympia Show.

Ivor Mutton continues: ... *in 1912, of course, they moved on to other things, they moved on to the big V-twin engines and what are generally known as Enfield sidecar combinations. The engine was 6hp or otherwise 770cc and it wasn't an engine of their own manufacture, again, it was a JAP engine which was made by J A Prestwich of London, again, this machine incorporated the Enfield two-speed gear, the oil change mechanism unit and an innovation which was the cush drive hub. This was a peculiar type of hub which contained about six rubber blocks which very gently took up the drive instead of having to snatch on it which you normally have to get off a chain and a solid back tyre. That lasted until the very last Enfield motorcycle was made in the latter part of the l960s, and it was a salient feature of Enfield's, right from its introduction in 1912.*

The 6hp had an overhead inlet valve, sprung forks and the improved Amac carburettor. Among the many tributes paid by the trade press is one from *The Motor Cycle* of 18th June 1914, 'The beauty of the Enfield gears is that it is impossible to damage the gears in changing, no matter how clumsily the operation be performed'. The *British Trade Review* of July 1916 gives the results of petrol consumption tests and concludes that the 6hp is 'one of the most economical motorcycles in the world'. The price was 80 guineas (£84) or £100 guineas (£115.50) if fitted with Lucas electric lights and horn and the overall cost per mile, including depreciation, was reckoned to be 1½d (½p).

Instead of a sidecar a tradesman's box could be attached 'of roomy proportions', which was used for every purpose imaginable, by bakers, plumbers, tea merchants, newspaper vendors, market gardeners, fruit pickers, laundry men, fire brigades – even furniture removal companies!

By 1914, 30 6hp combinations were being made weekly. They were tremendously popular at all levels of society. In September 1916, a gentleman walked into the Redditch office and told the management that he had had the honour of driving Princess Victoria in an RE sidecar combination. 'HRH expressed herself as being charmed with the ease and comfort of sidecar travelling'.

It made a very good racing bike and was even better in trials. It came first in the Australian Canberra Club Reliability Trial from Sydney to Bathurst, won the Cerrara Cup Trial in Spain in 1916 and several South African Reliability Trials. O J Prillevitz described his ride in the 200 mile Wiener's Day Reliability Trial in *Motoring* of November 1st, 1913.

On reaching the middle of the river we found the water both strong and high, completely submerging the sidecar and running over the tank of the machine. This necessitated some very hard pushing. On topping the rise, we saw a second river... No time was lost in letting the water out of the magneto and carburettor.

They were away with only a five minute delay and reckoned that this was the advantage that won them the race.

The catalogue lists the three cups, eight gold medals, two silver medals and two watches won in Great Britain during 1914.

Douggie Alexander rode this ohiv twin in the 1914 Junior TT. Lying second on the first lap, he crashed and lost his saddle, but he remounted and completed the race.

A year after the 6hp combination was launched, came the famous 3hp, the first bike to use Enfield's own engine. By now, Royal Enfield had standardised the colours, all parts were enamelled black with green tank and gold lines. Ivor Mutton described the new bike as follows:

In 1912 a Swiss named Guillon who had been at the Enfield for a number of years designed a 3hp which was a 425cc V-twin cylinder engine. It had overhead inlet valves and side exhaust valves but the most important innovation was that it had forced oil feed by mechanical pump to the big end bearing. Not only that, but the oil was returned from the crankcase to the glass oil tank... so, by watching this you could see that the oil was returning and that you were getting a continuity of supply. It was a very sweet running engine, the lubrication system of course was possibly eighteen years in front of itself because it wasn't until the late 1920s, and early 30s that this dry sump lubrication, as it was known, came into general use.

These were seen across the world. In Cairo, a Mr Flowers rode up Mount Olympus (6,000 feet) with a 14-stone passenger. A 3hp won the ten-mile road race organised by the Canberra Motor Cycling Club of Sydney, Australia, in 1913, achieving 54½ mph. In 1915, it won King Alphonse's Cup in the International Motor Cycle Trials in Spain together with every prize in the Swedish Motor Cycle trials. *Wheeling* of May 1st 1916 states, 'There are few motorcycles better known in Australia and New Zealand than the Royal Enfield machines'.

During 1913 and 1914 Enfield bikes were prominent at almost every race meeting. One of the work's riders was Ernest Keyte and his daughter gives a little pen portrait of him. He usually rode a reduced-stroke 3hp.

My father was 'Bones' Keyte who was riding in the TT races from 1912 to 1914. Everyone called him 'Bones' because he was so thin but his Christian name was Ernest.

An interesting Royal Enfield was advertised in 1912 which was not a big-seller and did not win any major races

Mrs Riley and her 6hp twin sidecar.

1912 bike for ladies. 2½ open frame two-speed free engine.

but was politically correct. This was a 2½hp with open frame, that is, without a cross bar, so that a lady could mount the bike without losing her decorum. These were the years of the suffragettes and women were making their presence felt. Mrs Mary Riley took her 6hp to the Lake District and embarked on a journey which incorporated The Wrynose, Hard Knott, Honiston and Blea Tarn passes, the first motorcyclist to complete the journey.

The chief concern of female 'bikers' seemed to be what to wear, and there is many a page of advice in the biking magazines. May Walker in *The Motor Cycle* of 2nd April 1914 recommended a costume with a divided skirt 'so as to fall each side of the tank, and a motoring bonnet with a veil attached to protect the face from wind and dust'. The men, on the other hand, seemed to be content with greasy overalls and a cap worn the wrong way round.

Royal Enfield even published a little booklet, *The Lady Drives*, a sumptuously-produced publication containing a number of letters and photographs of lady riders. It reached the dizzy heights of a review by The Queen in 17th April 1917 – 'There is one picture in particular of Mrs Douglas Prentice and another lady in a sidecar, which is the daintiest thing in its line that I have ever seen'!

All was going well at Royal Enfield and particularly so for R W Smith. His motorcycles were a success and his eldest son, Frank Walker Smith (later Major Smith) had joined the company in 1909 and was showing every sign of pursuing a brilliant career. In 1912 he had been promoted as joint managing director with John Davis and in February 1914, at the tender age of 25, he was given the vacant position on the board. No doubt his young exuberance was responsible for many of the decisions made, such as the introduction of an annual works outing. Over a hundred went to Matlock, Bath, they explored the caves, visited Haddon Hall, and ate lunch and dinner at the New Bath Hotel. It was intended that this should be an annual event but there are no other references to works outings for some years.

The order books were full, the employees apparently happy and content. Only one tragedy stirred the Enfield's placid waters. On Tuesday, 19th May 1914, at one of the last TT race meetings for many years, Fred Walker, the Enfield rider, was killed. He had been taking part in the Junior event and was leading, but on the third lap he had a puncture which caused him to crash. He repaired it and rejoined the field and although there now seemed no hope of him winning, he managed to catch up and to everyone's surprise, finished third.

As to the actual incident: ... *after passing the timekeeper's box, he overran the turning leading to the depot. His speed must have been close on forty miles per hour as he dashed down the Ballaquayle Road and too late he observed a pole which had been placed across the roadway to act as a barrier to the traffic. The rider made a great endeavour to get beneath the obstacle, but he failed and was thrown to the ground, while the handlebar*

The Maxim Gun as Enfield's advertising slogan that caused much offence in Ireland.

Royal Enfield's contribution to the Great War

1915. A consignment of military bikes await delivery outside the Enfield offices.

The machine gun combination.

The 6hp stretcher-carrying outfit.

and saddle of the machine were wrenched off. This race was bedevilled by accidents, Douggie Alexander turned a somersault on the first corner but remounted and finished the race minus a saddle.

The Enfield – 1914-1918

For advertising purposes, the Enfield publicity department had strengthened a 6hp combination chassis and replaced the sidecar with an old Maxim gun which they took round exhibitions to represent their slogan, 'Made like a gun'. The stand had been impounded by the Irish customs early in 1914 who found it too lethal-looking for their liking. At the outbreak of war, this display stand was rushed to the Ministry of Munitions and an order for 6hp's with strengthened chassis was received. Vickers guns were used on the sidecar chassis, they could be swivelled in any direction, forward, backward, sideways or even upwards in order to take a shot at a passing plane. A padded seat and backrest was supplied so that the operator could sit behind the gun. By 1915 eighteen of these had been supplied. Royal Enfield also manufactured 6hp combinations with a stretcher instead of a sidecar for Red Cross work.

The battlefield made tremendous demands on a motorcycle, it was estimated that the average life of a motor bike behind the front line was five weeks, although Royal Enfield was proud of the fact that many of their machines lasted for more than a year. Bikes were used by messengers because the wireless had not been fully developed, and to keep the front line supplied with ammunition and provisions. For obvious reasons it was safer to travel at night without lights. The ground was very rough and many a motorcyclist found himself in a six foot shell hole. A great many Enfields played a leading part in the war when many bikers, together with their machines, were recruited through the pages of *The Motor Cycle*.

Although the British Ministry of Munitions were reluctant to order the Enfield 3hp, governments overseas had no hesitation in using them. The first government order for British bikes for use at the front came to the Enfield from Belgium, who ordered 50, followed by orders from France, Denmark and Russia.

Not all the technology used at the Front was new. The good old basic British bicycle was very much in demand, and this was where Royal Enfield excelled. The *Redditch Advertiser* reports that they were making 500 a week for the War Office alone. The military bicycle had a 24 inch frame and 28 inch wheels with 1½ Dunlop or Palmer roadster tyres, slightly upturned handlebars and clips to hold a gun.

There was also an increased demand for bicycles from the home market, partly because of an acute petrol shortage. In 1917 German submarines were destroying a quarter of British ships, rationing was not introduced until 1918 and so anything which had to be imported was in short supply – this was when the French word 'queue' came into use. Attempts to get round the fuel shortage were often quite bizarre. Petrol was mixed with a variety of other liquids ranging from whisky to paraffin. Strangest of all were the contraptions which enabled a 6hp to be run on gas. The sidecar was fitted with all manner of strange balloons, often six times the size of the motorcycle, sometimes resting on the sidecar, sometimes raised on posts above it. The gas was introduced into the induction pipe midway between the cylinders, then a pipe carried the gas from the container to the engine which was fitted with a control tap.

Orders for motorcycles, too, poured in. Many had been donated to the war effort and needed to be replaced. Again, because of the petrol shortage, people were turning from cars to motorcycles. Several police forces, Tarbridge for example, changed from Ford cars to Enfield sidecar combinations. In London in 1917, a Women's Police Force was formed and officers were issued with a 2¼ RE 2-stroke. Women Police Officers had to learn to ride and make minor repairs, such as cleaning plugs, purifying the carburettor and repairing punctures – one female police officer recommended carrying a butt-ended tube and replacing the whole tube. They were rather nonplussed by the recommendation that, before going up a hill in first gear, the rider should smoke a pipe in order to let the engine cool.

As part of the war effort, Royal Enfield were also making shells, the *Redditch Indicator* reported: *…the finished articles have to pass through 12 separate distinct operations… Some of the most important parts of modern shells are now being produced, one part from solid brass bar, the other from special hot stampings …At the Hunt End works nearly three tons of finished munitions parts are now being made weekly.*

They had never been so busy. Before the war, the Enfield had expanded considerably, Givry Works at Hunt End had been re-purchased in 1912 (finally vacated in 1920) and new machinery installed. The following year the machine shop at Redditch had been considerably extended and a new block built for motor repairs and other sundries. Nevertheless, although every department was working to full capacity and some departments were operating a night shift, they were unable to satisfy the demand. By 1915, there was a backlog of 2,000 motorcycles, all of which had been ordered by private owners. The *Redditch Indicator* of 18th March 1916 said that delivery of a new motor bike from any manufacturer could be anything from eight weeks to more than three months.

On 17th August, 1915, the Royal Enfield factories were declared controlled establishments and their products were to be for war use only. Under these circumstances it was impossible to produce any new models, however, just after the outbreak of war a new 2¼hp had made its debut at the Coventry and Warwickshire Motor Cycle hill climb.

Ivor Mutton recalls: *In 1915 they did bring out a new model in the form of a 2¼hp or 225cc single cylinder two-stroke which was something that they'd never been concerned with before. It's rather interesting because, of course, the two-stroke of 1915 did stop in the range until about 1965 in various forms as required by its use.*

One of the few benefits of the war was plenty of work for the factory and full employment. Wages increased nationally, sometimes by as much as 500%. The profits for 1915 increased to £53,200 as compared to £32,700 for 1914. The Board issued a statement to say that the increased profits were not obtained by inflated war prices but by the gradual development of the business over recent years. The net profit for the three years 1916, 1917 and 1918 were published as a total in August 1918 and amounted to £71,642, however, the government decided it was eligible for a share and deducted an Excess Profits Duty and a Munitions Levy which reduced the balance to a mere £11,222.

In a statement issued at the end of the war, R W Smith said: 'The problem of reconstruction ... is not an easy one. My opinion is that this will best be met by producing existing models for the immediate future so that there will be the least possible delay in delivery.'

And so there were no more new motorcycles for five years and for some time after the war, the Enfield would only accept orders for standard bikes. There was one exception to this, the 6hp was very popular with ex-servicemen who had lost all or part of a leg because the gears were operated by hand. The factory therefore supplied the 6hp with the brake fitted on either side, as requested.

With the end of the war we come to the end of an era and into the scope of living memory so the ghosts in the archives can now be put to one side and the story of Royal Enfield continued by those who took part in it.

CHAPTER ONE
Hard times in the twenties

Body Building Department in the 1920s. Foreman is Jack George (in suit and apron).

VIC BOTT: from 1920 to 1968

In a few years time I shall be a hundred years old! I think of myself as living on borrowed time. Most of my working life was spent at Royal Enfield, consequently I am one of the few people alive today able to describe life as a worker at Royal Enfield in 1920 and the years that followed.

Like everyone else at the time, I left school at thirteen. I was apprenticed to toolmaking at Thomas's, at one time one of the largest factories in Redditch. Parts of the building was leased to other companies and round about 1912, Royal Enfield rented a section as a despatch department.

In 1915, having reached sixteen and being influenced by the patriotic hysteria of that time, I was stupid enough to leave my apprenticeship and join the Worcestershire Regiment as a volunteer. After a year's service I was transferred to the Machine Gun Corps and from 1916 until 1918 I served on the Western front. My memories are chiefly of wet, mud and desolation.

I was demobilised at the age of 20 when the ex-serviceman's rehabilitation from the army to civvies was a complete disaster. After four years of voluntary active service at a shilling a day, I had no job and no skills.

The management of Royal Enfield were very considerate and took on as many ex-servicemen as they could possibly accommodate, despite already having an adequately trained workforce. Most of the family of my wife-to-be worked at Royal Enfield. Her two brothers were there, her father had been a foreman for many years and she herself was a supervisor in charge of the accessories department. They managed to get me a job at Enfield's for 36s (£1.80) per week.

Even those in full time employment were under financial strain because of the low wages and the fact that even at Royal Enfield, you could spend a quarter of the year working only three days a week or even laid off altogether. The competition from other manufacturers of motor bikes was intense – Kings Norton had the Norton bikes, Coventry had the Matchless, Wolverhampton had AJS and there was a competitor in Redditch itself, the BSA. In addition to this, most of the local light industries were 'luxury' commodities and therefore the demand was seasonal. People tended not to go fishing or to buy motor bikes during the winter months. The short time usually came during the Autumn and we therefore called our lay-off 'our hay-making ticket'.

A momentous occasion in the 1920s was the formation of the British Legion. It was managed by the Smith family. At that time there were three main charities in Redditch which aimed at relieving the grievous poverty of the day. Of these three charities the British Legion was, I am sure, the liveliest. At its height, it had about 180 members and we raised thousands of pounds over the years. I was one of a fourteen-strong concert party, all from Royal Enfield, who went all over the county giving concerts. I used to do a Rolf Harris-type act, making lightning sketches in charcoal to such songs as the *Village Blacksmith*. I led such an active life outside work that my wife said that she was going to get my portrait taken and stick it on the wall so that she would see me sometimes.

A prestigious new factory

The Redditch site in Hewell Road was much more prestigious than the old factory at Hunt End. Across the front of the new building was an impressive suite of offices where about 150 people worked. The managing director was here, plus the works manager and the buyer, also the general office and the comptometer department which looked after the finances such as general accounts and wages.

Three parallel bays ran backwards at right angles to the offices. It is not possible to say what area was used for what, as the factory kept changing round, but there was always an enormous machine shop, plus a polishing shop and a plating department (nickel electro-plating only as chrome had not been invented). The first floor was a huge balcony, running the whole circuit, and open to the ground floor. The western side of the balcony comprised the various stores departments and the eastern side held the assembly departments. The whole of the rear part of the first floor was occupied by the enamelling department for cycles.

The assembly department was divided into different sections such as the frame assembly, where the frames were built and braised up and the wheel assembly shop where the spokes were fitted to the rims and the wheels 'trued'. The frames then went from the frame assembly to the enamelling department.

When component parts were finished they were sent to the stores, a large department which ran the whole length of the assembly department. The stores sorted these parts into individual bicycles or motor bikes, each of which was then issued as one unit.

Protruding from the front of the offices, to the north-west, was the toolroom. Parallel to this was a separate block used as a machine shop. Between this and the sports field was another separate block, the service department. Small ancillary buildings were used by maintenance personnel, carpenters and so on.

An enormous new building was erected in about 1920 which was almost as large as the previous factory and the test track combined. I believe I am correct in saying that the shell of the building had then been completed but no machinery had been moved in, because, soon after I was demobbed in 1919, a reunion of all ex-servicemen was organised and this was the only place in Redditch found to be large enough to hold everyone.

For some reason, probably because of the lie of the land, the rear half of this new building was about four inches higher than the front half. The rear half was larger and was one big shop containing a number of smaller departments such as the enamelling and the frame building departments and a huge machine shop over all the works. The new building was used chiefly for motor bikes; pushbikes remained in the older building. The motor bike industry was then developing but the majority of the population could not afford a motor bike and still relied on a pushbike as their main means of transport, so this industry continued to thrive. Royal Enfield were producing 600 or 700 cycles each week.

The bike-testing track was also enlarged and improved soon after the war. The test shop had two junior testers, three senior testers, a foreman tester and they came under a head of department. Every machine was taken round the bike-testing track, it then went into the factory for adjustment and this was followed by a thorough test on the road for twelve to fifteen miles. The petrol was removed from the tank, the machine cleaned and sent to the motorcycle despatch department where it was carefully wrapped by the ladies. Immediate orders were despatched, others were taken into stock and dealt with as required. Cycles and motor bikes were despatched either by train, when they were taken by lorry to Redditch station, or by our own haulage system which was a fleet of specially adapted lorries.

By the end of the 1920s, the site covered eighteen acres, eight of which were under glass.

Royal Mail sidecars ready for delivery in 1924.

The Royal Enfield factory, circa 1928.

The bikes of the twenties

There isn't really much that I can say about the motorbikes themselves in the early 1920s because Royal Enfield just continued to produce the two models which had been made during the war, the 2¼hp two-stroke lightweight and the 6hp sidecar combination.

As the site developed, so the range of models increased so that by 1924 we were offering four versions of the 2¼hp two-stroke, two new JAP-engined 350s and two versions of the 8hp Vickers-engined sidecar combination.

Those sidecars were a marvellous job, made from Armenian white wood and plywood. Sidecar manufacture was in a department of its own under the supervision of Jack George, the foreman. The design of the sidecar and chassis was quite revolutionary in that it could be detached in minutes by just undoing two bolts, one at the front and one at the back; very simple.

During 1925 or 1926 I worked on the last thirty of the 424cc (3hp) ohiv V-twin models with the Swiss Motosacoche engine. The only model of this bike which I know to be in existence today (and which was probably assembled by me) is in the National Motor Museum at Beaulieu. The bike was too advanced for its day and the management couldn't charge enough to make it a viable concern. Assembling these was the worst job in the factory. They were the most difficult to assemble and the lowest paid, you couldn't get your money on them.

Pride in the job

I found, at Royal Enfield, a loyal, enthusiastic and committed workforce. Everyone took a pride in their work, for example, if you went to talk to the women who were putting spokes on the wheels they would hold their work up for you to admire. We took great pleasure in the knowledge that our bikes were exported to countries all over the world. We used to say that the sun never set on an Enfield bike.

My first job was that of fitting linoleum on to each motorcycle footboard, which was suspended on two bars. This work was considered to be the lowest of the low but I did not mind, I was grateful for any job. However, I was determined not to remain there and to acquire sufficient skills to obtain a job in the engine assembly department. I therefore paid a senior member of that department to teach me the various necessary skills such as valve and ignition timing. When I had become proficient I approached the head of the motorcycle department, George Wakelam, for a job in assembly, with the vision of a gradual climb upward.

When I first started, everything was quite primitive. If you went into the workshops you would see a great many whirling belts driven by overhead pulleys. The girls had to wear caps because if their hair became caught up in a belt they would have been more than scalped. The belts were made from leather and the ends were laced together with metal clips. You had to be careful that you didn't catch the sleeve of your overall in them. Occasionally the clips used to come apart and the belt thrashed dangerously about. We all did our own shoe repairs in those days and we used to try and get hold of a bit of leather belt to resole our shoes. There were still a few of these old belts left in the 1950s.

It must be remembered that the bike industry, especially with regard to motor bikes, was relatively new and therefore the assembly line was very basic. Each assembler collected a frame from the frame stores, two wheels from the wheel stores and a box of components from the general stores, and stood at a trestle table and put them together. They were then wheeled up a ramp to another department to have the tanks, saddle and handlebars fitted. The sub-assembly was now complete and from here they went to the main assembly for the engine and gears to be fitted.

We started at eight am in the morning and at five to eight the bulls (hooters) would sound for all the main factories – Enfield, BSA, Alcock's, Terry's, Abel Morrall's and Henry Milward's – and would go on, making a great racket, until eight o'clock. Each bull varied slightly in the noise that it made so that you always knew which one was yours. Each factory employed several hundred people, both male and female, so that before eight o'clock in the morning, the whole of the centre of Redditch including Prospect Hill and Mount Pleasant, would be crowded with people hurrying to work, it was worse than Blackpool beach on a hot day, then after work had started the streets would be empty.

At eight o'clock the gates were locked and if you were late you had to go through a little wicket gate at the side. You were fined 1d or 2d, according to how late you were, and this was docked from your wages at the end of the week. Discipline was very strict, there was no smoking and the pay was deplorable, the average wage was between 30 shillings (£1.50) and £2 10s (£2.50). The latter was a hell of a good job.

The washing facilities at the end of each working period consisted of one bucket brought on to the shop floor. There were thirty-six people on the floor and the thirty-sixth person to use it was washing his hands in a bucket of sludge. However, it wasn't long after the First World War that proper washbasins were installed.

Of gears and cush drives

Each section was supervised by a chargehand, over him was a foreman and he, in turn, was responsible to a superintendent who was in charge of the whole department. The factory was run by the works manager, these days he would be called the chief executive. At the top there was, of course, the managing director, R W Smith.

R W Smith, one of the founders of the company, was a prominent engineer of that time. If there was a problem on

The original Enfield test track, probably before 1920.

1924 8hp twin, with Enfield's own engine. The prototype machine.

the shop floor, it would be investigated by the managers concerned, but it was usually solved by R W Smith. He would look at it for a couple of minutes, then he would have it solved.

He was always bursting with new ideas and would visit the design department, rapidly draw a squiggle or two and give it to them to sort out. Two of his inventions revolutionised motor bikes, the one was the cush drive, which improved starting and the other was the cam-operated two-speed gear which was used on motor bikes for many years until it was superseded by the Sturmey-Archer three-speed box. R W Smith also designed a ladies' motor bike which was really revolutionary, the fact that it didn't have a crossbar meant that the whole frame had to be redesigned.

He was one of the engineering elite of that period. It was rumoured that he was well in with Henry Ford. I have no idea as to whether this was true or not but I do know that he was always going over to America. I also know that Lord Nuffield was a great buddy of his who came regularly to the factory. I think he acted as an agent for us. Lord Nuffield always wore a navy-blue suit which looked as if it had been polished.

When R W Smith retired, he had a little office made for himself within the offices at the front of the factory and he spent his days there with an industrial chemist by the name of Gibbs, with whom he had worked in Coventry in his early days.

His eldest son, Frank Walker Smith, joined Royal Enfield in 1909 at the age of 21, then at the outbreak of war he left to join the Royal Artillery and returned as Major. We all knew him as Major Smith. From then onwards he virtually ran the show.

From the end of the First World War until about 1960, the works manager was Tommy Guise. He was a typical hard case and a stern disciplinarian. We had to ensure that we were not doing anything out of line when he was around. The workers signalled his approach by coughing twice. Guise was

Tommy Guise, the efficient works manager, and Lou Hadley, recruited from Wolseley, on a military 6hp.

35

tough as old iron on the outside, but he could be quite soft on the inside.

I remember one incident where a man who worked in the sidecar department was found guilty of smoking and sent to Guise for disciplinary action. There had to be a very strict prohibition because of the highly inflammable solvents used, such as cellulose and amyl acetate. Guise said that if this man was found smoking once more, he was to be dismissed. The foreman again found him smoking and sacked him on the spot. When Guise was told, he said, 'You can't sack that bloke, he's got a son who's mentally subnormal', and so the punishment was rescinded.

A well-known face at the factory during the 1930s was Walter Freeman, the Olympic star marathon runner. He had just an ordinary job on the shop floor in motor assembly. When he was about to depart for his Olympic run we had a whip round and bought him a bottle of sherry to see him on his way. Later, the management presented him with a motor bike in recognition of his successes.

Both the assembly shop and the testing department were under the supervision of Fred Bicknell. He was one of the most eminent trial riders of his day and so he was often away at national and international events. He could always be relied upon to put a Royal Enfield bike amongst the leaders. The top speed of a trials mount was only about 50mph but the bikes were considered to be phenomenal. Technology was being stretched to its limits.

Fred did so much for the company that we nicknamed him 'Mr Royal Enfield'. He made Royal Enfield what it is. He used to come back from these various events saying something like, 'I don't think the rear springing on this bike is quite right'. Then he would take the bike to pieces, alter it and put it together again. That's how the swinging arm developed.

In later years I was sometimes persuaded, against my better judgement, to be a sidecar passenger; including the time when Fred Bicknell took part in the TT races. I would see some great obstacle and call out, 'Surely we're not going over that!' and over we would go! Racing with a sidecar was much more difficult than racing without, so with the usual perversity of humanity, the courses were made even more difficult for combination racing.

Many of those who worked at the Enfield went on to found their own businesses and companies and some did very well in life, for example, John Hill who set up an MGB/Triumph centre in Lakeside, and the head of our service department, Jack Spencer, who later became Chairman of Redditch Borough Council.

GILBERT HUNT: from 1922 to 1933

I can remember, when I was about five or six (I was born in 1908), sitting at the side of the road opposite the Enfield factory and watching all these strange black vehicles drive out of the factory. They had large wheels, a long body and a small hood at the rear end. I realised in later years, that these had been the early cars.

For some strange reason which I could never understand, when I was thirteen I was allowed to

Capstan Section. Aluminium turning. Foreman (in suit) is Solly Knight.

leave school providing I worked on a farm for a year. By the time I was fourteen and able to leave farm work, I was motor bike mad. My parents were then, in 1922, renting a house in Callow Hill and a neighbour of ours was Major Smith who was living at Callow Hill House. He now found me a job at Royal Enfield in Redditch, 2½ miles away, a distance which I had to walk twice daily.

Like my brother, Major Smith wanted me to go into the toolroom but I was having none of that. I wanted to work on the bikes themselves so I went into the assembly department under George Wakelam where I worked with Vic Bott. We fitted the magneto with chain and timing to the 8hp engine which was bought in from J A Prestwich.

I'm proud to say that I had a part to play in the 1925 Isle of Man TT races, as I helped to build the bike which was ridden by Stanley Woods. It was a 3½hp, fitted with a JAP overhead valve, Sturmey-Archer 3-speed gear box and expanding hub brakes. It would have won but Stanley fell off and bent the handlebars so that the bike was disqualified and he was waved off the course. I later bought a smaller version for my own use, with a 23/4hp engine.

For some years after the First World War, Royal Enfield only mass-produced two models, one with the twin JAP engine and one with the 2-stroke 225cc engine. The management then decided to start work on another model which they called the 'Z', later rechristened the Cycar (see p53). This was a cheap but sturdy little bike, with a two-stroke engine and a gear box with two speeds only and as it was only 146cc it qualified for tax concessions brought in by the Government round about 1932. It was quite different to any other bike at that time as the engine and all the central working parts were covered by a pressed steel frame and it was, perhaps, the first streamlined bike to be launched. The price was only about £24. A more expensive 8hp version was made with handlebars which were fitted with springs and bounced up and down.

Despite working on motor bikes all day, I never lost my fascination for them and every Friday evening I used to go up to Hall Green dirt track and watch Jack Booker ride, he was one of our testers. The craze for dirt track racing started in Australia and when all the races had finished, the course was cleared for an Australian (I think his name was Dick Smythe) on a Douglas machine, made at Bristol, to have a go at the world speed record. The cycling boom was on in the early 1930s (I was 25 or 26) and cycle assembly had more work than they could cope with, whereas we were only working three days a week on the motor bikes under Fred Bicknell. I did not want to move from my work with motor bikes but when I bumped into Tommy Guise and he offered me a job working all hours, I felt that I had to accept.

I can recall quite clearly R W Smith, the co-founder and managing director. When I

Gilbert Hunt on a 350cc JAP engined model in 1925. This was the first Enfield to be fitted with internal expanding hub brakes. The picture was taken in front of Major Smith's house.

worked there he was a very slender man, and he always wore a smart, light suit.

In 1914 R W Smith's son, Major Smith, was appointed joint managing director. I am sure that R W Smith was an extremely proud father, especially as Major Smith's teenage years had been quite turbulent, he had been a lively teenager and fanatical about motor bikes but these were attributes which stood him in good stead when he joined the army and he did very well there. The last time I saw him he must have been in his seventies and he was riding a 692cc Constellation, still going to work.

MAJOR SMITH: by Jean Russell-Jones, his daughter

My father was the eldest of four sons of R W Smith and was born on 7 August 1886. He was educated at Bourne College in Quinton and Birmingham University and served an apprenticeship with R W Ward and BSA, joining the Enfield Cycle Company in 1909. He served in the Royal Artillery Territorials prior to 1914 being taught to ride a horse by Mr Langley who later taught me, and in 1915 became a pilot in the Royal Flying Corps. A local paper, under the heading, 'Prominent Trade Men in the RFC', described him as 'one of the many motor-cyclists in the Flying Corps'. He was in the Territorial Army for many years, receiving the Territorial decoration for 25 years' service and he commanded the Company's Home Guard during the war.

My father became joint managing director of the Enfield Cycle Company with R W Smith in 1914 and sole managing director on the death of his father in 1933. He became chairman in 1935. At that time, too, he was President of the Birmingham Chamber of Commerce and a member of the Council of the British Cycle and Motor Cycle Industries Association. We had badges saying 'Buy British and Support British Trade'. During World War II the company made armaments as well as bikes. In recognition of this, my father was awarded a CBE in 1949.

He took an interest in everything and everyone connected with the Enfield Cycle Company. He was a strict disciplinarian who extolled the benefits of military service. For instance, he was very proud of the works Fire Brigade but said it was a pity they had not all been in the army! He had respect for the feelings of the employees who were not exactly overpaid. While he, obviously, for the sake of the business, liked to appear prosperous, he did not wish to appear ostentatious.

My father was a keen motorcyclist all his life and I imagine in his youth he was a bit of a dare-devil, driving motor bikes and cars as fast as possible. On one occasion he rode a motorbike down Unicorn Hill to see how fast he could go and still turn right into Windsor Street. Unfortunately, there was a coal lorry in the way. He was lucky to escape with a broken nose. He encouraged us to ride bikes, horses and motorbikes. He had a small motorbike made for my brother when he was six. Later he acquired a small French one which we both rode round the garden. They were amalgamated into one small bike which all the children of the family rode until about twenty years ago.

It was my father's dare-devil attitude and casual approach to his well-being that brought about his final illness. At the ripe age of 73 he was trying out a new golf cart at Stoneleigh Golf Club and was pushing it uphill when it fell back on him. Although he was in pain, he insisted on attending a director's meeting. A few days later he was admitted to Leamington Hospital with septicaemia but the medical team couldn't find the source of the infection. By the time they discovered that he had broken his hip, it was too late to save him.

My father was much loved by friends and family who were greatly saddened by his death. Five hundred people attended his funeral with hundreds more outside the church. The vicar said, 'Life had many honours and distinctions for him, but he was a kindly and friendly man and this was greater than all the honours which came his way. I can pay no finer tribute than to say that'.

WALLY POWELL: from 1917 to 1962

Wally Powell gave this contribution in January 1995, a week before he died. Although he was very ill and in some pain, he was still making amusing comments. Many people remember him as one of the characters of the Enfield, always ready with a smile and a joke. He said:

Everyone at Royal Enfield knew my face, in fact I was well known everywhere because I was the groundsman. I knew R W Smith and Major Smith very well. They often called me into their office to ask me to look after their gardens. At that time there were only four groundsmen and this meant that we had a lot of work. We were responsible for all mowing, the removal of litter, tree maintenance, reed cultivation and so on.

I was born in 1902 and was one of sixteen children. Allowed to leave school at thirteen, it was on condition I worked on the land. When I was fifteen I left farm work and joined my father at the Royal Enfield factory in Redditch. The site was then only about six acres but the following year they bought another two or three acres and the year after that they added another couple. When I first went there the site was very disorganised with piles of stuff everywhere but they soon pulled themselves together and got things running smoothly.

We were provided with a good range of implements to help us in our work. Of course, we always had a Royal Enfield mower. Our first mower was a tiny thing, no bigger than a large piece of writing paper but as time went on the motor mowers got bigger and better until eventually I had one which ran on four small wheels. Mowers were made at Redditch and I remember them being loaded a dozen at a time on to lorries and taken to the station.

I stayed at Royal Enfield until I retired in about 1962, by which time the site covered about 30 acres and its maintenance had become quite a large enterprise.

Wally Powell (nearest camera) doesn't look too happy about helping out in the motorcycle enamelling department. Foreman, in hat, is Tommy Chapman, ex-racing cyclist.

CHAPTER TWO
Almost a Life Sentence

The toolroom, 1926.

DOLLY: from 1928 to 1953

Most of the famous bikes have been wrapped by me, I wrapped Prince Charles' pushbike which was presented to the Duke of Edinburgh in 1953 and the bikes which went off to compete in trials. Jack Booker liked me to pack a large box of spares to go with his trials bikes.

I worked at Royal Enfield for twenty-five years in all, from 1928 until 1953. My home is only a stone's throw from the factory site. I was born and bred here, one of eight children. On top of this my mother took in our three cousins when they lost their mother, they were going to have to go into an orphanage but she insisted that they lived with us instead. Our house only had three bedrooms, one large and two small. My parents slept in the large bedroom with my sister and me in the corner (we were the two youngest), while a smaller bedroom contained one bed with six children in it, three the one end and three the other! When we were older the boys slept in one room and the girls in the other. We were not all at home for long, one elder sister and a cousin went into service at thirteen then other members of the family got married. However, one of my cousins was so happy here that he stayed with my mother until he was over forty!

Although there were eleven children and my father was only a farm labourer, we were never short of food. We had a garden and an allotment looked after by the lads which provided vegetables all the year round. We kept two pigs and we always had a fitch of bacon hanging down the stairwell with muslin over it. My dad often came home with a couple of rabbits and we also kept fowl.

Two of my sisters, Edith and Florrie, were also wrapping bikes at Royal Enfield. We didn't all work there at the same time, Edith and Florrie were at Enfield's first, then Edie left to get married in 1928 and I took her place. Florrie left after a dispute – the management wanted her to work over to wrap an important bike but she had had nothing to do all day and the bike arrived at five thirty just when it was time for her to go home, so she went. Tommy Guise gave instructions that she was to be sacked, but I must say that she was re-employed some years later. When she left I was the only employee wrapping motor bikes but I coped, I could manage twenty-five or even thirty a day.

Vic Bott used to inspect the motor bikes, then Jo Adams would wheel them out of the assembly shop, down the yard and into the despatch department where I wrapped them. Sometimes, the work was very heavy, especially when they had to be boxed and crated, but Bert Harris was very kind and helped me a great deal. After the bikes had been packed, Harry Andrews drove them to the station.

1953. Major Smith presents the Duke of Edinburgh with a child's bike for Prince Charles.

A farthing a bike

Wrapping a bike in the early 1930s was quite complex. Every part was wrapped in brown paper and, in addition, the number plates and tank were covered with corrugated paper, the lights had to be covered in felt and the tank had a special cover fitted. For doing all this I received 15s 7½d (78p) per hundred. I told Oliver Wythes that I wanted a rise. He said, 'Why? – You've been happy with your pay so far,' and I answered back, 'Yes, and I'm just waking up!' He did give me a rise – a farthing per bike!

The bikes for export were packed differently and for these I received 3¼d (1½p) per bike. Each one had to be taken apart by Jack Moss, who worked with me, then fitted either into crates or boxes. For a crate, the bike was packed almost complete with just the headlamp, rear lamp and handlebars removed, whereas only the frame, engine and tank went into a box.

During the war the radio was switched on for half-an-hour in the afternoon for 'Music While You Work'. It used to scare me when the sirens went. I just used to carry on working. I heard the bomb which dropped in Glover Street one Friday afternoon.

I worked there for twenty-five years in all and I enjoyed every minute. Although the managers were very strict, they were quite compassionate, for example, when my sister was ill in Barnsley Hall Hospital, my foreman, Joe Yates, let me have Monday afternoons off for ages so that I could go and visit her. Royal Enfield was just like a big family. When I go up town now, I bump into people that I used to know there and we always stop and have a chat, it's like meeting a long-lost relative. Everyone was so friendly and we all used to help each other.

HARRY HUGHES: from 1921 to 1969

My brother, Les, and I clocked up 100 years of service at Royal Enfield between us. Les had a gold watch for fifty years' service but I was made redundant just six months before my fifty years was up. My brother was older than me and began working as an apprentice at Enfield's when he was only 13 during the First World War, making shell cases which then went off elsewhere to be filled.

Working at Royal Enfield meant that you had a fairly regular job and were not in and out of work as in other firms. The company also had a reputation for a happy environment, although some of the pranks went a bit too far. One day, some blokes caught hold of my brother and

put itching powder down the back of his shirt. It nearly drove him mad. My mother had to strip and bath him and wash all his clothes. In the early days the toilets were a row of twelve cubicles with no doors on them and a gulley of water running along the bottom. Occasionally, someone used to fold a newspaper into a boat and let it sail along the gulley, having first set fire to the top. There used to be a shout from first one cubicle, then another.

By the time the Second World War came, I had graduated to the cost office where I handled the claim forms which came from the Ministry. Filling them in was a full-time job as Enfield's made a terrific contribution to the war. They had developed various brilliant devices, among them the oil units for Bofor guns which were operated by the sound of a plane. Whichever way the sound came from, the gun faced that way and fired at the noise.

Eventually I was put in charge of the cost office. Mr Wagstaff (the son of the works policeman) and I did the wages for the workers, there were just over a thousand from the 1920s onwards. The workers were on piece work, they had time on the job plus whatever they had done. Only the labourers had standard wages. In the 1920s the average wage was about £2 10s (£2.50), and this was about the same in the 1930s. In the 1940s and 1950s the average wage had gone up to about £4 10s (£4.50), rising to about £11 in the 1960s.

Nothing changed very much over the years. People seemed quite happy with what they had got, they didn't have the expectations which they have today.

The pre-war cost office.

'KIPPER' GIBBS (Les): from 1929 to 1968

One of the difficulties in working at a local family company is that once you get a nickname, you never lose it. When I was a toddler, my next-door neighbour called me 'Kipper' and as Vic Mountford and Oliver Wythes lived in the same road, together with a few other Enfield employees, everyone continued to call me 'Kipper' when I started work at the Enfield factory. To this day, and I'm approaching eighty, everyone calls me 'Kipper' and no-one knows my Christian name.

In total I worked for Royal Enfield for 28 years, starting in 1929 and finishing in 1968, with a ten-year gap during the war. I just fitted in where I was needed, I think I have done every job except spidering (fitting spokes to wheels). My first job was greasing the motor bikes before they were despatched.

After the war, one of my jobs was to put 250 miles on the clock of all the old G-type 350s which had been manufactured for use in the army. These bikes were very popular with the soldiers in Cyprus, and if the mileage was over 250 they didn't have to pay tax on them.

Another job of mine was fitting the sidecars on to a J500 motorbike for the Milk Marketing Board. We did hundreds and they went all over England. The MMB collected them as fast as I managed to assemble them. I found that I had to teach some of the riders to drive a combo. More than one turned the first corner and went straight into a wall!

Sometime during the 1950s I spent about twelve months working on three-wheelers. I assembled these on my own in my own department. They had a little two-stroke engine and they were rather like a stop-me-and-buy-one. We sold a few to local people, for example there was a newsagent from

The assembly line in the 1940s.

Feckenham who used to deliver the papers in one. They were only in production for about twelve months.

A big change came in the mid 1950s when an assembly track was installed and I was one of about ten who worked on it. As each bike came off the track I fitted the exhaust pipe and finished it off, giving it a quick check over and fitting any parts that had been missed off.

The competition shop had a crisis in about 1965 and I was asked to help out. One of the drivers from the despatch department had taken all the competition bikes down to Earl's Court, but he hadn't bothered to fasten them in with the wooden struts which separated each bike. Just before he got to Earl's Court he had to brake sharply and the bikes, which had taken many months to prepare, all ended up in a heap at one end of the van. The driver had to bring the bikes back to Royal Enfield and we had to do them all up again. It was a terrible rush to get them ready for the show. The driver got the sack.

I owned a 500cc Bullet which had a very interesting history, it was a prototype of the 500 Bullet which was supplied to Madras. As I had helped to build it, I had an affection for it so I bought it. The registration number was, I'm fairly sure, AUY 317. It was a lovely thing, one of the managers got us a sidecar specially to match and my wife and I went all round England on it.

When Royal Enfield closed down I went to work at Dunlop's. By a strange coincidence, the Redditch branch of Dunlop's was using Givry Works, the first Enfield factory at Hunt End. Here comes my claim to fame. I was the last person to work in Givry Works. I had been working there for about three years when, one very ordinary Saturday afternoon, I was working late and was the last to finish. I locked up and went home, and later that day, the works went up in the most spectacular fire. That was the end of the Hunt End factory. The site was cleared and is now a small industrial site.

JACK POWELL: from 1923 to 1967

I started work at the Enfield in 1923 when I was about eighteen. My wages then were £2 a week and that was a lot of money in those days. I had to hand most of it to my mother to keep me. Times were hard in the 1920s. If you looked up from your machine for a moment the foreman would come down and tell you to keep your eyes on your work. You had to keep your machine spotlessly clean and oil it five or six times a day.

First I was milling, then grinding, after this I was asked go into the toolroom. Enfield made quite a number of models and each one required a lot of jigs, fixtures and tools to be made. The toolroom foreman was a very important person, a great deal depended upon him and from 1920 until the factory closed these were, in order, Harry Robinson, Les Purser, Reg Gibbs and Jack Clements.

I did quite a lot of competition work for Charlie Rogers. I liked him very much, he was a decent fellow, a friendly chap

Milk Marketing Board J2s with sidecars leaving factory.

and very popular, He was tallish, about five feet ten with brown hair and he was a very good trials rider. Later in life he was in charge of the competition shop and he worked on the bikes for the trials.

Even in 1923 Enfield's had excellent sporting facilities, which just suited me, as I was very keen on the sporting side. There was a football pitch, a cricket pitch, three tennis courts, a bowling green and they even had a shooting team. I was a member of the cricket team and the angling club. Royal Enfield owned waters at Hillborough and I used to go over every weekend during the season on my bicycle. I fished at several all-England championships, representing Redditch, from the Enfield.

During the war most of my time was spent grinding big ends for the military bikes – I used to grind about 600 or 700 a week, besides other work for military purposes. We all used to work very hard during the war. We would start at seven in the morning and not finish until seven in the evening or even later, I've often worked until eleven. Although we were supposed to finish at one on Saturdays, I've often worked Saturday afternoons. Then one night a week we would have to be back at seven to be on duty for the Enfield Auxiliary Fire Service.

I worked at Enfield's for a total of 43 years and during this time I bought several bikes. My first was an '148cc overhead', followed by three 250cc's one after the other, then a CO army bike which had been returned unused when the war finished. My last bike was a Royal Enfield prototype single cylinder 250 Crusader, registration 131 GWP, with airflow enclosure at the front end and with the rear half enclosed in a fibreglass casing which could be raised and used as a boot. Reg Thomas designed it but it never went into production. I sold it and a few years ago a motor museum in Japan paid £1,500 for it.

The Enfield Cycle Company closed on 21st November 1967, and, after thirty years in the toolroom, I was made redundant. My wages then were just over £18 a week. Before the factory closed, we were allowed time off to look for jobs. I was offered, and accepted, a job in the toolroom of BSA, but I much preferred Royal Enfield.

LOUISE CHALLICE: from 1926 to 1942

About twenty or thirty people worked in the welding and brazing department, both men and women. I was one of the female welders. I started in 1926 when I was 14, welding, spot welding and brazing. While we worked, we sang. During the twenties we would sing the Flanagan and Allen songs and the Gracie Fields songs. During the war it would be Vera Lynn. Although we could sing, we were not allowed to talk.

When you worked at Enfield, you were allowed to buy a cycle at cost price so I bought a racing bike on graduated payments and had 2/6d (just over 12p) stopped out of my wages every week until I had paid for it. In those days, if you possessed a bike you were considered to be rich. I joined Redditch Road and Path Club. About twenty or thirty of us from Enfield's would be in the club, but then perhaps we might join up with BSA or another firm.

When I met my husband I changed my racing bike for a tandem. Tandems were very popular in the late 1930s, many couples bought one and they remained very popular for about ten years. Then, when my daughter was born, I changed it for a single bike with a carrier on it which held my daughter.

I really enjoyed my years at Royal Enfield. We used to get up parties to go to the theatre. In the 1950s the *Sound of Music* came out and a coach-load of us went to see that. We used to go to the pantomime every Christmas. I was sorry to leave in 1930 when I had my first baby, and I went back part-time in 1938 for four years. Royal Enfield had a happy atmosphere and, although you were on piece work, the speed was not as fast as it is today. They wanted quality, not rubbish.

WALTER DEAKINS: from 1926 to 1966

When I left school in 1926 you had a choice of three jobs, it was Enfield's, Terry Springs or Heath Springs. I went to the Enfield. I was 14 and started as a labourer in the enamelling shop under Tommy Chapman, taking the finished work out of our shop and into the stores. I stayed in that department for 40 years and eventually became foreman.

Many of the motor bike and cycle parts could not be dipped in the enamel tank for various reasons, either the part was too small or, if it had small holes they would be clogged up. Those parts had to be sprayed with a hand-held spray. Motor bikes were mainly dipped although the smaller bits and pieces had to be sprayed: the spraying department was to the right as you went in.

Next was the lining department where Harry Knight worked, he put the lines on the bikes for over thirty years. He was a short stiff man, a very nice person and all the lines were done freehand. Then came transferring, where four or five women fixed the transfers on the bikes. The badges for the petrol tanks were also painted here, in the early 1950s we tended to get behind on this work so occasionally I had to take them home with a tin of paint and spend the evening painting them. I would say that we did approximately two hundred motor bikes but can't say how many push bikes each week, perhaps a thousand.

My wages hardly went up at all in 1952 when I was made foreman because, like most other workers, I had been on piece work which pushed my wages up and when I was made foreman I was on a flat rate.

For two years during the war very little enamelling was done and so I was transferred to the shell-making department where I was grinding 2lb shells to size, working from 8am until 7pm every day, then I had my duties in the Home Guard. My wife was working and we hardly saw each other, I went out just as she came in. I had to go on Fire Watching, evening meetings, Sunday morning parades and practice drills. The Home Guard was drilled with great enthusiasm by Edward Spiers from the wheel-building shop. He was a full-blown Sergeant Major!

The Enfield cycles were excellent. My brother-in-law had one forty years ago, I recently noticed it in his garage and I thought it was a new one, it was in such good condition. My wife and I had an Enfield bike each which we bought for just under £4. When we had the children we changed to a Royal Enfield tandem and we put a sidecar on it. Yes, the Enfield cycles were excellent, particularly with regard to the enamelling!

The prototype Crusader, with Airflow front fairing and fibreglass rear enclosure designed by Reg Thomas.

JOHN LATTER: from 1926 to 1939

Redditch in 1926 was set in lovely countryside; a small town on the side of a hill. In those days, if you couldn't get a job when you left school you could go back to school for a bit and this is what I did. I wanted an office job but as I couldn't get one I went back for three months. Then a message came from 'Bones' Keyte in the engine shop that he had a lad off sick if I wanted a job for a week. At the end of the week I was put in the motorcycle assembly shop, this was above the lad that I had stood in for which I didn't think was fair but there wasn't much that I could do about it.

The actual tyre fitting was the 'star show', as this was one of the things that visitors to the works were shown, and most of them couldn't believe their eyes. You put a bit of wind in the tubes, tucked the tube into the tyre, put the valve into the valve hole and with a circular sweep of your left hand you scooped the tyre on to the rim on the one side, then you had to do the other. It took a long time to learn how to do that. I didn't use any levers and the management seemed to think this was worth showing off! The stark reality was that

Welding and brazing department shown here in 1926. In the foreground is Louise Challice. The Foreman, Mr Cale, is in the centre of the photograph in a suit.

I had no time to use levers, since I was paid between three farthings and two pence per tyre, depending on size – but this included getting the tyres and tubes from the stores and then, after fitting them, inflating to the correct pressure.

I could fit about 30 tyres per hour but I didn't do these all day. I would finish a batch in a couple of hours then I would go on to something else. Sometimes I was on hubs, when I had to put the spindles and bearings in with Enfield's patent cush drive, which contained six rubbers. You pushed these upwards so that you could drop them into the hub, then you banged the sprocket in with a wooden mallet which forced the cush drive home.

I worked mainly on the 2¾ and 3hp's, then the 8hp's came in which were rather better paid, thanks to a bit of subtle negotiating on my part. Nobody had done them before and no price had been set, so they had to be booked as day work. The trick was to book enough day work to make up the amount you lost by not doing piece work.

Royal Enfield made all kinds of other odds and ends. They supplied Brough Superior with complete wheels and New Imperial with hubs only, as the Enfield cush drive was patented. It's probably not commonly known that Royal Enfield also manufactured lawnmowers, and I worked on the assembly of these for a while too.

The Brough Superior wheels were one of the worst, they were very low-priced and difficult. When a batch of these came through, I worked really hard that week and I earned less than a pound. Mr Bicknell said that he would book day work to make my money up but he would have to see Tommy Guise, the works manager, before he knew how much it would be. My money was made up to £4 or £5, I was very pleased!

I was on one job where I fitted the bits such as filler caps on the tanks, which meant that I often had to go to the enamelling department. In that department was the man who painted the gold lines on the tanks. He was a bit of a tippler and his hands shook. He would pick the paintbrush up and the paintbrush would be shaking, dip it in the paint and as it came out you wondered what was going to happen but he would then line the tank perfectly with a nice, regular oval.

The Enfield was a good place to work if you were keen on sport – they had about half a dozen soccer teams and excellent facilities – along with a soccer field, they had a bowling green, tennis courts, etc. They also had a field hockey team, in which I was one of the stars – we had the best works team in Birmingham district.

We also had, as you know, another motorcycle firm in Redditch – this was a division of BSA, and you can imagine the rivalry between the firms, especially on the sports field. Most of the time it was good clean competition but one game in the 1920s got so vicious with so many injuries that it had to be abandoned.

For about ten years, between about 1930 and 1940, I was very keen on cycle racing. My dad had been Midland Counties Champion for cycle track racing (one mile and five miles) and had won stacks of prizes which he sold to offset his expenses. The foreman of the enamelling shop was Tom Chapman, a well-known Midland racing cyclist, and he took an interest in me. He heard that I was going to buy a special light-weight racing bicycle and he suggested that I got one from the Enfield. I pointed out that the Enfield didn't make one, so he got one specially made for me, the Enfield bought in all the materials specially. The frame was much lighter and the wheels were made from wood and cane. The tyres were stuck on with a special glue. I had to pay for the materials but they only cost £3 whereas the bike I had thought of buying was £13.

I won a great many local club races on that cycle, many of them organised by the Redditch Road and Path Club. My proudest moment was, I think, when I won the President's Cup, presented and given by Major Smith, a 25-mile race from Astwood Bank to Evesham and back.

Before I left, I was asked to show Kipper Gibbs how to do my job as he was taking over. Although you didn't use levers to put the tyres on, sometimes wheels were returned with a fault or a puncture, then you needed a pair of levers to get them off. I gave him my good pair which had belonged to my father. A fortnight later I happened to bump into him and he had a black eye. He told me that when he tried to remove a tyre, the levers had slipped and hit him in the face.

EDDIE WRIGHT: from 1925 to closure

The Enfield factory buildings were as familiar to me as my own home. I have had a hand in most of the building work since 1925 when I started as an apprentice in the carpenter's shop, learning joinery and general building work. I moved to the Enfield from the Birmingham Small Arms Company in Lodge Road, Redditch (originally the Eadie Manufacturing Company) because BSA moved and the wages were so low I could not afford to travel to Small Heath. After experiencing the tough conditions of BSA I couldn't believe how lax the discipline was at Enfield's. There I saw people floating around with teacans and all sorts of things, this would not have been allowed at the BSA. Royal Enfield was much more free and easy.

I worked on the bench until 1936 when I became foreman, of what was known as the carpenters shop but it carried out all general building work. Then in the early 1940s I was appointed senior staff manager and sat on committees such as the forward planning committee. When the works engineer was dispensed with, I had half his work. Eventually, I also became manager of the packing department. By the 1950s I had a team of almost fifty working for me, including five bricklayers and ten painters.

I don't know how some people existed on their wages in those days. Enfield's was the sort of place where you were on short time for long periods. From about Easter to August you were working flat out from six in the morning until eight or nine at night but then during the winter months there were long periods when people were on half time or only working two or three days a week. When you were working full-time you weren't paid much, £3 or £4 was an excellent wage and the labourers got less than £2 a week.

Amongst our efforts was the huge decorated arch which spanned the centre of Redditch during the 1935 Silver Jubilee. It stretched right across the road, from where McDonalds is now, to Saint Stephen's Church. Two Belfast roof trusses were supported on a scaffold, placed side by side about eight feet apart and covered in sailcloth, then decorated with shields carrying the royal coat of arms, flags and bunting. The message was – what else but, 'Loyal Enfield Greetings to their Majesties'. These public events, such as the Silver Jubilee, the Coronation and the annual Redditch Carnival, were really something in those days.

Progression of building work

When I first joined the company the site covered about twenty acres and the office block and three large blocks of two-storey workshops had been built for some years, in 1906 or thereabouts. The main block

'Clocking on' – *as seen and drawn by Vic Bott.*

was nearing completion, having been built with temporary sides and ends which were moved as and when necessary. I helped with the final replacement of the temporary end and sides with a permanent structure, then with the fitting out of that building as an expansion of the machine shop, inspection area, service office and repair shop.

1930 saw further new building when the factory was extended over the other side of the work's road to occupy part of the allotments at the rear of the sports ground. The main purpose of this building was to move the sidecar shop etc from the main block and to provide a better service office and a larger export packing and despatch area. By this time, synthetic paints had arrived so that the sidecar shop required dust-proof paint and varnish rooms and a first attempt at air conditioning.

With the sidecar shop moved we were able to take the motorcycle assembly into that area, giving them much needed space. The tool room was then moved from number one machine shop into the area vacated by the motor assembly. All this created a lot of work for my department, building benches, stores, racks, bins of pigeon holes, etc.

Prior to 1934 we had our own source of power, a gas-producing plant on the south side of the test track. Coal was burnt using the slow combustion method whereby the resultant gas went through filter beds into a gasometer which provided power to drive three Westinghouse Electric Generators; Callow Baker was in charge of this operation. Each one must have been about eighteen feet long, eight or nine feet wide and about ten feet high, complete with steel ladders up to platforms at the top, all kept in pristine condition. I still remember seeing these splendid generators working away on their last Saturday morning and the sense of outrage I felt on Monday when the scrap men arrived to do their damndest.

The scrapping of the generators meant, of course, more electricity from the local power company, SWS at that time, and that meant upgrading the sub-station. This was done by dividing the old power house into two, one part to serve as the Number One sub-station. Therefore a number of cables and trenches had to be cut through the foundations of the generators which were made out of very strong concrete. By this time I was in charge of the works. I well remember the reluctance of our staff to keep going with the pneumatic drills when I was checking with the plans and I had to keep saying, 'Just another three inches deeper'. This sub-station is still in use.

Later in the 1930s we extended the plating and enamelling shops, also the cycle and despatch shops. A new polishing shop and a new wheel building shop were built. All these were two-storey buildings.

With the 1939-45 war came various extensions to the works: air raid shelters, new fire station and first aid rooms. Glass roofs had to be treated with bitumen and hessian, all to be camouflaged. It was found necessary to take over and convert other factories, and I had to supervise the conversions. A factory at Feckenham had to have new floors in and Compton's old needle mill in Clive Road had to be strengthened to hold heavy machinery, but our greatest test of ingenuity was the conversion of the old stone mine at Westwood, near Bath, seventy feet underground, into an efficient factory. One of our problems was that the floor level in the large, main chamber was not even, parts of it were ten or fifteen feet below other parts so that two-thirds of the machines were in a pit. We had a lot of fun and games with that.

For years it had been obvious that the work's canteen was getting out of date and needed replacing. Inspectors for the Ministry of Supply were very unhappy about it. Plans were produced and approved in about 1942, the appropriate building licenses were obtained and work started. A very smart new canteen with first class stores and kitchens was built, using a very good type of material. The bricks were Baggeridge Rustic multi-coloured facing bricks and the general appearance was very pleasing. It was awarded the Building of the Year certificate, Major Smith liked the bricks so much that he had a matching frontage added to the next building, which is now Trentham's.

About 1959 it was decided to scrap the various heating chambers and build a central boiler house with three large high pressure Thompson steam boilers. The site chosen was the former petrol and oil stores which meant the removal of seven large underground oil and petrol tanks.

I often bumped into R W Smith at the factory. I can remember a conversation that we had in the early 1930s, only a year or so before he died. The first was when I was supervising the moving of the boardroom and I was standing on the bare floorboards of the old boardroom, deep in thought, when R W Smith came in and said, 'What are you thinking about?' I explained that I had rolled up the carpet and had found a beautifully-made trap door between the joists, with brass hinges and a little brass ring handle. I couldn't think why on earth it should have been put there. R W Smith said, 'Oh I can explain that. In the early days we only had one telephone so on 'Board' days we just pulled it up through the floor.'

I also knew Tony Wilson-Jones, the technical manager, quite well, I remembered him from the BSA. Under the BSA apprenticeship scheme I had to do a month in different departments and I had one wretched spell in the sales office where Tony also worked. I didn't get on with the manager neither did Tony Wilson-Jones who wrote to Commander Herbert telling him how he (Wilson-Jones) could do a much better job than the manager. For this he got the sack. When I went to Enfield's who should I bump into but Wilson-Jones who had been appointed technical officer. He worked in a small area off the engine shop devoted to test beds, to put engines on for tests.

There is a story about Tony Wilson-Jones' first day at Royal Enfield. Tommy Guise introduced him to Harry Bowkett, the manager of the engine shop, then Tommy said 'I'm going to take Mr Wilson-Jones on a tour of the works and while I am away I want you to get together the sort of tools that you think he will need to do the tests on the engines'. When the tour had finished, Tommy Guise said to Harry Bowkett, 'Have you got the tools?' 'Oh, yes!' replied Harry and produced a bucket, a broom and a wheelbarrow. Tommy Guise let fly with appropriate language.

By the time the factory closed on 31st March 1867 the building had become dated. The cast iron columns in each bay restricted access for the larger modern vehicles and the ceilings were not high enough for fork lift trucks to stack stillages. The main staircase was late Victorian and really old-fashioned, furthermore, there was a problem with the foundations of the office block which was five inches out of the vertical so that the first floor sloped downwards towards the centre of the building. This was first noticed in the 1930 and although the slippage seemed to have stabilized – I measured it regularly and it never altered – the Redditch Development Corporation thought it best that the building should be demolished.

The powerhouse generators.

CHAPTER THREE
Into the thirties

The Cycar of the early 30s.

BERT WEDGEBURY: from 1928 to 1967

For over ten years, from 1928 until the war, I was a member of the 'Chainwheel Gang'. We did the basic work on the cycle assembly in the cycle finishing shop. We really were a gang and there was a great camaraderie among us. We all earned the same wage – because we were on an assembly line the office pooled our money. We worked like hell and if we got £3 a week apiece we thought we were rich.

I worked on the bikes on and off from 1928 until the factory closed and in all that time the basic method of production in the chainwheel department remained the same. All ten of us stood in a row, in front of us was the track, a wide belt moving along with bikes fitted upside down on pegs. The bike started off by the chainwheel being trued and the back mudguard fitted, the next chap put the chain on the wheel, put the back wheel in and adjusted it, tightening it down and making sure it was aligned. Off to the next member of the gang who fitted the front forks and lamp bracket, he also fitted the front mudguard, then the next man fitted the front wheel and two brakes (back and front). The bike was lifted off the track and stacked in racks in batches of 25 or 50. The handlebars were put in and connected up, then it was viewed. Afterwards they were taken in their batches to forwarding for despatch.

We were the mainstay of Royal Enfield. The popularity of the motorcycles waxed and waned but there was always a steady demand for cycles, we were rarely on short time. Each employee was allowed one bike a year a bit below the normal retail price and we were plagued by workers asking us to get them a bike.

Although there were about fifty models in all, from the Coventry Cross to the de Luxe models, Royal Enfield were

Where 'the Chainwheel Gang' reigned supreme. The bicycle assembly line.

always developing new ones. There were the dropped handlebars of the 1930s racing bikes, the lightweight bikes, then there was a flat bar with calliper brakes – because it was a lightweight cycle it needed a lighter brake. The cheapest bike was the Coventry Cross at £3.19s 6d (£3.98), on the handlebars it said 'Coventry Cross' and underneath, 'Made like a gun'.

I had worked at Royal Enfield for six months before I joined the chainwheel gang. I had been unemployed in 1928, you couldn't get a job anywhere. Fortunately, Oliver Wythes was a friend of the family and I was up town with my mother when Mr Wythes happened to come along. My mother asked if there was any chance of a job for me and Mr Wythes said, 'Send him down'. I started in the cycle stores, working from 7am until 6pm each weekday and from 7 until 12 noon on Saturdays. For those hours I received 9s 3½d per week (41p). I gave the lot to my mum and she gave me sixpence back. I went to the pictures for 3d and spent the other 3d on a bag of monkey nuts.

When I'd been in the stores for three months, I put in for a rise to make my wages up to 9s 6d (45p). I thought that was a lot of money, it seemed to go further in those days. After six months I applied for a change and that was when I was put in the chainwheel gang.

The cycle finishing shop was rarely on short time but strange to say, we were out on what we called a 'spiv' day when war was declared. All the chainwheel gang had gone fishing at Hewell Grange. I was in the local artillery and when I got home that same day there was a letter telling me to report to the local barracks. My mother greeted me with, 'There's a letter for you and I've put your uniform out ready'.

During my army years I went to Northern Ireland, to Italy with the Mountain Regiment, Castel Benito (Mussolini's stronghold), Cairo, then Sinai on the Great Western Front, joining up with Monty's Ironsides. However, my army career was interrupted by eight or nine months in 1941 when Enfield applied for Frank Masters and me to return for essential war work.

This essential war work was the testing of army motor bikes. We were a ragtag outfit, all ages, and abilities, anybody they could get hold of. You should have seen our outfits. Over our boots we would pull a pair of waders that had been handed down from tester to tester, as for coats, Reg Steel used to tell us to sort the best out from a pile of old clothes and they were all tattered and torn. We were often working until ten at night to get the military bikes through and these were the days of the blackout, the only lighting we had was a tiny little spotlight on our front and on our back.

For testing each bike we received 3d (6p) and for this we had to fetch it from assembly, take it into the test shop, set the tappets, see if the tuning was correct, put the petrol and oil in, get the bike going and run it for a bit, then get the bike warmed up round the track, set the tappets for the road test and give it a ten mile test on the road. If we went along the Slough into Studley and back down the Holloway it would put nine miles on the clock, then Reg Steel would put the extra mile on going round the track. He tested every bike before we got our money. We would have to take it back to the shop, drain the tank, take the oil out and remove the slave exhausts.

Reg Steel was a case, although he was alright really, I got on with him. He certainly knew his job, he had a wooden-handled screwdriver which he placed against the pot of the motor bike and after a second or two listening to it he would know straight away if the bike needed a new piston or a new barrel. I shall never forget the time I saw him go to start a bike and it kicked back, going up in the air, catching his leg. First he hopped round on one leg, then he took off his cap and slammed it down. (This was very unusual because Reg had a lump on his head and was never seen without his cap). As a grand finale he gave the motor bike a good kick with his hob-nailed boots.

Each dinner time he would choose a bike to go home on, he would say to one of us, 'put my number plates on that bike there', then he would get his old coat on, jump on the bike and go flat out. He had no mercy on the bikes, he would be in top gear as soon as he came out of the gates. Many a time he conked out, then the phone would go and one of the testers had to go down and bring him in. You'd go out on an 1140 twin with a coil of rope.

When I was demobbed in 1947, I eventually found myself back at the Enfield on cycle viewing, sitting outside the gaffer's office. Every cycle had to come to me to be viewed before it went out and from the tallies, I noriced that between 500 and 1,000 per year went to each of two places, Jan Lausanne of Switzerland and J P Burney, of Ireland who had the 'Irish Girder' built specially.

I was paid £1 per hundred, I viewed 80 or 90 a day and in all about 500 a week. I had to take a measuring stick along each bike, adjust the brakes, see the wheels were in true, tighten the wheel nuts and make sure that everything worked, then turn the bike over and try the three speed gear and the brakes. Every frame was stamped with a different number, I had to write the serial number in a book with a note as to what model it was. I filled a book every two weeks.

Everybody was on piece work and in a great hurry so that mistakes were often made. I used to have to stop the track, get the cycle off and send it back to be altered. Usually, if one cycle was found to be wrong the whole batch would be faulty.

The Time Office, where Eric Gibbs began, under Mr Moss (third from right).

In 1963 I was made redundant, but I managed to find myself a job at the High Duty Alloys, grinding, polishing and scurfing jet blades. If the Enfield paid me £3 I thought I was doing well, but at HDA I could make as much as £14 a week if I worked nights. The job was quite interesting as the technical expertise was in its infancy. However, I hated it. I was doing high temperature work and I couldn't stand all the hammering and banging. I was among strangers and I missed my friends at the Enfield. I stuck it out then I took voluntary redundancy just before I was 65.

ERIC GIBBS: from 1931 to 1947

When I was fourteen and due to leave school, my dad said to me, 'What are you thinking of doing lad?' I said that I wanted to work at the Enfield. So he said, 'Well, if I were you, I would go on the stool because that way you'll never be laid off and you will have fifty-two weeks' work'. That was in 1931, in those days, if you worked in an office you sat on a high wooden three-legged stool so it was called 'going on the stool'.

I started in the time office, a little brick building just to the right of the main gate, under the head commissionaire, Mr Moss. Many a time I've seen a fellow come cycling to work at 8 o'clock just as the bell went, but the big wooden gates were shut dead on time, his front wheel would hit the gate and he would be locked out for two or three days for being late. If he came the next day he wasn't allowed in.

Mr Moss lived just over the road from the main gate and every day at round about 10 o'clock his wife used to bring me over some thin arrowroot biscuits and cheese.

After two or three months I left the time office and became a progress clerk under Oliver Wythes. There were several progress clerks and we each had certain departments to look after, I was looking after the bikes. I had to keep an eye on them, making sure they went from one department to another without being held up.

I stayed there until I was almost twenty-one. I'd joined the company on the staff side and so the work I was doing wasn't really in my line. I asked Oliver Wythes if I could have an apprenticeship and he said that it would cost too much, so in 1938 I left to work as a grinder at BSA (Guns) down the Holloway in Redditch and I stayed there through most of the war.

My brother, Reg, worked at Enfield all his life and it was he who told me, in 1944, that they wanted a grinder at the Enfield and so I returned for three years to do production grinding under Billy Keyte, boring and honing all cylinder barrels. I also had a floating commission for Bob Lucas and did a bit of work for him.

I bored and honed four cylinders for the first lot of twins for the bikes at the underground factory – and they were scrap. There's a story to tell about that. I did these cylinder barrels and I said to my inspector, Vic Barker, 'We ought to have a mandrel on these two cylinders to check that they're running true'. These four cylinder barrels went off to Westwood and a week later, Mr Guise came to see me. He pointed to a notice at the far end of the workshop and said, 'Did you read that notice? I wish you had done, those cylinder barrels were scrap'. The notice said, 'Each component in each batch must be inspected'. Anyway, when Mr Guise had gone I looked at the notice and thought, 'I can't see that with my left eye' so I went to the optician who told me that I had a lazy eye and from that day onwards I wore glasses.

Once, I had a real roasting from Gilbert Baker, the works manager. Just before the Easter holidays they had an urgent order come in from their agent for six motor mowers. I was given the job of doing six con rods. When I machined the six con rods I bored the small end out a bit too big. Gilbert Baker had a go at me and my brother said, 'You b... kid, you made a b... mess of it!' They found me some bronze and I was sent to the lathe in the bottom machine shop and made to turn six bushes oversize to fit. There was no arguing about it in my days. You just had to go and do it.

In 1947 I could see that the orders were dropping so I found myself a job with Rolls Royce, as their aircraft division had come to BSA (Guns). There have been nice people at every company but at Royal Enfield there was something that seemed to make it that little bit different. It wasn't only how other people treated you, it was also in yourself, the way that you treated other people.

Boring the cylinders.

KEN SOMNER: from 1936 to 1937

In 1993, as Mayor of Redditch, I was privileged to present a telegram from the Queen to Tommy Guise's widow on the occasion of her hundredth birthday. I felt that it was a great honour to do this, particularly so when I remembered that 47 years earlier, in 1936, I had been a 16 year old working on the shop floor of the Royal Enfield factory. Tommy Guise, the works manager, had been so far above me that I hardly ever saw him and certainly never spoke to him.

My job was that of making front hubs on a lathe and I was very good at it. Although the pay was only 10d (4p) per 50, I managed to earn £2 10s (£2.50) per week which was good money in those days. An apprentice would only earn about 15 shillings (75p). I earned more than my father. I gave my mother 7s 6d a week which left me very well off, I was able to go to Burtons in Redditch High Street and buy myself a nice made-to-measure suit for £2 10s.

A pint of beer was 6d (just over 2p) and 1s 6d (just over 7p) bought you the best seats in the cinema. Five Woodbines were 2d (nearly 1p), and the men would be waiting for their wages on the Friday afternoon so that they could buy their next packet. Although there was a strict non-smoking policy in the factory and you got the sack if you were caught smoking even in the toilets, most of the men smoked but not the women as it was considered 'common'.

The gates were closed at eight promptly each morning and if you were late you had to go through the commissionaire, Frank Clark, an ex-Sergeant Major who had never forgotten his army training, if you were persistently late he wouldn't let you in and sent you home. When we got to work, our coats were put on a hook on a rack, then the racks were hoisted up into the roof, if you had a pass to leave early you had to get the foreman to lower the racks so that you could retrieve your coat.

My number one enemy at the factory was the son of Major Smith, Barry Smith. There was nothing personal in this, in fact today we are good friends, but we were both active members of opposing political parties. We used to collect a few friends then go along to each other's meetings and heckle to try and disrupt the meeting. Sometimes we got as far as fisticuffs on the pavement outside.

Although the factory workers used to have political arguments, no-one dared to be politically active. You would have been sacked on the spot and once you were dismissed from one job, it was impossible to get another in Redditch.

Putting hubs on wheels day after day held no prospects for me and I left before the year was out to go to another Redditch motorcycling firm, the BSA. During the war I joined the RAF and served in the Far East. After a long career in engineering which took me up north-east as chief production engineer in ship-building, and down south as general manager of an engineering works in Essex, I retired and came home to devote the rest of my life to the citizens of Redditch. My name had been put forward at the Borough Council elections some years previously, I was then elected and became Mayor in 1993.

An ironic touch was that my first election speech in 1951 was made from the balcony of Major Smith's old home, which by then had been turned into the offices of Redditch Borough Council.

I have yet another association with Royal Enfield. My great-grandfather was George Wiggett, a name which has gone on record, but posthumously, as he lost his life in an industrial accident at the old Hunt End works. He was helping to install a boiler, back in 1891, when it slipped and crushed him.

VERA: from 1934 to 1938

I went straight from school and started in the post room, then after I had been doing that for a bit I asked to be put on the cycle wrapping – that would be in 1934. Cycles were brought into the department and I had to put each one on a stand and wrap it all over with this special paper, then the delivery man collected them and put them in his van.

I was on piecework and the money was quite favourable compared to Terry's Springs and the fishing tackle trade

Royal Enfield paid quite decent money. I was working under Eddie Wright for most of the time who was a really pleasant man; first I worked for his father who was quite dour but then all the foremen were in those days.

My husband had the biggest motorcycle that Royal Enfield ever made. How he managed to keep it on the road I do not know. It was 1,000cc and it had a double adult sidecar. We had the sidecar built specially to match the bike, we were friendly with the couple across the road and we used to go out together, the two wives sat together in the sidecar and her husband sat pillion behind my husband. When the four of us went out we were really something. However, it was always breaking down, to start with there was a fault with the design of the primary chain.

I was wrapping bikes in about 1938 when Royal Enfield produced its first lightweight sports model pushbike, called the Firefly. Before then, bikes were very heavy. This was *THE* bicycle. I told my friend about this new sports bike that was coming out, with celluloid mudguards, black enameled frame and Enfield Comfort dropped handlebars. She asked me how much it cost and I said £5 15s 6d (£5.77). She said, 'Oh my golly, we shall never have that amount saved up!' Anyway, we saved hard and managed to get the money together. We joined the Redditch Road and Path Club but were told that we would have to ride at the front with our lightweight bikes. Seven miles from Redditch my friend's front wheel touched my back and off we both came. Worse still, we fetched many others off as well. We were in terrible trouble!

BERT HARRIS: from 1934 to 1959

I started at Royal Enfield when I first left school in 1934. Although the wages were low, Royal Enfield was a very friendly place and you were never out of work. If the work dried up in your department you could always go and help somebody else. My wages were fifteen shillings a week (75p), of which I gave my mum 12s 6d (62p) and kept half-a-crown (12p) for myself.

When you walked in through the middle entrance you were faced by a row of enormous clock-faces, about half-a-dozen in all, raised on stands about two-and-a-half feet off the floor, with numbered holes round the edge. These were the clocking-on machines and you had to grab the handle in the middle of clock, swing it round and push the point into your clocking-on number. I can still remember mine, 681. You didn't have to clock off when you went home unless you did overtime.

I was first working in the carpenter's shop where I had an accident with a bandsaw and cut the tip of my nose off. After a stitch or two I was back at work the same day.

I packed hundreds of cycles. They were packed for the home market in crates of any number, but the motor bikes had to be dismantled to fit in the crates. The parts couldn't be supplied straight from stores as the bikes first had to be tested. I was mainly packing RE2's, hundreds of them, two to a case, mainly for the American market.

I packed about 25 a month of the big 350 motorcycles which were carted off to the goods station and from there to be shipped to Lausanne in Switzerland. We didn't send all that many bikes to Europe, most of them went to the Middle East, especially India.

I used to work all hours, often from eight in the morning until eight or nine at night if a load needed to catch a boat. My wife didn't mind, she was glad of the extra money.

"FIREFLY" LADY'S MODEL

CHAPTER FOUR
Enfield at war

The Flying Flea in action.

JACK CLEMENTS: 1943 to closure

At the outbreak of the Second World War, the production of all motor bikes and push bikes for civilian use had come to a halt. Fortunately, Royal Enfield was able to switch its workforce into providing such a large range of munitions that the original site at Redditch expanded and additional factories were required. Because of the labour shortage in Redditch, the other factories were sited elsewhere and by the time I joined Royal Enfield, there was the Redditch site, four main satellite factories and various small workshops.

Redditch was always known as the number one factory and was the largest by far, eventually covering some 27 acres! We continued to manufacture bicycles and motor bikes but these were now for army use, and were mainly the 250cc and 350cc side-valve and the 350cc ohv. Our technical expertise was tremendous. One of our developments was a lightweight, 125cc bike, known as the 'Airborne' which was capable of being dropped by parachute with airborne troops. This was known as the 'Flying Flea' in its civilian guise.

We also pioneered the production of specialised oil units and, in 1942, the works manager and foreman of the oil unit assembly department were asked to go to America to advise on the production problems they were having with their oil units.

We were also at the forefront in the development of the air-cooled diesel engine. This was quite new. In the early 1940s Royal Enfield had made a water-cooled diesel engine for a firm in Coventry under licence but in about 1944, Frank Nossiter, the head designer, produced an air-cooled engine.

Redditch was also the centre for the production of diesel engines, generator sets and other munitions including armour-piercing shells.

Number two factory was at Westwood, in Wiltshire, about five miles south-east of Bath. The site was a great triumph for Royal Enfield and the technical team because, in only seven months – from December 1941 until June 1942 – a network of underground quarries, which had been abandoned in 1895, were converted into an efficient modern factory, 90 feet below ground. It was a tremendous feat, even more so when you realise that they were making intricate and delicate precision instruments such as predictors for the accurate control of anti-aircraft fire. Three of the men from the toolroom, where I worked, had been among the first to go down in 1941 to help establish this factory. Harold Middleton and Charlie Mead were young, single men in their mid-twenties but Gilbert Baker, who was installed as works manager, was an older man, with a family.

Most of the workers at Westwood had never seen the inside of a factory before. I went there several times on errands. It was a strange place; in the middle of the open countryside a rough track suddenly dipped quite sharply and you found yourself at the entrance. They had every amenity there, even suntan beds, the only way you knew that you were underground was that the ceilings were quite low. This factory continued after the demise of the Redditch factory.

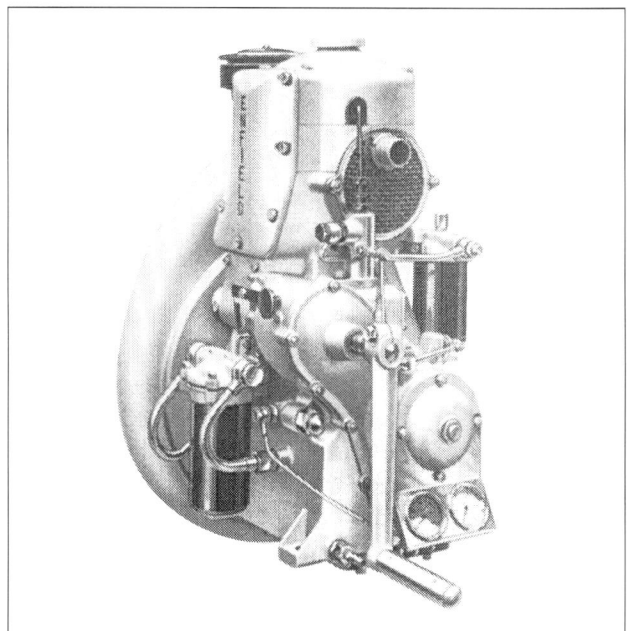

The single cylinder diesel power unit.

Number three factory was a fairly small, modern development sited at Edinburgh, the works manager was Les Hughes. It was equipped to make motorcycle frames and tubular crates, each airborne motorcycle had to be packed in one of these crates to ensure that it would land safely after parachuting.

Number four factory overlooked the village green in Feckenham, a little country village about five miles south-west of Redditch. This was by far the most picturesque of the sites, being a little old needle-making mill, just large enough to hold a few small capstans and drilling machines. They made small parts for stationary engines and motor bikes under the management of Charlie Wardle. The factory has now been converted into a private house.

A fifth factory near the centre of Redditch was a small section of the old Alcocks Fishing Tackle Company in Clive Road. Works manager was Bert Aimes and most of the workers were women, operating capstans and drilling machines to make small machine parts. Royal Enfield also had a small factory at Droitwich which I visited with Stanley Smith (Major Smith's brother). Again, it contained capstans and drilling machines.

When I started work in the toolroom in 1943 on bench work, virtually all the tools required by Royal Enfield were made in the toolroom – reamers, special drills, form tools, gauges, press tools, taps and dies, jigs and fixtures. I worked from eight in the morning until seven at night, but then I hadn't finished. I was on Home Guard duty one night a week, on parade every Sunday morning and I had to attend practice drills during the evenings and weekends.

You would think that the long hours of factory work would make life very depressing, but in actual fact we had a good many laughs in the toolroom. We were always playing jokes on each other! Most of them are too trivial or complex to tell but I remember one dinner hour when it was bonfire night, someone had got hold of a rocket of the type which leaves a trail of stars and he shot it straight down the toolroom. The man standing at the far end had quite a shock.

Jack Clements.

There was a lot of light-hearted bantering on the floor, if you had anything a bit out of the ordinary you knew you were sure to have your leg pulled about it. Little anecdotes were popular which showed a person's character in an amusing way. Jack Field, the foreman of the press shop, came to work on a motor bike each day but never indicated when he was about to turn into the factory gate. Someone asked him why he never indicated and he said, 'Why should I, everybody knows that I work here!' That one went the rounds of most of Royal Enfield!

MARGARET CLEMENTS: from 1943 to 1945

To get to my workplace at the Royal Enfield I had to pass the toolroom, and sometimes I could see, through a long window, this very nice young man standing at his bench. I was therefore on a nodding acquaintance with him and I got to know him better when I started going to the dances held in the canteen on the Saturday night – they were quite popular and about 150 people went. I was a real black country lass and Jack was fascinated by my accent. I thought his Worcestershire accent was peculiar as well, he seemed to add an 's' on to the end of each word. It seems strange that our accents were so different and our home towns were only 23 miles apart.

Despite its romantic associations, I didn't like working at Royal Enfield at all. I hated being away from home and I hated working in a factory. Before war broke out, I was happily working in a gent's outfitters at Walsall, but when I was seventeen I was called up and sent for sixteen weeks training at Handsworth Training Centre. I was taught inspection and the reading of verniers, but I was put on a capstan lathe at Royal Enfield which had gauges so my skills in vernier reading were not used.

I had never even seen a machine before I went to the training centre. At Royal Enfield, I had to stand at that machine from eight in the morning until seven at night, with only the dinner break and a couple of other short breaks. Everyone did their best to make me feel at home and I was very lucky because I didn't have to stay in a hostel. The personnel officer, Mrs Wareham, found me lodgings with Graham and Madge Beszant in Rookery Road, who were very kind to me, but I was so homesick!

I usually went home on a Saturday, as soon as I had finished work I would wait for a Midland Red bus to take me the twenty miles into Birmingham, then another to take me the ten miles out to Walsall. I would do the return trip on a Sunday evening, catching the 6.10 from Walsall. I was much more fortunate than some of the other girls who came from Wales, Scotland and even Ireland who were billeted in a hostel and were, of course, not able to get home for weekends. Before I moved to the Enfield factory I was a member of the NFS (National Fire Service) in Walsall, where I helped to man the switchboard one night a week, so I was transferred to the NFS in Redditch. I was on duty fire watching one night a week, down at the Fire Station in Red Lion Street.

I made many friends at the factory. I had my 21st birthday while I was working there and although I held my party at home, nine of my friends travelled all the way from Redditch to Walsall on a Midland Red bus, in and out of Birmingham, in order to come to my party. Despite everyone's kindness, I never settled to factory work and I was not sorry when I had to leave the Enfield in 1945 through ill health.

When Jack and I were first married we lived with my mother in Walsall and Jack had to catch three buses a day to get to Royal Enfield. Then Tommy Guise, the works

A wartime 350.

manager, said that the company owned two houses in Walkwood Crescent at Hunt End and we were offered the use of one of them.

After living in Walsall, Hunt End seemed to me to be a different world! It had not then been developed and seemed to me to be in the middle of the country. Our house was modern with all mod cons but some of the cottages were still lit by oil lamps and one family even drew their water by a pump in the garden!

BARRY CLOUGH: 1941 to 1944 and 1947 to 1961

Although general events during the war years were dramatic and exciting, life on the factory floor was extremely dull. We ordinary people just did what we were told, we got our heads down and worked. Everybody worked long hours, I worked from eight in the morning until seven at night every weekday, then on Saturdays I worked until four-thirty or five. We had a ten minute break at ten o'clock, an hour for lunch and a fifteen-minute break at five thirty. By the end of the day, we were just glad to fall out of the factory and on to our bus.

Special clips were fitted to this model to carry an army rifle.

I began my working life at Royal Enfield in the rear number two machine shop on the small capstans making motorcycle parts under Harry Hay. The management did their best to make our lives less tedious. We had a good canteen which provided a choice of meals including a hot dinner for about two or three bob. The management also provided very good sports facilities, we had bowls, cricket, tennis and football. When I first joined Royal Enfield, I was surprised at the number of elderly men, some as old as eighty who were working in the factory, they had returned from retirement to help in the war effort. Towards the end of the war and just after, conditions in the factory improved tremendously. The majority of the factory machines were changed from the noisy overhead belting to a little electric motor at the side of each machine. This made a tremendous difference to the noise and to the safety aspect. The Royal Enfield wheelwrights and electricians converted the machines one by one, gradually working through the factory so that production was not interfered with.

After the war, Royal Enfield continued to manufacture bicycles and improved versions of the two motor bikes which had been most popular with the army, the 125cc two-stroke and the 350cc ohv machine. The latter was now painted a different colour and fitted with a new development – a hydraulically damped telescopic fork. When the war finished Royal Enfield found themselves with a surplus of this rather heavy machine on their hands which they sold to employees at about £60 each.

The Royal Enfield was a happy factory. Even those who left expressed a tinge of regret. It was almost like being in a club. Everybody got to know each other and if you met someone from the Royal Enfield later in life you always recognised each other and got talking about the good old days. The place was so friendly.

The only complaint which everyone had was about money. The workers were so badly paid but then, all the factories in the area paid low wages.

Quite a few people spent the whole of their working lives there. If you had served fifty years, then you had a gold watch. You also had a Certificate of Gratitude after twenty-five years. In some years, only a small number of people qualified for an award, then they were just called into the managing director's office for a glass of wine and a sandwich. However, sometimes over a dozen people would qualify, then an evening would be set aside for a Presentation Dinner and the canteen would provide a sit-down meal.

In 1964 Redditch was designated as a new town and the Redditch Development Corporation was instituted. They eventually bought the whole site, demolished the entire factory and converted the site into a trading estate of small factories. The prestigious offices along the front of the building were the last to be demolished.

LES ONIONS: 1946, few months only

The Flying Flea played a large part in my life for several years. I rode and maintained them in the army, then after the war I assembled them on the shop floor. The Flying Flea was a little lightweight 125cc bike, probably designed by Jack Booker and Tony Armstrong-Jones in about 1940. The armed services asked Royal Enfield to design a bike which could be dropped by parachute with airborne troops and which was light enough to be carried, if necessary. When dropped by parachute, it was held firmly in a tubular crate made at the Enfield factory in Edinburgh.

The Flying Flea was in competition with BSA's Bantam. Although the Bantam had a slightly larger engine and frame, I think it tended to be more widely used.

If you were a despatch rider, you were handed either a Bantam or a Flying Flea according to where you were stationed, the depot at Ashchurch in Gloucester seemed to hand out Bantams whereas the depot at Ashford in Kent provided you with a Flying Flea.

I spent the first two years of the war as a Staff Sergeant Fitter working on motor vehicles and guns, mostly 25 pounders, stationed on the Salisbury Plain, at Spennybridge in Brecon and in the Sperrin Mountains of Ireland. When I wanted a break I used to ask if I could substitute as a despatch rider, trolling back and forth on the Flying Flea between observation posts and batteries. I then joined the REME and spent three months in West Africa as a full-time despatch rider on the Flea, our unit had four or five riders.

Some of my friends saw active service in France and they said that the Flying Flea was a great boon. It was very versatile for getting from A to Z and if they were stuck anywhere, they could just pick it up and carry it. To take just one example, the Flea was dropped with troops behind enemy lines after D-Day and the bikes enabled them to travel some way across country in order to regroup.

It was a robust little bike which stood up well to the ill treatment it received. However, the forks were sprung with rubber bands and with continual use over rough ground there was a tendency for them to snap so wherever I travelled, I made sure I had a pocket full of elastic bands.

Another problem was that it was difficult to balance the flywheels without special equipment. It was a simple operation if you had the correct equipment which was only a pot with four pillows, you just dropped the one flywheel in and the big end, then dropped the other in, tightened it up and hoped for the best. At the Enfield works, of course, they had special machines to check it.

When the war was over I found myself a job at Royal Enfield, first in engine assembly and then in the top shop,

The Flying Flea, in its parachuting crate.

assembling the bike itself. I collected the parts from the stores, put the frame on a stand, dropped the engine in, passed four bolts through the frame, then put the wheels and frame in, tightened it all and added the tank. I was quite amused when I saw a recent BBC documentary on the Enfield India, because there they were, putting a bike together in exactly the same way that we did in the late 1940s, all hand-assembled on separate stands with no moving assembly track. An assembly track did run round the shop but this was for pushbikes.

There were five men working in the department and we had to put together eight bikes a day to earn our money. We received 8/6d (about 42p) per assembly, very poor pay but the whole area was badly paid. It was on a par with the battery factories and better than the fishing industry. Despite the pay, people were very happy at Royal Enfield and tended to work there all their lives.

While I was there, one outstanding character ruled the factory and that was the industrial nurse, Nurse Ralph. Her word was law. Oliver Wythes, the works manager, walked in fear and trembling of her, she used to tell him what to do and what not to do. In those days, there was no Health and Safety Officer and Nurse Ralph had to do the lot. The sight of a trailing flex or a poorly guarded machine brought Nurse Ralph's wrath down on the foreman's head! She was a legend! She had brought many workers into the world – me, for instance.

After a few months at Royal Enfield I left to work on the Sunbeam prototype – but that's another story!

VIC BOTT: His war

In 1939 I was still on the shop floor and my next chance came with the outbreak of war. There was a government order that 80,000 men had to be elevated from the shop floor and their talents devoted to the furtherance of implements of war. Our motorcycle section was closed down as such and I was re-assigned to help develop a government metallurgical department for the sole manufacture of 2lb anti-tank shells. I was the head viewer on the metallurgical side which sometimes involved advising on the design. I had a department of twelve girls directly under my control. Although I didn't know anything about metallurgy at the beginning of the war I had to learn all about it – and fast.

BARBARA SEVIOUR: 1940 to 1946

Royal Enfield sometimes asked me to model for them. I'm featured in two 1941 advertisements sitting with a young man on a motor bike. The illustrations are sketched from photographs. I would hasten to add that I was used as a model not so much for my looks but for the simple fact that, as Tony Wilson-Jones' secretary, I was on hand. He was the technical manager of the experimental department which looked after buyer's interests and he therefore worked closely with Fred Bladen in the publicity department.

Tony Wilson-Jones was a very imposing man, tall and broad, and distinguished looking with a military bearing. He had this rather pompous attitude which made him a little difficult to know, but I always found him kind, helpful and considerate. He gave me the confidence to cope with his work, which was extremely difficult. The problem was that part of Mr Wilson-Jones' work was replying to letters from people who were experiencing problems with their bikes. He wrote long technical missives in reply, with detailed explanations, often two quarto pages and it was said that if you could take shorthand from Tony Wilson-Jones you could take it from anybody.

I remember that Mr Wilson-Jones went everywhere with his slide rule. He said to me once that he was so used to using it that he would reach for it when he only wanted to multiply 4 x 4. He was best man at my wedding, I met my husband Harold, through Royal Enfield. Harold lived in Bradford and was making gear boxes, we had some correspondence with him and he called in to see us several times. Then Major Smith asked him if he would like to work at Enfield's where he started the industrial engine department.

Tony Wilson-Jones, Technical Manager of the experimental department.

It was so exciting working there during the war. You had all these interesting people dropping in. A lot of them were army personnel arranging inspections for the war department bikes. I remember one of them, Captain Briggs, asking us to think about him the next day as he was going to do a dangerous parachute jump. I heard afterwards that he had broken his leg but had survived. Richard Illingworth, an army Lieutenant, arrived to help Mr Wilson-Jones write an army manual to cover the servicing and repair of the army bikes. First they listed all the different parts, then Mr Wilson-Jones began to dictate that this, that and the other should be done. Lieutenant Illingworth changed 'should' to 'must'. He explained, 'if you don't say must, they just won't do it'.

Mr Wilson-Jones' office was on the first floor and I was idly looking out of the window one day when I saw a plane moving across the sky with flack bursting all round it. I was out of the office and down the stairs so fast! My shelter was an old building across the road, opposite Dixons. On the whole though, people didn't seem to bother about the war. We got used to planes being overhead and went to and from work as usual. To us, the greatest inconvenience was the blackout. My brother, before he was called up, went out to see one of his friends one night and walked into a wall. He came home with his nose bleeding.

I made the biggest mistake of my life in 1946. I had worked for Enfield's for eight years and felt that I needed a change so I applied for the post of secretary to the export manager at BSA, Small Heath on the eastern side of Birmingham. There, instead of a quiet office for just my boss and myself, I had to work in a large general office and I found it very noisy. The work was much more complicated

Looking towards a peaceful future. Barbara Seviour featured in this 1941 advertisement.

as the three companies, Sunbeam, Triumph and BSA had merged and I had to be careful to use correctly headed paper with correctly coloured copies. I hated travelling all the way into Birmingham every day and it was a great relief when my aunt told me about a house for rent in Studley. Not only were Harold and I able to get married, it also meant that I could leave work.

MARY McGOWAN: 1940 to closure

Working in an office during the 1940s was very different to today. To begin with, it was much more formal. We wouldn't have dreamed of calling our managers by their Christian names. Discipline was very strict and we were not allowed to stop working for one minute, despite the hours being much longer. I found myself with three other shorthand-typists in a huge service department, exporting spare parts all over the world. We were kept in order by Frank Cooper, the service department manager, who had the most piercing blue eyes, they stared right through you!

We took great delight in outwitting Mr Cooper whenever possible. The service department was in a block on its own away from the main office and behind the tennis court. The ladies' lavatory was situated to one side of the court. During the summer months we used to take it in turns to go into the Ladies, open the door wide, spread ourselves out on an old box in there and sunbathe for ten minutes at a time. When Mr Cooper banged on the window and said, 'Where's Miss So-and-so?' the other girls in the office used to look at him innocently and say, 'She's gone to the toilet'.

One afternoon, we heard the sound of gun fire and we ran out of the office to see a German plane circling overhead being fired at by our guns which were then stationed at Brockhill Lane. I climbed up a heap of something (I think it was coal) to get a better view and the men in the offices shouted at me to go back inside. One of the managers was sitting under the desk; we laughed about that afterwards. The German bomber circled round for much of the afternoon then, as I watched, I saw a bomb falling from it. I heard later that the bomb had fallen in the BSA grounds, uprooting a tree, and blowing out some of the BSA windows. The plane was eventually shot down over the East coast.

As soon as the war was over, a friend of my mother's managed to get me a post as a managing director's secretary on a factory estate on the outskirts of Birmingham. After a couple of years there, I saw a little advertisement in a local paper asking for a secretary and giving a box number. I replied, not knowing that I was applying to Major Mountford the sales manager of Royal Enfield.

Now, my father, Louis Hadley, was working at Royal Enfield and had been there for many years, in fact he was one of the original Enfield Autocar workers. When R W Smith had decided to go into car manufacture at the turn of the century, he had asked my father to join him.

I don't know why R W Smith chose my father. He came from quite an ordinary background, having been born in Nechells, Birmingham in about 1879 but he did attend

A Royal Enfield family. Lou Hadley, Mary McGowan's father.

Birmingham Technical College, probably at night school. He met R W Smith when he was working in Coventry, something to do with Daimler's.

After my interview, Major Mountford went to my father and said, 'By the way, your daughter has just been to see me!' My father didn't know anything about it, which was quite embarrassing. Anyway, I was appointed secretary to Major Mountford. The war had not long finished and he was travelling all over the world with Major Smith, trying to get orders, and it was quite exciting to see the export market expanding. I remember we were exporting to Belgium, Holland, America – and India, of course. We even had an agent in Australia. My language skills came in useful, particularly when the export manager left when I spent a lot of time translating into French.

After a year or two with Major Mountford, I was appointed as secretary to the managing director, Major Smith. The two were great friends and were extremely nice men. They were rather similar in appearance and character. They were quite tall and well-built with a little moustache and both had this military air, they were always very formal and correct. Major Smith was one of the old school – you knew he was the head – and he came complete with chauffeur by the name of Sid Parsons.

There was no chance of sharing a joke with Major Smith unless you were a very close colleague. Nevertheless, he was a kind, pleasant and even-tempered man and I enjoyed working for him. I had my own office, but I would be called into his office for dictation. My shorthand speed was 120 words per minute so I found the work very easy.

Royal Enfield was a really nice place to work. It had a happy, friendly atmosphere. Perhaps this was because it was a family business, it does make a difference.

MARGARET: from 1951 to 1952

I was brought up on a farm in Tipperary in Ireland but when I was eighteen, in 1951, I found myself working in the spares parts department at Royal Enfield. Everyone was so kind and friendly, if anyone had any biscuits or sweets, they would share them round. I appreciated that. However, I did miss the fresh air and found it difficult to get used to being cooped up indoors all day.

I was the packer (the only one) in the spare parts department. I had to get a part from the stores next door – it was only a short distance away – take it back to my bench, wrap it in brown paper and gummed tape, and box it. The parts were quite heavy but not too much for me, I was a good strong lass.

Work was my whole life. I was only young so I didn't go out in the evenings except that once a week I went to the pictures. That was all I could afford! On the other evenings I usually read books bought from a second-hand bookshop in the centre of Redditch.

I enjoyed work – and I loved the bikes. One thing that stands out in my mind is the collection of exhibition bikes. These were given a special finish and kept separately to the main production. When we went through one of the shops we could look into the next unit where they were built, and I can still see them in my mind's eye, shining and gleaming. They were beautiful.

Funnily enough, I was given a Royal Enfield bike for my eighth birthday, which I thought the world of. It cost £3 10s (£3.50) and was a 26 inch wheel, my mother had to put wooden blocks on the pedals so that I could ride it. It was still in use four years ago, then I gave it away. I didn't realise it was an antique!

GERALD COLEY: 1940 to 1948

Royal Enfield was a good place for an apprenticeship in those days. You gained experience in every field. We made all our own drills, taps and milling cutters, we were self-sufficient in everything. When people left Royal Enfield and went to BSA they were at a loss, because if they had wanted, say, a mandrel at Enfield's they just went and got one from the stores but at BSA they were non-existent. You either had to make one or codge one up.

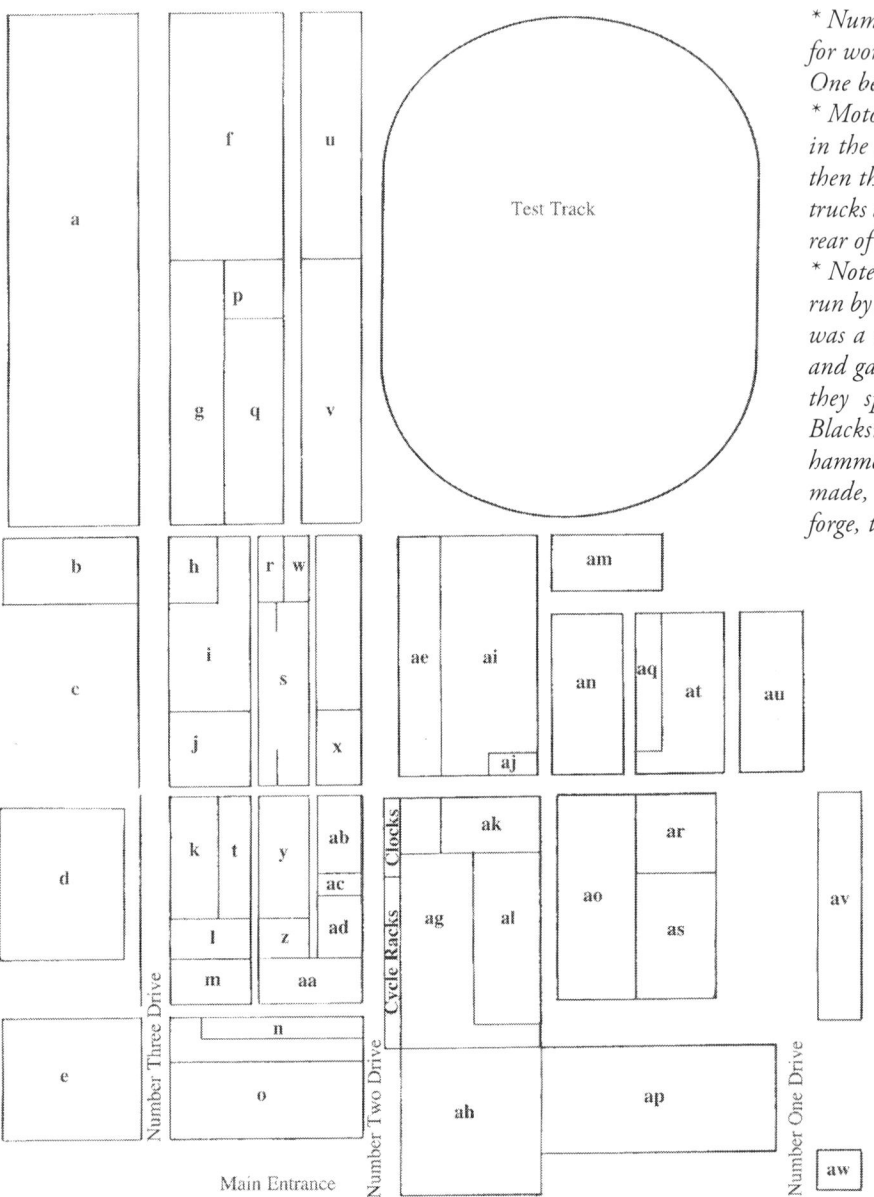

* *Number Two Drive was the main entrance for workers but cyclists were allowed in Drive One because cycle racks were there.*
* *Motorcycle frames were assembled upstairs, in the autoshop at the front of the building, then they had to be transported on hand-held trucks all the way to the brazing section at the rear of the building.*
* *Note the Blacksmith's shop off Drive Two, run by Frankie Day and Ernie Twitty. Frankie was a large pot-bellied man, Ernie was thin and gaunt. They both chewed tobacco which they spat into the fire at intervals. The Blacksmith's had a small foot operated drop hammer and a forge. If someone wanted a tool made, he would have it bumped out in the forge, then get it ground in the tool room.*

Diagrammatic Layout of the Enfield works in about 1945
(Not to scale)
Based on a plan by Gerald Coley

a	Oil Unit. Predictors and Diesel Assembly	aa	General Stores: *A. Layton*
b	Bowling Green	ab	Progress Office
c	Sports Ground	ac	Jig and Tool Drawing Office: *Jack Hassall*
d	New Canteen	ad	Steel Stores
e	Lawn Mower and Service Department	ae	Motorcycle Test: *Reg Steel*
f	Welding: *G. Bayliss*	af	Blacksmith Shop
g	Motorcycle Engine Test	ag	Lower Floor: Cast Iron Section: *L. Hartridge*
h	Diesel Test: *Frank Edwards*	ah	Auto Shop: *J. Lucas*
i	Capstans: *L. Hughes*		First Floor: Pattern Shop: *Mr Foster*
j	Grinding: *W. Keyte*	ai	Millwrights Maintenance: Manager *T. Lacy*
k	Aluminium: *H. Hay*		Foreman *C. Baker*
l	Small Capstans	aj	Nurse
m	Shell Section	ak	Lower Floor: Press Tool Store
n	Toilets	al	Lower Floor: Press Shop: J. Field
o	This building did not belong to the Enfield but to Terry Springs. Major Smith tried to buy it but was not successful		First Floor: Cables, Frame Sub Assembly
		am	Old Canteen
		an	Hardening Shop: *G. Strain*
p	Finished Engine Stores	ao	Plating: *H. Anderson*
q	Motor Cycle Engine Assembly		First Floor: Cycle Wheels: *E. Spiers*
r	Engine Store	ap	Offices
s	Inspection: *H. Mole*	aq	Experimental Department
	Motorcycle Assembly: *F. Bicknell*	ar	Generator Assembly
t	Drilling Section: *C. Freeman*	as	Cycle Despatch
u	Brazing		First Floor: Cycle Assembly: *J. Yates*
v	Paint Shop	at	Polishing: *H. Stockley*
w	Motorcycle Wheel Assembly	au	Carpenters: *E. Wright*
x	Motorcycle Stores: *S. Neale*	av	Cycle Racks
y	Tool Room: *L. Purser*	aw	Time Office
z	Tool Stores		

Among the wide range of jobs given to an apprentice was that of making the tea. I had to go to the canteen carrying twenty or so billy cans on a piece of wood. This was a grim building, made from corrugated iron and painted brick red, right at the back of the hardening shop. The water came from a big geyser and it was always greasy. The workers complained so much that it was eventually decided to clean out the cistern and a dead rat was found in it.

There was quite a bit of larking about among apprentices. One of the workers in the tool room had a hot water pipe running high up above his bench, and he used to hang his umbrella from it. Every time one of the apprentices went past he would throw something up into the umbrella. I was in trouble over one incident. On Friday afternoons we used to have to go in pairs to empty the rubbish, using this little mobile platform on four rubber wheels with a handle to pull it along. If you put a large box on it you could get a person inside and we had a lot of fun with that. On the return journey I managed to knock a fire hydrant off the wall.

When I had been at Enfield's for five years, I heard about a six month residential course at Loughborough College to gain HNC. The entry qualifications were City and Guilds and Ordinary National, which I already had from my day release at Enfield, so I was accepted on this intensive training course, where we did two year's work in six months. This enabled me to move, in 1944, from the tool room to the department for testing diesel engines.

During the war Enfield's had a contract from the Ministry to make the Coventry Victor Cub, to put into a generator set. Fred Farley was the foreman of the diesel engine shop, he was fortyish and very volatile. Frank Nossiter was not only the designer of the diesel engines, he also designed a motorcycle with an engine which didn't vibrate. The design was brilliant but it was never produced. He had a J2 engine machined down to the dimensions he wanted. The engine was a horizontally opposed flat twin with a shaft drive and it didn't vibrate at all, you could stand a pencil on it and the pencil didn't move. I often wonder what happened to it.

The foreman of the shop testing these engines (my boss) was Frank Edwards. He was about 26 years of age, shortish with black hair and of Welsh origin. Both Frank Edwards and Frank Nossiter had been seconded from the Austin Motor

The postwar motorcycling boom. The Royal Enfield stand at the 1948 Motorcycle Show, the first to be held after the war.

Company and both were extremely nice fellows. After the war I went into the jig and tool drawing office where I worked on the tools for most of the new developments, the one which I found most exciting was, I think, the pressed steel cycle frame. I did all the tools for doing the lugs for that.

Not many people realise that we also worked on new designs for cycles. The cycle designer was a chap called Stan May. We produced the Coventry Cross, which was a very cheap bike; a bright red bike known as the Bullet; and a twin-topped tube bike, the Firefly. Stan also designed a very flashy bike, the Continental, which was all chrome plated and finished in bright blue lacquer.

I remember Bill Lomas working in the Experimental Shop. He was nineteen or twenty, about five feet eight or nine inches tall, very slim with his hair sleeked back. He had heavy lids to his eyes so that he always looked sleepy. He was a very agreeable chap and married a girl out of the canteen.

I bought the famous Enfield bike, which is now in a Japanese museum, from Jack Powell for £20. I hated the sight of it. The clutch slipped and it was susceptible to side winds. It wasn't my type of bike – it wasn't fast enough. I sold it to one of the testers, Nigel Buckingham, and within a few weeks he had sold it for £1,000.

Riding an Enfield round central Birmingham was deadly, the rigid forks would catch in the tram lines and the wooden blocks, and you would either come off or spin in a circle. I was carefully making my way along Suffolk Street in Birmingham one day when a Douglas bike came sailing past at great speed without any difficulty. I decided that that was the bike for me.

I left Enfield because of the money, they never paid well. I also felt that I was in a rut in the jig and tool drawing office, so in 1948 I moved to Lockheed Brakes at Leamington.

Enfield's Home Guard on parade. George Fairgreave (office manager) leads the convoy.

CHAPTER FIVE
Of diesels, atoms, rockets, gun mountings and radar predictors, with compulsory sun tan

Frank Nossiter, Chief Designer, shows twin-cylinder diesel engine (air cooled) to Gilbert Baker (right) and Swedish visitor (left).

FRANK EDWARDS: from 1944 to closure

In September 1944, together with a small team, I joined Royal Enfield to help set up the Enfield Industrial Engine Company as a separate division to produce diesel engines. The idea was originated by Tom Hobbis, the then lively sales manager of Royal Enfield, who had accepted a nice fat contract to produce diesel-engined electric generators for the armed forces. Enfield's were already producing, amongst other things, little flat twin two-stroke horizontally-opposed air-cooled engines for generator sets etc for the war office. The problem was that, at that time, there was no-one at Enfield's who had experience with diesel engines, hence the reason for taking on us new boys, as it were.

The new staff were made up of Harold Seviour as commercial manager, Frank Nossiter as chief designer, being a brilliant engine and automotive engineer, and yours truly as chief test engineer in charge of experimental work, production assembly and testing and servicing. Some time later Frank Nossiter moved on and I became chief engineer to embrace the design work as well. We were provided with the machine shop and office facilities of the main factory and gradually became more and more independent of the cycle and motorcycle side.

The first engine, produced only for the services, was a horizontally-opposed, water-cooled unit based on a pre-war Coventry Victor design. Then a new contract was made with the Air Ministry to produce lightweight air-cooled diesel engine generators. This engine was a completely new design and formed the basis of a very successful range of single and twin cylinder units procured for the post-war period.

The engines were capable of operating at high temperatures (tropical) and low (sub-zero). Extensive and exhaustive tests were carried out in the works, at the Lucas Research Centre in Birmingham and the Admiralty Experimental Department at West Drayton. A special treatment which included anodising the engine castings and spraying with zinc chromate paint prevented corrosion by sea air or salt water.

We built up a strong home and export business using these engines for industrial, agricultural, automotive, military and marine purposes. They were used, for example, in road rollers, industrial tractors, mud pumps and dual pumping units for rotary or diamond drilling. They were very much in demand by boat-builders in both this country and across Europe for a variety of sea-going vessels such as launches, yachts, barges, lifeboats and fishing boats.

The employees were a grand bunch of people and the atmosphere generally excellent with a high degree of loyalty. Many employees were inter-related so that almost everyone you spoke to would be someone else's cousin, uncle or what-have-you. The talents and expertise were many and varied.

Amongst my close motorcycle acquaintances were people like Tony Wilson-Jones, the technical manager; Charlie 'CN' Rogers and Fred Bicknell, both trials wizards; Jack Booker who was no slouch on the race track; C A E Booker, the service manager (he came from Ariel's originally); and Ted Pardoe, the Designer, who used to ride an interesting V-twin

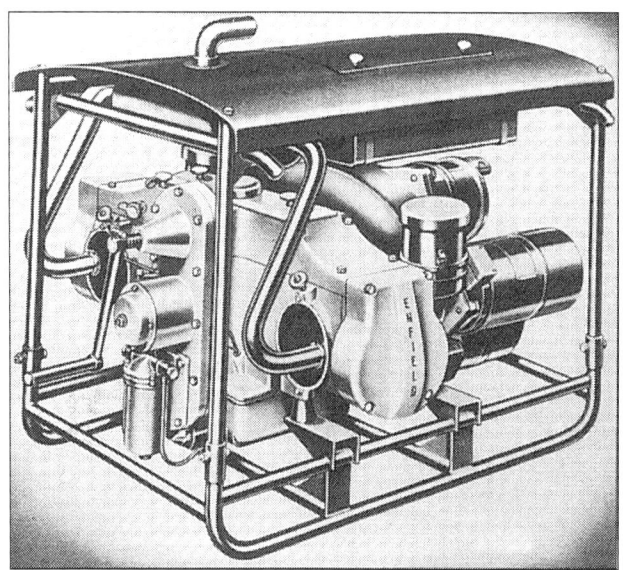

Generator set with Enfield designed diesel unit.

ohv experimental combination to and from work and on local weekend fishing trips complete with pipe and trilby hat! Bill Lomas was with us for a while and used to occasionally break any daily monotony by testing a racing machine up and down the works road – I can smell the Castrol R now!

All good things come to an end and unfortunately, by 1960, some of us had moved on to pastures new. It was not long before Major Smith passed away, in 1962, and from then onwards Enfield's fortunes changed. The industrial division embracing diesel production was taken over by a private buyer in the Isle of Wight. A few of the staff followed over where they all soldiered on for some time.

BILLY CAINE: from 1912 to 1950
by Walter Caine, his son

In the middle of the last war, in 1943, four managers from Royal Enfield were decorated for their war effort. Tommy Guise (works manager) and Vic Young (manager of the underground factory) became Members of the British Empire and two others received the British Empire Medal; one was Mr Robinson, an inspector, and the other was Billy Caine, my father.

My father was a remarkable man and a very accomplished industrial engineer, and after serving his apprenticeship with the Sunbeam company, he began working for Enfield's as a machine tool-setter in Hunt End in about 1912. I can remember going to see the old factory down at Hunt End, the windows were low down in the outside wall so that you could look down on to the heavy machinery such as lathes and automatics.

At the beginning of the war in about 1938 or 1939, my father was involved in the setting up of the huge new extension in the Redditch factory to make oil units for tanks and predictors. These oil units were quite a thing and they had been perfected in Redditch. They contained needle bearings and once they were sealed, they never needed lubrication again. The predictors were high precision instruments for accurate control of anti-aircraft fire.

It took my father and his team about two years to draw up the complete ground plan and put the department into full production. From what I can remember, it was his responsibility to get the machinery into a production plan to provide a continuous flow and it involved supervising the laying out of plans, installation of machinery and training of staff. He had one lot of toolsetters nicely trained then they went off to Bath to the underground factory, and he had to train another set.

We lived in St George's Road, near the centre of Redditch, Jack Booker, who rode in the Isle of Man TT, used to come to our local recreation field with his bike and he used to join in kicking our ball. He was our local hero. I often used to see him come striding out of the Enfield works, he was a stocky sort of a fellow and we always got a smile out of him. He was a great guy.

When I was about ten years old my older sister and I had to take my dad's dinner as there was no canteen at Royal Enfield in the 1930s. We were given one-and-a-half hours'

The prototype predictor – code name Red India – undergoing test with paraboloids.

lunch-time from school, long enough to walk the three-quarters of a mile from St George's Road to the Enfield factory in Hewell Road and back. We had to carry this basin with a towel round it, tied at the top. Sometimes it was a hot dinner, sometimes a cold. At first we left his dinner at the gate but then he moved to another department and we were allowed to walk along the gangway between the buildings providing we didn't go anywhere near the machinery.

We used to go down and meet him on Friday afternoons when he got paid. Just inside the main gate in Clive Road was the timekeeper's office and he collected his wages from there in a little tin on his way out. It amused me the way that the empty tins were just tossed into this big box on the floor.

In 1945 my father received a certificate for working at Royal Enfield for 33 years but he continued working until he was seventy. He only gave up then because his second wife was ill and needed a lot of his attention.

My father got me a job at the Enfield for a few months in 1942, while I was waiting to join the Air Force. I worked from six in the morning until eight at night, Saturdays and Sundays included, with only half-an-hour for dinner. Before the war the gates were locked three minutes after the bull had stopped blowing and if you arrived after this you had to go back home. The three minutes were given, they said, because it took you two minutes to get to the clock, find your card in the rack then shove it into the machine to clock on.

However, during the war the rules about lateness were relaxed, the management had to do this because of the shortage of skilled men. By the time I went there, the gates were reopened and you just lost fifteen minutes pay. On a Friday night you were allowed to go half-an-hour early, at seven-thirty, which just gave you time to reach the shops before they closed at eight.

I took a day off from Royal Enfield to go to Buckingham Palace with my dad to see the Queen give him his medal. A great many military decorations were presented but only half-a-dozen civilians received medals. As you may guess, that evening we celebrated with a party at home. When I arrived at work the next morning, rather the worse for wear, I was met by a disgruntled manager who threatened to report me to the Ministry of Labour for having an unauthorised day off. If you were in a reserved occupation and were late or absent you could be reported and then your permit would be withdrawn and you would have to join the services. I couldn't have cared less, as I was waiting to go into the Air Force anyway.

EDDIE BAKER: from 1942 to 1968
Enfield Precision Engineering

When the manufacture of armaments began to get under way at the beginning of the last war, Wimpeys built and ran a camp for 200 Irish labourers at Westwood, which is about two miles south-west of Bradford-on-Avon, near Bath. It was also within half a mile from the entrance to a vast maze of old stone quarries. These men, under the direction of the Ministry of Works, converted the mines into an underground factory, known as Enfield Precision Engineering. Adjoining the factory and using the same entrance was a large area where the contents of the Victoria and Albert Museum were stored. This also housed an emergency suite for the royal family. Hostels,

The twin cylinder diesel power unit.

houses and other buildings were built on the surface. It was a tremendous feat and you can see how important it was by the fact that it was visited by Queen Mary in 1943.

I was in charge of assembly, fitting and experimental work. I had moved to Westwood in 1942 from the Bristol Aeroplane Company, who were not very pleased. However, I knew Royal Enfield well, I was born (in 1912) only a few houses away from their factory at Hunt End. The whole of the Baker family seemed to work there, my father, older brother and uncle who was the export manager! I went there straight from school but I only stayed two and a half years then I went to the Austin where I had to work a lot harder, but I could earn more money. I married in Redditch but in 1936, together with half-a-dozen other Austin workers, I answered an advertisement for skilled engineers, fitters and turners with the Bristol Aeroplane Company.

Anyway, in 1942 Les Young, the managing director of the underground factory, and Gilbert, my brother, who was works manager, decided that my expertise would stand them in good stead. They therefore requested through the Ministry of Instrument Production (who was in overall control of the mine) that I should be transferred there. That's how it was that one week I was building the engines to send the aeroplanes up, and the next week I was working on equipment to shoot them down.

One of our headaches was the training of this large workforce to operate the machines and to build and assemble the units, especially when so many men were at the front. 70% of our workers were women. Some turned out to be brilliant machinists and fitters. They had to be. Most of the work was highly specialised and extremely technical and all was very hush-hush. It fell roughly into these categories:

Work for the Atomic Energy Authority at Aldermaston:

Although we didn't realise it at the time, we were doing precision instrument work for the mighty atom. Once atomic energy had been developed, the equipment was needed to control it. I visited Aldermaston several times and you wouldn't believe the number of badges you had to wear – I had already had stringent security clearance. You could say, loosely that Royal Enfield helped in some development of atomic energy. There were very few manufacturers with the machinery and the expertise to undertake such very high precision work.

The missile control mechanisms for the Bristol Bloodhound rocket:

The standard required was so high that you not only had to have top quality machines but the people who were using them really had to know what they were doing. This was troublesome from day one and we were just beginning to make a success of it when the war came to an end.

Hydraulic Control Equipment:

Towards the end of the war we were working on a specialised type of hydraulic equipment to control the fire of Bofors anti-aircraft guns for use against the V1 bomber, commonly known as the Doodlebug. The guns were frequently failing to hit them and we went down to Kent to see why. One of the problems was that they flew so low the normal equipment could not cope. As well as this, we found that as long as the girls could see the doodlebugs they could fetch them down but in the early morning there was a lot of mist so the girls just fired and hoped. We worked 24 hours a day for ten days to alter the position of the gun so that it would be on target.

Those girls worked night and day shooting down doodlebugs and were out in all weathers. Sometimes the girls were only 250 yards away from them. The doodlebugs would drone away overhead, then when they cut out, you never knew where they were going to land. They could drop there and then or they could carry on some way or even go into reverse for a short way. You just had to sit and wait. Thank goodness Hitler never really got his V2 under way, if that had come out twelve months earlier we wouldn't be here today.

Oil Units:

Although these were being manufactured at the Redditch works, further quantities were required so another section of the quarry was opened up to increase their production. They were only a small part of our total production, we specialised in oil units to power quick-firing, short-range anti-aircraft guns, such as the Bofors. Other people were also making them, Woolwich Arsenal, an armaments factory at Nottingham and Reyrolls in Newcastle.

Ericsson Predictors:

We made more predictors than anything else, hundreds of them, forty girls were working full-time on them. The Ericsson's were Scandinavian design. The predictors increased the accuracy of anti-aircraft fire by calculating the angle and the time at which the anti-aircraft gun could be fired.

Radar Controlled Predictors:

During the last years of the war, we got an order to produce an experimental predictor controlled by radar. Radar was just coming out and was obviously top secret. Nobody was allowed to speak of the project except to call it the Red Indian. This predictor was huge, about four feet square, and very, very heavy, carried on huge transport vehicles. A pair of paraboloids, rather like satellite dishes, were mounted on top. Other paraboloids were also mounted on a high tower. So that the radar predictor could be tested, a metallised balloon was sent into the air. A signal was sent from the paraboloid on the high tower to the balloon which was bounced back and picked up by the paraboloid on top of the predictor which controlled its movement and enabled it to turn towards the balloon. It could move in azimuth and elevation, ie it could move in any direction. That was quite a big project, but by the time we got around to doing what they were looking for, the war ended and so that project finished.

Special gun-mounting equipment for naval guns on warships:

This was a special semi-hydraulic spring mounting for small, very fast AA guns, designed to remain steady when positioned on a swaying deck.

Automatic Fuse Setters for the 4-5 inch anti-aircraft guns:

We had one of these guns at Westwood on the surface for experimental purposes but it was so huge that in order to house it half the length of the barrel was sawn off! The shells were enormous and it took two men to lift them. By the time the fuse had been manually set for point of travel, the shell loaded in the breach tray, pushed up the gun barrel and fired, the object was often out of range. We were therefore asked to make timed fuse setting equipment so that the fuse could be set very quickly. It was tested at Manorbier in Wales and proved quite successful.

At the end of the war at least 3,000 bikes came back from the army. They arrived in their hundreds. We were storing them anywhere, old buildings – anywhere we could find space. Part of the old mine at Westwood had been used for mushroom cultivation and that was now empty so we stored seven or eight hundred down there. We carried them all through the factory and out the door at the rear. It was a different world in that old mine. There was water everywhere, when you walked through you had to have a good light because it was nothing to walk into a six foot deep miniature lake. After a few months it was decided to start stripping and we discovered that the bikes were white all over except for patches of a green growth. After that, we stopped storing them down there and found somewhere in the Bath area.

After the war, the Ministry contracts petered out and we started reverting to commercial work to provide employment

Pump units for operating gun turrets of tanks.

and to keep the machines going. We manufactured the Constellation 750cc engine at Westwood. The Meteor and the Meteor Minor were first produced at Bradford-on-Avon. I went there for a spell as manager, we were making motor mowers as well as the big twins.

Ultimately, when the Enfield was taken over by Smith's, Bradford-on-Avon was closed and everything went to Westwood. Reg Thomas, the designer from Redditch came down in 1966. At the tail end, for the last two years, we were building the complete machine with Roger Shuttleworth in charge of all assembly. When Redditch shut up shop, we had quite a lot of work on a contract from the Bristol Atomic Energy, we were also doing top quality work for Lucas's, nothing for Enfield.

JACK NORMANDALE: from 1940 to 1961

In 1942, a notice went up asking for volunteers to go to a new underground factory opening at Westwood, near Bath.

By that time, I had been working at the Enfield for two years, moving there from the Alkalide Battery Company. I had worked on a drilling machine but I was experienced in all types of machining – grinding, milling, lathe-turning – so if somebody on another machine was off sick I could take over their job. Anyway, my wife also worked at Royal Enfield and we felt that we were in a rut. Going to Westwood would be a nice change.

The underground factory was a converted mine, this was where all the stone came from to build Bath. It ran underground for miles and branched off in all directions. A couple of times while I was there we had a fire or bomb drill, when we would go out through double doors at the rear of the factory into the unconverted mine where it was cold and wet with dripping from the ceiling. We were taken along the mine for about a mile and a half, then we came up in a field just south of Bradford-on-Avon. Part of the passage was used for commercial mushroom cultivation and there was one area where you could see all the mushrooms growing.

The factory itself was a marvellous place. It was ninety-eight feet underground with brick pillars every few yards. Although it was a large, open area you couldn't say that it was one big workshop because it wasn't a regular shape, you would see a row of machines then you would go round a pillar and there would be another row of machines round the corner. Walls and ceiling had been whitewashed and

Leaving work at the underground factory at Bath. The entrance tunnel ran for 150 yards before dividing off into the Enfield works.

everywhere was spotlessly clean. First thing every morning a vacuum was run over everything, even the walls. Every day a man came round tapping the roof to make sure it was safe. In my department, cracks appeared in the ceiling so they were cemented over and painted. We all wore bib and brace overalls which we bought ourselves, there was none of this supplying you with industrial clothing which they seem to go in for these days.

Here and there was a large round tin cylinder sticking out from the ceiling, this was an air shaft which was bringing fresh air in. Occasionally, for devilment, one of the men would give it a bang with a stick to frighten all the women. The noise would roll along the air duct all the way through the factory. Then one of the managers would come along and tell him off.

I was making the housing for predictors and other parts, we also supplied parts for other firms such as Hymatic. My machine was huge, it took up an area about the size of a small living room. Accommodating the machine had been quite a problem and a pit had had to be dug in the floor, I had to go down two steps to get into the machine.

Although we all worked hard, we were well looked after. The place was kept warm and dry. The doctor came down once a week and suntan treatment was compulsory, although we were glad to get it after being underground that length of time. We had to go off for our tanning session once a week. You couldn't stay under too long or you were burned, the lamps were very powerful.

In 1953, after I had been working underground for eleven years, I was asked to go to a huge old warehouse right in the centre of Trowbridge to work. All the army bikes and spares that had been returned from the army were stored there. I had to take them out of the crates and strip them down. The bikes were rebuilt using engines which, I believe, had been reconditioned at Redditch. They were then repainted and sold for £57 each. I spent between six and eight months stripping bikes, then I was sent back to the underground factory on the radial drilling machine again.

When I was moved to bike-stripping in Trowbridge, I had had a salary drop. I now resumed my old job but the management refused to reinstate my wages. I therefore left

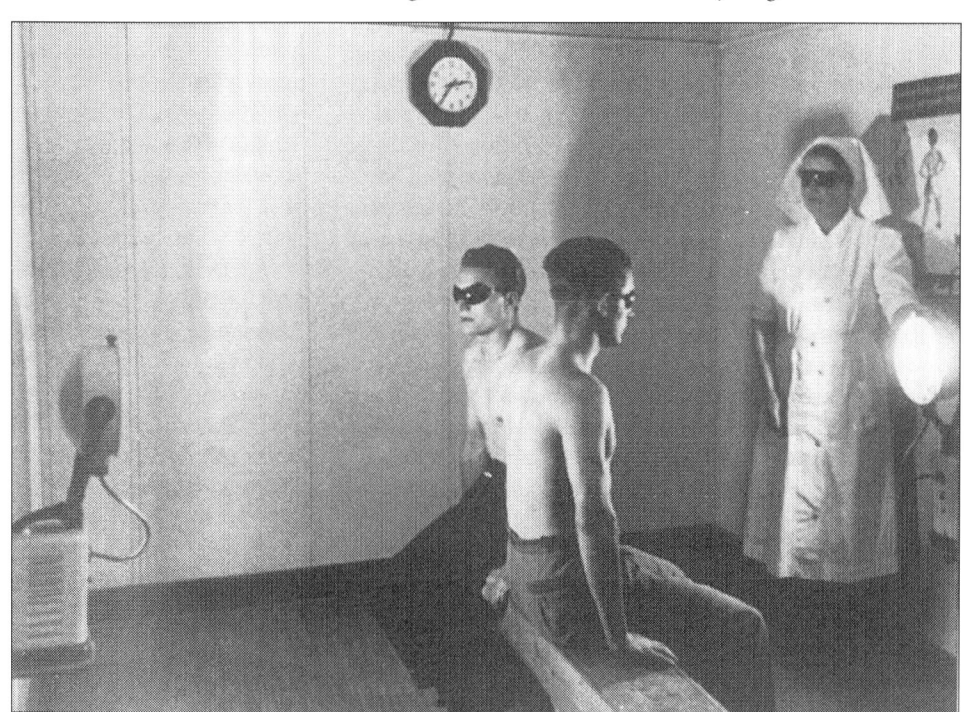

The sunray lamp room.

after a couple of months and returned to Redditch. I left Royal Enfield in 1961 because work was obviously getting short and my old job was going at the Alkalide Battery Company, so I moved there, the wages were roughly the same but the job was more secure.

ROGER SHUTTLEWORTH: from 1947 to 1970

For as long as I can remember I have had an interest in motor bikes. I bought a Velocette 250cc and gained first class awards in both local trials, such as the 1954 Wye Valley Traders Cup, and national trials, such as the British Experts and the Southern Experts. I was Wessex Trials Champion in 1952.

In 1945, I left the RAF and a couple of years later I was working in a garage when we were hit by the petrol shortage. A friend told me about a job going at the Trowbridge branch of Royal Enfield so I lost no time in applying for it. I found myself working in an old warehouse in the centre of Trowbridge, on the WD (ex-army) bikes. We stripped them down and removed the army green so that they could be re-enamelled black and sold as new. Then, in about 1948, I was asked if I would like to go to Bradford-on-Avon to work on the engines for the big twins.

Royal Enfield had taken over Greenland Mills, an old five-storey weaving mill in the centre of Bradford-on-Avon, the other side of the level crossing and next to the river. They were in the process of converting it into a factory for the manufacture of the big twin engines. The original factory was very basic and we even had to install a lift. A great deal of specialist machinery was being brought in to make the parts. The ground floor was the machine shop, the first floor was the stores, the second floor was the assembly and the top floor was bicycle storage.

The Enfield didn't have the whole site, three other companies used some of the out-buildings. When the 250 Crusader came out, a small new out-building was specially erected for the manufacture and assembly of the 250cc crankcases and crankshafts which were then despatched to Redditch.

I believe that first of all we just made some of the engine parts at Greenland Mills, then as the factory became established and further machinery was installed, we took over more and more of the production until we were producing the complete engine.

Our lorry made two trips a week to take the engines to Redditch. When the work got under way we were able to manufacture somewhere between twenty and fifty engines a week although, to avoid resetting machines, this varied and occasionally there were no engines at all for despatch.

When I first joined Bradford-on-Avon I was balancing crankshafts and was just 'one of the boys' but I progressed to experimental work. I had my own little department where I could run the engines to test any innovations I had made. The prototypes were then sent to Redditch for road-testing, usually by Brian Crow.

The biggest problem was that the cylinder heads used to leak. I couldn't make a seal between the pushrod tubes in the cylinder head and the cylinder barrel. The main trouble here was the use of an alloy cylinder head and a cast iron cylinder barrel. The rates of expansion of the two metals were so different that it was almost impossible to maintain a seal. I tried putting a little grommet round the pushrod tube and I also tried a compression ring round the top of the cylinder but although I got the leak down to a minimum, I was never able to cure it 100%.

The original engine was made with sand castings which were very heavy and had to be polished. We changed over to die-castings which were much better, they were lighter, with a better finish and didn't require polishing.

I also worked on the adaptation of the engines for other projects, perhaps the most interesting was the experimental work for the use of the 700 Twin in hovercrafts, although this never came to anything.

From 1959 we were supplying the Indian Sales Corporation in the United States with the 700 Twin Constellation-type bikes. We had a problem with the big end seizing up and so I had to go out to Springfield, America, to see them about it and try to find out why. I discovered that, because the con rods were made and bolted straight on to the crankshaft, when the engine heated, they seized up solid. We fitted shell bearings instead which alleviated the problem.

We also had a problem with a dozen machines which we supplied to the Argentinian Police in 1964. I had to go out there, but I discovered that the problem was due to the cheap petrol they were using which was detonating the engine and causing pinking. All I did was tell them to use better fuel and the problem was cured.

There was some talk about my going out to India. The Madras Motor Company were having problems with the first lot of gear boxes to be made out there but I told Mr Nightingale, the manager of Westwood, that I didn't want to go. I had spent four years in India during the war and I knew what it was like.

One of the foreman, Bob Webb, left in about 1957 to start his own business and I took over his job. In addition to the experimental work I became foreman of assembly and of stores, about five people worked in each department. About fifty worked in the factory altogether and they were a nice crowd, one big happy family. We did have one strike lasting a few days but it wasn't a dispute within our factory. It was called by the Transport and General Union and affected all the local factories. I wasn't a member of this union so I could carry on working.

We used to get quite excited when our engines were used in the big races and Trials, especially when we were directly involved. A local dealer, Syd Lawton, had Bob McIntyre riding the 700 Twin for a year, he rode it in the Thruxton 500-mile Production race.

In about 1963 the Enfield vacated the mill and transferred production of the big twins to the underground factory at Westwood. Mr Nightingale, who had been a manager of Alpha Bearings in Dudley, came out to take charge of the mine. Previously, Les Young had been the manager. He was one of the older employees (one of Major Smith's right-hand men) who came out from Redditch. Both Mr Nightingale and Les Young were very pleasant to work for.

The Enfield underground factory had previously been engaged on top-secret work for the Bristol Aircraft Company and the Ministry. AID inspectors were calling there for years. When the aircraft side finished we had to do anything which came our way. I remember the grinders altering the huge metal trays used in the production of Cadbury's chocolate bars to make the bars a little smaller. One of my jobs was reconditioning Villiers' engines to go in invalid carriages. I had to strip the engine down to the last nut and bolt and rebuild with new parts, then send them to the invalid carriage manufacturers.

By the time the factory closed in 1970 I had been the manager of the motorcycle department for three years. I was therefore the last to leave. The underground factory had already been vacated, I had to pack up the final bits and pieces from the surface buildings at Westwood and send them to Matt Holder in Birmingham. By that time, the Enfield had become part of the Norton Villiers group.

The underground factory was kept scrupulously clean for years afterwards but it has now reverted to its original condition. As for Greenland Mills, they burned down in the early 1990s.

CHAPTER SIX
The new designs

Vic Mountford (Major Smith's right-hand man) selling the 350 Bullet to their Australian agent, George Bolton.

REG THOMAS: from 1945 to closure

It was 1945 when I wrote to Enfield at Redditch seeking employment and they arranged for me to be interviewed at their No 2 Underground factory at Westwood, which was nearer to my home at Taunton, Vic Young was the manager there and he must have sent in a good report. I moved up to Redditch in September to start as a design draughtsman in the motorcycle section.

The Enfield works were quite extensive but I was surprised, and I believe a lot of Enfield owners would be, at the small size of the design section. It comprised the chief draughtsman, three design draughtsmen, a tracer and schedule-clerk on motorcycles and bicycles, two design draughtsmen and a tracer on diesel engines. Edward (Ted) Pardoe was called chief draughtsman but was really chief designer – Major Smith would never give that title to anyone as he looked upon himself as chief designer because he said he made the final decisions on what machines should be produced and their general characteristics. Ted is best remembered for his design of the 346cc overhead valve engine, the original 125cc model RE and the 500 Twin. He was a very nice person, sometimes known as Snowball because of his round head topped with snow-white hair. He had one annoying habit, he was a pipe-smoker and when leaning over your drawing very often blew ash on to it. He would then take his handkerchief which he carried up his coat sleeve and attempt to clean it off but in fact making it a darn sight worse!

The motorcycle/cycle design section comprised Stan May, Mr Sealey and myself. Stan was an Enfield ex-apprentice about the same age as myself, who worked mostly on bicycle design. Mr Sealey was never called by his first name, he was about 50 years of age and in those days people often preferred it that way. He was mainly engaged on frame design. I thought I had the most interesting work with engine and gearbox design.

I started in the office by making detail drawings from Ted Pardoe's designs for the 350cc G2 and 500cc Twin engines. This was followed by some redesign work and detailing of the Twin. The early design had a built-up crankshaft with centre-bearing, three part crankcase and a gear-type oil pump in the sump and driven from the rear camshaft. The crankshaft was changed to two castings with centre bearing and finally to the one-piece design without centre bearing.

Later I was given the job of designing a two-stroke engine and three speed gearbox for the Australian market. Major Smith was pleased with the result and asked me to write the specification for a unit construction utility engine and gearbox for general use. I designed and detailed this and one prototype was made and fitted to a modified G2 frame. Price was the main consideration in the design of the unit and main features were: cast-iron crankshaft with plain main

Ted Pardoe, designer of the original Bullet, discusses a point with George Neal, then foreman of the experimental department (1949).

bearings, narrow angle valves with cross-over pushrods, one shaft at the front of the engine carrying cams, breather, oil pump, contact breaker on the mainshaft with idle spark, and cross-over three speed gearbox.

Royal Enfield owners may not have heard of this machine, Registration No KWP 707. I rode it myself for over 20,000 miles before it was stripped and one gearbox bearing was replaced. It had a tough life because much of my spare time then was spent helping Reuben Hunt (test shop) and Dick Bolton (repair shop) prepare sections for local trials and the bike went through most of them!

The first design on which I was engaged, to go into production was the Model RE2 which came out in 1953, Ted Pardoe did the first lay-out and I had the job of redesigning it to take a different generator and other modifications. This gave me the opportunity to make it look different and re-shape it as it went into production.

The manufacture of the crankcase and side covers for this unit were a departure from the usual sand and gravity castings used by Enfield's for previous models. They were to be made by J V Murcott & Sons as high-pressure die-castings, a method suited to high volume production. The initial equipment costs were much higher but component price was less. The castings could be very accurately made needing less machining. Joe Murcott gave me a lot of help regarding what could or could not be done with this process.

One thing bothered me though, we had never made a prototype of the new design and the die equipment was very expensive, Joe said the high quality steel alone for each die was £1,000, a lot of money in those days (my annual salary would have been about £400) and the dies were to be made direct from the drawings. Drawings were never checked by anyone else. When I expressed my concern to Major Smith he told me not to worry as the responsibility was his. Everything turned out OK but I have often wondered what would have happened if they had not!

The first six machines built were used by members of the staff for extended testing, I was one of the six, the first works machine I had, so I felt my efforts had been appreciated.

In the latter half of the fifties, car prices were coming down and the main interest in motorcycles was changing from utility to sporting. Major Smith then decided that we should drop the idea of the simple 250 we had made in prototype form earlier for KWP707 and go for a completely new machine; engine, gearbox, frame, forks, the lot! This kept me occupied for 18 months or so and went into production as the Crusader – a name chosen by Jack Booker.

Another project that I remember clearly was the birth of the Airflow streamlined moulding. Laurie Watts, the Motor Cycle magazine artist had designed an enclosure late in 1956 called the Dreamliner and made it to fit over the frame of the Enfield 350 (Bullet) Model G. We had the machine at the works, it was very impressive but I found it difficult to manoeuvre in restricted areas and the steering much affected by side winds. But it set me thinking of how I would like to do the job.

I had in mind that I would make a glass fibre moulding at home and firstly, I built up a ¼ scale model in plasticine. However, Major Smith got to hear of this and insisted that I brought the model in. He liked what he saw and said we could go ahead and make moulds at the factory. This meant I had to make some drawings, and body designing was a lot different to the sort of drawings I usually did. So I bought a book called 'Body Engineering' showing the method of proportional development of curves used on cars and I was

The Ted Pardoe designed 500 Twin.

Geoff Hay, foreman of the developments department, on the Laurie Watts designed Dreamliner.

able to scale up from the model and make full-size drawings of sections at various positions. At that time, we had our own wood-pattern making shop next to the drawing office and Ron Pearson, the pattern-maker, made the sections in wood and built up a full size replica of the plasticine model. It was finished with scrim cloth and plaster.

The mould then went to the prototype machine shop, another department next to the drawing office, and George Neale had the job of making glass fibre moulds to, eventually, make the finished mouldings. The materials and resins used were all strange to us but he made a very good moulding and the same moulds were used for the first production enclosures.

Later, various specialist companies made the same enclosure for us. At one time the Bristol Aeroplane Company attempted to semi-automate the process but it wasn't successful, the edges of the fairing were resin-rich and could crack away. But our connection with that company gave us the opportunity of getting the Crusader Airflow in their wind-tunnel. It showed up well on tests in the tunnel but the design was not influenced by them. The shape was just a matter of 'what looks right usually is right'.

Every bike, except for the Crusader Super-5, could be supplied with the Airflow enclosure to give it a streamlined appearance. We also made up a rear enclosure from the model but only two mouldings were made, one for the Crusader, the other was put on a Meteor Minor for my own use, this one had indicator lamps front and rear and I used it for a number of years.

Ted Pardoe retired in 1957 and I became chief draughtsman of the motorcycle section. Tony Wilson-Jones

Reg Thomas on prototype Crusader Airflow with Ron Pearson, pattern maker, who made the original wood/plaster masters from R.E.T. drawings.

was technical manager and responsible for development. He was a pleasant chap with a good technical knowledge, very useful if you had plenty of time to listen, but he rambled on a lot and rarely gave a straight answer to a direct question. If you could spend an hour or so to listen to his opinions then it helped you to make up your own mind.

He was fond of writing in the motorcycle magazines and it sometimes gave the impression that he was Royal Enfield's chief designer, which he was not. He once told me that he had never worked on a drawing board and he didn't have one in his office. However, that is not to say he didn't have an influence on design but it was more indirectly through development work as opposed to directly at the design stage.

Geoff Hay was foreman of the development department for some time before moving to engine assembly. For a number of years, Geoff, Charlie Rogers (foreman of the competition department) and I spent a week or ten days supporting the sales staff on the stand at the Earl's Court London motorcycle show. This experience helped very much to get an immediate reaction from motorcyclists on the latest designs and gave us an opportunity to see the latest models from other factories.

Charlie Rogers also had a big influence on design, particularly trials machines as these were modified to suit the competition riders and formed the basis for the production trials machines. Jack Booker was competition manager but he later moved to sales manager and Vic Mountford became managing director on the death of Major Smith.

Great changes took place when the E & H P Smith personnel took over. Leo Davenport became joint managing director with Vic Mountford until Vic died. I was then put in charge of all design, including diesels, jig and tool, development and competition and given the title – chief of design and development, rather a mouthful, I thought. Today it would be called 'engineering manager'.

Although this was a very frustrating time for many, I was given the opportunity by Leo Davenport to prepare some very interesting new designs. Unfortunately, as things later turned out, these never went into production although we

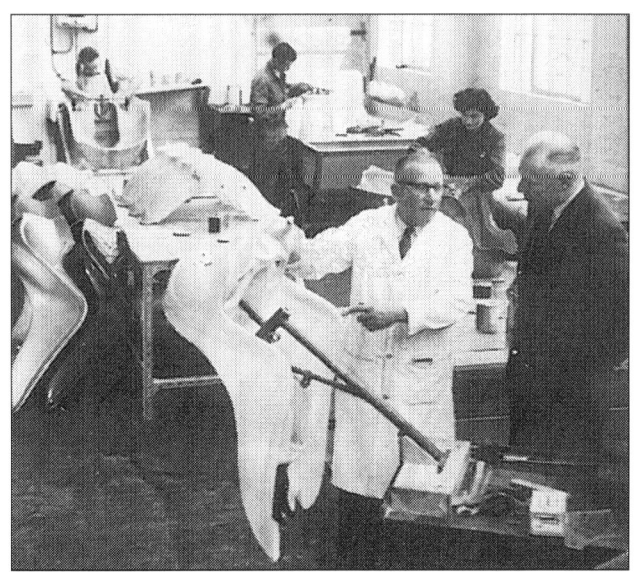

The Airflow production line.

did make prototypes. Six sets of the 175cc OHC unit were made although only two were built up, and one machine. This has been the subject of articles in the motorcycle press. Another interesting model was a 98cc 2-stroke engine with 6-speed gearbox – from memory I think we only made one prototype of this.

Production ceased at Redditch in 1966 but I was fortunate to be able to move to Bradford-on-Avon and take over design and development there on a five-year contract. The main factory was underground, with some offices and workshops such as the buying office and the bike assembly, above ground. We didn't think twice about working underground all day, we were working so hard that we didn't notice it. The mine had been hewn out of stone and you had to go down a long tunnel to reach the heart of the factory. A few rooms, such as the engine-testing room, branched off from this tunnel.

The main factory was one very large chamber where most of the operations took place. The only way that you would know that you were underground was that the ceiling was very low and it was supported by massive stone pillars. When the larger machines were installed it was necessary to take them underground in pieces. They were then reassembled in holes hewn out of the floor to get the necessary height. Set into the walls were several doors which led to the manager's office, the jig and tool drawing office and a few other offices.

I had redesigned the bottom half of the Interceptor engine before leaving Redditch and it went into production at the Westwood underground factory as the Series II model. We were now a very small unit with little money for development. The Norton forks and front brake were grafted on to the Enfield frame and this appears to have become a very desirable machine for collectors. If we could have been allowed to develop the 800cc engine we had in prototype form it would have been even more desirable! However, it was not to be.

So I was introduced to Royal Enfield's at Westwood and ended my twenty-five years there. I agree with another employee who remarked, 'It was a nice company to work for but the wages were very poor'.

The prototype Bullet, ridden in the 1948 ISDT.

CHARLIE ROGERS: from 1933 to closure

I was never interviewed or trained as a foreman at Royal Enfield, I just drifted into the job. A carpenter by trade, I began riding Royal Enfield bikes in trials in about 1933. At that time I didn't work at the Enfield factory but the management supported me, which meant that they provided me with a bike for trials and paid all my expenses. I was able to book myself into a hotel of my choice and send them the bill. There was a bonus for winning and a first prize brought me in an extra £25 with additional payments for the various class cups and team awards. We had a good team and won nearly every team event. I was also paid a retainer in the final year before war broke out. I rode 350's, usually the Bullet, and I was lucky enough to win two or three times.

During the war I worked at a motorcycle school in Keswick as an instructor, then after the war I continued riding Enfield bikes in trials. I then went into the competition department of the factory to prepare my own bikes and eventually, Major Smith asked me if I would take charge of the department. We did not design the bikes, this was done by the experimental department, but we tested the new designs and tried to iron out any faults.

The most hectic competition was the International Six Days Trial held in Italy in September 1948, not long after the end of the war. The bikes had to be assembled quickly so that they would be ready on time. The organisers had also had a rush to prepare everything and had not been able to work out the times, so it was more of a race than a trial. We just went flat out for the whole week. We were riding prototype 350 Bullets fitted with a new sprung frame which was heavily criticised by our competitors but they then went away and tried to copy it! We won the six-day trials that year, plus the ACU, and the following year we again won the International Six Day's Trial held in Wales. Royal Enfield bikes always did well in trials and there were usually at least two bikes with a team trophy.

Royal Enfield was a very friendly firm. Very few outsiders joined the company, it was mostly manned by workers who had started there as young boys, and their relatives. Everyone said it was run more like a church fete than a factory.

JOHN F SMITH, C Eng, MI Mech E, FIED: from 1936 to 1950

After matriculating at the County High School, I was apprenticed to Royal Enfield in 1936. In 1941 I joined eight others in the jig and tool drawing and planning office as a design draughtsman. Later, Vic Bott became a member of the department. There were two drawing offices, the motorcycle design office and ours – we worked out the best methods and means of production for the parts which the other office designed. They would issue new components such as cylinder barrels and crankcases and we would plan the method of production, deciding what operations should be carried out on what machines. We designed milling jigs and fixtures, press tools pressing components, in fact any production aid.

The chief planning engineer and draughtsman was Jack Hassall who should be put on record as one of the men who helped to build Enfield. He was responsible for all the jig and tool plant layout in the works after 1920. He came in the 1920s, soon after Tommy Guise had been appointed as works manager, and together they built up the engineering side of the firm. He was a fairly tall, thin, athletic man who had been trained as a toolmaker at Thomas's, one of the largest engineering complexes in the district. He went to South Africa in 1946 or 1947 to found a cycle factory but he died after only six months out there. Tommy Guise was incensed with rage when he heard that Jack Hassall was leaving him and later declared that Jack had died of a broken heart after leaving Enfield's.

Jack was succeeded by Les Whittaker who unfortunately suffered from ill health and was absent for long periods. By this time, I had become deputy chief draughtsman so I was left in charge for a great deal of the time. Mr Guise kept a paternal eye on me, he used to pop his head round the door and say, 'Everything under control?'

Looking back over a period of years, Mr Guise was one of the outstanding men of Royal Enfield. He was an exceptional character and an extremely shrewd engineer. He ran the works on a clever, low-cost basis, for example he bought a lot of second-hand machinery for very low prices which did years and years of useful work. He was very mean on money and I know that this in particular made him disliked by some, but it is my personal opinion that he literally held the firm together from 1920 until he retired in 1950. I believe that, from then onwards, Royal Enfield began to go downhill.

As a draughtsman, I was a member of the only Union at Royal Enfield, the Union of Amalgamated Engineering and Shipbuilding Draughtsmen. I was a Corresponding member

Producing the first batch of all-welded cycle frames, which made a lighter, more rigid and stronger frame, 1950.

and we used to hold Union meetings. Tommy Guise attended one of them and even gave us a rise as a result!

I worked on motorcycles from 1941, beginning with the two models used extensively during the war, the 350cc CO and the 98cc 2-stroke Flying Flea. When the war was over, the CO was developed into the 350cc commercial motorcycle fitted with telescopic forks and the Flying Flea became the Baby Royal, made for the Dutch market. Princess Juliana had just had her first baby, hence the name. That particular machine could be sold on the English market and a fellow in the tool room bought one for just £26!

Another interesting development on which I worked was the all-welded motorcycle frame. I did all the tools for that. Previously, the frame was made by malleable lugs pushed into tubes but after 1948 the frame was all-welded at each joint.

I also witnessed the development of telescopic front forks. These came into production in about 1945, but there was a great need to develop something similar on the rear wheels to absorb the jolting when going over rough ground. It was always said that you couldn't have a chain drive if the rear of the bike was sprung as the tension in the chain altered considerably. Royal Enfield were the first to overcome this problem to produce a sprung rear end, known as the swinging arm frame. The design department worked out that if the rear wheel was pivoted near the centre of the driving sprocket than it would move in an arc which naturally preserved the constant tension of the chain. It proved so successful that all English and German manufacturers followed suit. Of course, the chain manufacturers were delighted as it gave them a new lease of life. Later, the Japanese developed the idea even further and pivoted right on the centre of the driving sprocket.

My oldest sister, Lily, worked in the offices from 1916 until she married in 1934, then she continued part-time. Major Smith sent for her and said that he had this young sixteen-year old, the son of the owner of the Madras Motor Company, coming over from India for engineering training. He needed a lady who could be a second mother to him and, as my sister had a nice big house in Bordesley, would she take this young man as a lodger? Sundaram lived with my sister for two years while he attended Bromsgrove Engineering College where I was teaching. He was a very bright student indeed, he took his HND and, in fact, won a State scholarship but unfortunately, this was not awarded to foreigners. After leaving my sister he went to Aston University, then to India. They corresponded regularly and in about 1988, Lily's daughter was invited to his daughter's wedding in Madras, spending six weeks there at Sundaram's expense.

When Sundaram returned to India, an older man, Harry Sandford, came out to continue the link between Royal Enfield and Enfield India. The model now manufactured by them, the 350cc with overhead valve, is, in almost every respect, the model designed by Ted Pardoe and it is a great tribute to him that, fifty years on, it is still in production.

Ted Pardoe was an extremely clever design engineer who produced a whole range of bikes from the 1920s until the 1940s. He was a distinguished looking man who wore a white raincoat and trilby hat. He spoke very quickly and quietly and, as a result of a war injury, he had a slight impediment in his speech so that it was often difficult to catch what he said. He drove backwards and forwards to work on a twin 660cc motorcycle and sidecar which he designed but was never put into production. Royal Enfield could afford to produce about five experimental designs every two years. Some bikes came to nothing, others were wildly successful. The 660cc was not developed because an even larger bike, the KX V-twin 1140cc, was put on the market.

Ted Pardoe was succeeded by Reg Thomas, a gifted designer who even improved the strain of Enfield design.

CHAPTER SEVEN
The competitive Enfields

Enfield riders in the 1948 International Six Days Trial, from left: Charlie Rogers, Vic Brittain, Tom Ellis and Jack Stocker. The British Trophy and Vase teams remained intact despite Charlie Rogers sailing over a hedge. Rogers and Brittain were the only two riders of 350cc machines to win Gold medals on this trial.

RAY KNIGHT looks at the Royal Enfield Road Racers

> *Ray Knight started a 36-year racing career on a Royal Enfield Super Meteor in 1958 and rode a works Constellation in the Thruxton endurance races in 1961/62. A contributor to motorcycle magazines for 25 years, he has published five books on motorcycle racing and won a Production TT in 1968.*

Royal Enfield machines have featured in many branches of motorcycle sport, but in road racing, it has to be conceded that they were not the first choice for a rider, given the ready availability of purpose-built and very successful models from the like of Norton, Velocette, AJS, Matchless and all the rest.

Nevertheless, they certainly were fielded at the highest levels even if victors' laurels came their way infrequently. That the company actually designed and built a model specifically for the job, is a story in itself, involving as it did famous names – six times world champion Geoff Duke and respected two stroke designer and tuner, Hermann Meier.

The Isle of Man Tourist Trophy Races are, arguably, the most famous road races in the world. In the early days of the races, Royal Enfield machines did in fact feature quite prominently, in spite of the relatively small numbers of them entered.

The Royal Enfield riders in the 1914 TT. From left: Alan Hill, Douggie Alexander, Fred Walker, H. Hanks (non starter), 'Bones' Keyte and F. H. Wasling.

It was back in the dim and distant days of 1911 that an RE first made its appearance in the fledgling TT programme – in fact there were two. It was in the Junior event in which H Greaves finished a most creditable fifth; the other succumbed to those 37.7 miles of, in those days, deeply rutted unmaintained roads that broke the early cycle-derived frames and reduced riders to near physical wrecks.

In 1913, the Junior race distance was upped to 225 miles, in which there were five Enfield's entered. The official works team consisted of H Greaves, E Keyte and Bert Colver, while C M Down and D Alexander were amateurs. Perhaps inauspiciously, they achieved 16th and 17th places, with the others mechanical fatalities in the race. The following year there were no less than nine entries and F J Walker achieved the distinction of finishing on the rostrum, in third place. A further seven finished from eighth to 26th places, a pretty good example of reliability.

There seems to have been something of a lack of enthusiasm in the intervening years up to 1925 when, in the Junior race as usual, four machines were featured in the entry, riding the new twin-port ohv, JAP engined models. One of the riders was no less then Stanley Woods, later to write his name in the hall of motorcycling fame. But the best result was Charlie Young in 17th. Incidentally, there was never more than one RE retirement in any year so machine stamina was a feature of the early Enfields.

In the years through to 1960, there were a total of 46 Enfield's entered in TT races. A particular highlight was the record of Cecil Barrow who achieved second place on a 250 and eighth in the 1935 Senior event; interestingly, this model was a four valve Bullet.

A recap of the results shows that from the 46, two finished on the rostrum, seven on the leaderboard and 33 completed the course. Along the way Royal Enfield won the Manufacturer's Team Prize in the 1927 Junior. Hardly a bad record.

The Manx Grand Prix too provided successes for Royal Enfield machines and a notable one at that – of which more later. The races were started in 1923 and soon established themselves as the stepping stone to the World Championship at that time, Tourist Trophy Races. The races were the pinnacle of their racing careers for many an aspiring Clubman.

Enfield's were raced in the Manx from 1926 with varying degrees of success, quite frequently until 1948 when rising star W A (Bill) Lomas finished in seventh place in the Lightweight Race. His bike was something of a mechanical masterpiece, based on a 1938 model, he contrived double overhead chain driven camshafts. He was to go on to win Grand Prix and become a world champion.

The Newcomers race was an event added to the programme in 1987 and was the route taken by many riders to winning Manx Grand Prix and TT races. It was to provide Steve Linsdell with a notable ride to a magnificent second place in the 1981 Senior Class. This was a substantially re-engineered Bullet with Alpha bottom and large capacity oil pump. His 'old' Enfield embarrassed a host of Japanese multis.

A talented mechanic as well as an excellent rider around the Mountain circuit, Linsdell started his affair with Royal

H. Greaves with a 3hp twin, the first Royal Enfield to be fitted with their own engine.

Enfield machines when he fielded a 350 Bullet in Vintage races from 1977 and throughout the next three years with considerable success and against machines originally sold as specialist racing machines.

Not content with that, he next produced a big twin racer from an early Meteor, effectively two 350 Bullets sat upon a common crankcase. With this he regularly blew off the Triumph and Norton twins that had been the bikes to beat in the big classes. The 692cc Enfield twin was housed in a Colin Seeley racing frame and transmitted the power through a five speed Norton gearbox.

The story of Royal Enfield's foray into marketing a racing machine specially built for the job is probably one that they would have preferred to have forgotten, in that reliability was a constant problem. Perhaps less than 20 machines were actually sold to customers though records seem to conflict.

The story began in 1963, and the bike, like the Cotton and several others, used the Villiers Starmaker engine. This version, however, was only a prototype to enable the Enfield to proceed in developing the machine's chassis.

The chassis design involved the vast experience of Ken Sprayson, a man responsible for many a special racing frame

Percy Tait heads the field on the experimental GP5 at the 1965 Hutchinson 100, before being passed by the works Yamahas after developing piston trouble. He finished in third place.

design. It employed a single top tube and duplex loop thereafter. A particular feature was that the left front down tube had to be cranked to clear the exhaust pipe. The swinging rear arm employed a split clamp end which used alloy spacers of varying sizes to achieve chain adjustment.

The cycle was interesting in that it employed the leading link type front fork originally designed by Reynolds for Geoff Duke, intended for his lightweight Norton and reflects his input to the project. Of particular note was the one-piece fuel-tank-cum-seat aluminium alloy fabrication, to be replaced by a fibreglass version in production model, of almost six gallons capacity, fuel being stored throughout the full length of the unit. Benefits of the design were the reduction of the overall height of the tank and distribution of the weight of the fuel load over the length of the machine.

After having employed the Villiers-inspired engine firstly in a scrambler and then in the GP5 prototype, they worked on developing their own engine. Again a single cylinder two stroke, it used the Alpha bottom end, Alpha are a company long-established in the supply of components to the motorcycle industry, particularly big-end flywheel assemblies.

From Roy Bacon's excellent book, *Royal Enfield, the Postwar Models*, the technical details show that the bottom end conformed to their usual designs, it did differ in that the front cylinder studs were more widely spaced and the crankcase halves had cooling fins around the outside. Internally it had the normal Alpha pressed-together crankshaft with full circle wheels, oval section connecting rod and caged needle roller big end bearing.

The rest of the bottom end was a pretty straightforward Alpha, but the top end of the unit was totally Royal Enfield. Barrel porting, like the rest of the engine, was designed by Hermann Meier, though within a brief that excluded a rotary inlet valve.

Six times a world champion, Geoff Duke had been invited by the then managing director of the Enfield Cycle Company Leo Davenport, winner of the Lightweight TT in 1932 on a New Imperial, to assist in designing the machine and Geoff spent a year with them working on it. It was he who was instrumental in bringing in Hermann Meier, the highly regarded two stroke development engineer, to ensure that the Enfield power unit would provide 'adequate motivation'. A formidable name indeed that led to the launch of the machine designated the GP5.

That Meier succeeded in his mission is amply borne out by the appearance of Percy Tait in the Hutchinson 100 at Silverstone. He kept the prototype Enfield racer in front of

Geoff Duke tries the GP5 for size, aided by John Surtees.

the field for three laps, which included works Yamaha riders Phil Read and Mike Duff. Piston trouble eventually relegated him to a nevertheless creditable third, but to prove the considerable performance potential, he did manage to break the lap record on the way. He was also recorded at 132mph in the 1965 North West 200 International race.

Meier, aware of the engine's mechanical limitations when developing the quoted 34 brake horse power at 8,250 rpm, proposed an engine with twin cylinders in line with liquid cooling and with the inlet controlled by disc valves. However, financial cramp precluded the expenditure that would have been required to take the project forward. One more example where Japanese designs might have been matched if only the financial muscle had been available.

There were several instances of racing the production road machines that were always, I feel, underrated in terms of performance potential. They were quite capable of holding their own with models from other manufacturers with the emphasis on top end performance.

What had started life as the Thruxton Nine Hours Race staged by the Southampton and District Club in 1955, became the Motorcycle 500 Mile Race in 1958 and was to

Ray Knight (1956 Super Meteor) at one of his early race meetings at Brands Hatch.

be the scene of several manufacturers inspired entries in the long distance production machine race. The likes of Mike Hailwood and many another great names of the time raced production machines entered by dealers which were in reality works-prepared machines, including Royal Enfield.

It was the sight of one of the Super Meteors competing in the Thruxton Production Machine Endurance Race in 1958, ridden by the great Bob McIntyre contending for the lead, that was instrumental in my making my own competition debut. The sight was sufficiently inspiring for me to acquire a Super Meteor, which I soon found to be the equal of current big British twins when ridden with elan on the open roads; there was no 70 mile per hour speed limit in those days.

The Motor Cycling Club staged meetings on the Silverstone Club circuit in the late fifties and indeed still do. Whilst there was no structured production machine racing at the time, it was about the only place where road machines could compete without entering the competition arena against purpose-built racers. It was the scene of something of an annual 'bash' for aspiring road racers and the competition was fast and furious.

My own inauspicious competition debut took place in the Hour High Speed Trials in 1958 where the 'bog standard' Meteor proved to be pretty competitive as it was. However, disqualification for 'over exuberance' resulted.

It is relevant to mention that a certain Mr Collander won the Southern Area Sidecar Scrambles Championship on a 700 because it was that bike, prepared by ex-Norton works rider and dealer Syd Lawton of Lawton & Wilson of Southampton, that I was to purchase from Syd in October 1969, to supersede my own standard model.

Fitted with the pistons and camshafts that were to be standard on the later Constellation model, it was competitive enough to hold the production machine lap record at the Silverstone Club circuit for three years against the Tiger 110s, BSA Super Rockets and Lightinised Vincents of the day. Even so, with a long string of places, I never quite managed to get 'under the linen' first.

1958 was McIntyre's first try at winning the '500' on a 700 RE, but it was marred by a leaking petrol tank and misfire. However, although frequently lapping faster than any other machine in the 50 strong grid, second place surprised many who would not have considered the Meteor a competitive mount. In that year, a certain Mike Hailwood ran out the winner. A couple more tries in following years ended with a spill and a broken connecting rod.

In 1961, I was riding a Constellation entered by the Royal Enfield Owners Club, one of five competing that year, so the marque was gaining recognition among keen clubmen. My machine was in fact loaned by the factory, while the cycle details were supervised by Syd Lawton. However, an error in calculating the fuel consumption meant that I had to push back to the pits for something like two miles, which somewhat spoilt the result; 13th.

The Crusader 250 four stroke single fared rather better though. In 1960 it won its class, ridden by R Prowting and M Munday. It was a popular model for club-production racing for several years and has since made something of a comeback in Classic racing.

Royal Enfield may not be a name that is always associated with road racing competition but raced they were and the standard product was at least as competitive as the other machines of the day.

Certainly in the later years there was never enough money in the kitty to fund a serious racing effort. I was to race an Interceptor for the works during the 1970 season but the company folded before I could take up an offer that many production racers of the time would have given their right arm for. I remember a conversation with Jack Booker when he revealed that he had actually to get a Board approval for a new inlet manifold casting to enable the Constellation to be fitted with twin carburettors. Indeed the purse strings were very tight. It wasn't very long before the take-over by Norton Villiers, but one more symptom of a failing industry, one that when it did have the resources, failed to invest in new models and technology to compete in world markets with the Japanese.

BILL LOMAS

Bill Lomas became double world and British champion in 1955 and 1956. He worked at Enfield's from late '47 to the end of '49 when he left to go into GP racing, first with Velocettes and AJS, then going continental and riding for NSU, MV and Benelli. He finally ended up living in Italy by Lake Como and working as development rider for Moto-Guzzi, for whom he won two world championships and many races including the Isle of Man TT, as well as breaking world records using the Moto-Guzzi V8.

In mid 1947, having had racing successes at Cadwell Park which included winning the 350 championship on a pre-war 250 Enfield Bullet fitted with a 350cc JAP engine, I was asked by Jack Booker if I would like a job in the experimental and competition department. I accepted and he found me digs at the Abbey Hostel alongside Charlie Rogers, who ran the competition department at the factory.

Tony Wilson-Jones was a larger-than-life character, weighing about sixteen stones and big with it. He used to run around on a little 125 RE. When he wore his big gabardine motorcycle coat and waders you had a job to see the motorcycle. Tony Wilson-Jones used the experimental department to try things out so that he could write a thesis to read to the Society of Mechanical Engineers. One such idea as the depreciation of rubber. The 125 RE had rubber-band front fork suspension, so a 125 RE was available to be used as a test bed for the rubber bands.

He was very kind to me and allowed me the use of the competition shop and dynamometer after working hours. As you can imagine, I spent most of my spare time there in the evenings. After many complaints from local residents about noise in the evenings, I had to finish Dyno testing by 9 pm.

I was coached by Charlie Rogers in the art of trials riding, and rode in many Redditch club trials. When the works riders came to collect their factory bikes before each trial, we would usually give them a practice run on the Enfield test ground over the old air-raid shelters.

The factory did try running 125 RE in trials, but due to it only having a hand change and a three speed gear box it was not very successful.

Jack Booker and I did a lot of experiments with the two-stroke porting. I managed to get one to do about 75-80 mph, and made a positive stop foot change for it. I raced it once at Cadwell Park finishing second after a bad start. Jack

Booker then raced it in scrambles with some success.

I developed the original pre-war 250 engine so well that it enabled me to win many races and championships from 1948 to 1950 including the Cadwell Championship. I made a twin front brake for it, using two standard Enfield brake drums. This was later copied by the factory. Finally, I made a double overhead camshaft head for it in late 1949. A 500cc engine was later fitted in the bike to win the 500 championship.

One morning I surreptitiously fitted a modified cylinder and head to Tony Wilson-Jones RE. He came back after lunch, enthusing about the new petrol oil mixture he was using, saying that it had put more than seven or eight mph on the bike. It went up one hill in second gear instead of bottom. During the afternoon I replaced the original head and barrel. He was rather late coming into work the following morning. It transpired he'd been running backwards and forwards trying the RE out to find the reason for the loss of performance. It was suggested that it could easily have been the change in the wind direction. This placated him a little, but he was forever puzzled.

When I first started, I noticed that two beautiful-looking black 125cc DKW motorcycles were forlornly leaning against the back wall. They had apparently been annexed at the end of the war by the military, ending up at Enfield's for their appraisal. Obviously, the view was that the design might be copied at some future date, DKWs being the world-leaders in two-stroke technology at that time.

One day, a van from BSA's picked them up, and a year later the BSA Bantam appeared for sale. It was more or less

Bill Lomas at Cadwell Park, 1949. Photo: George Schofield.

an exact copy of the DKW except that the gear and kick-starter levers were on the right-hand side of the engine. This was to become the best selling bike BSA's ever made. Why Enfield's decided against doing this I'll never know. The new Enfield-designed 150 RE which later appeared never hit the sales jackpot because of its many basic design faults.

It was only Jack Booker's engineering common sense that kept Enfield on the right road, although the Board designers who had never ridden a motorcycle could over-ride him and his ideas in the end.

I must add that my time at Enfield's, and the kindness shown to me, remains one of the highlights of my career. I found a wife, Kathleen, and many friends there. The things I learned there have stood me in good stead throughout my world-wide travels.

VIC BRITTAIN
by Pat & John Brittain

> *For fifteen years the two brothers rode together in competitions and worked side-by-side in the family business during the day. They won countless trials in that time and really put Royal Enfield on the map.*

Dad could do anything, he raced and he took part in trials and scrambles. We only rode in trials. He was well-known internationally as well as nationally; he was a member of the winning British team in the 1948 International Six Days Trial when it was held in Italy. Great Britain won the International Vase and the International Trophy. Dad and Charlie Rogers were on 350 Bullets and were in the winning Trophy team, they also won gold medals.

He originally rode Nortons, but one of the directors had a disagreement with the Norton family and walked out. Dad left at the same time and it was suggested that he rode for Enfield. In those days Fred Bladon was in charge of the competition shop. Dad rode Enfield bikes for over twenty years, right until the early 1960s.

When war broke out on 3rd September 1939 Dad was competing in Germany and he had to race home.

PAT BRITTAIN

I was never a megastar like my brother, although I did manage to beat him in a number of events, he just had the edge on me.

John was a few years older, and was riding in trials when I was fifteen. He would be at work during the day, so when I came home from school I would, unknown to him, have a ride on his trials bike. There was a cinder track running alongside our house in Walsall leading to some allotments, I used to take his bike up there and practice. Luckily he never found out.

My first trials bike, when I reached sixteen, was a DMW. Suitably sporting L plates, one of the first national trials I entered was the Clayton Trophy in the Buxton area and like John a few years earlier, I found it very tough, although in later years I found the Bemrose and Clayton run in this area very enjoyable.

In 1953 Enfield's offered me a little 150cc Ensign, at that time it was one of the bikes they were trying to sell, and they thought the publicity might help. Also, being a lightweight person when I was young, I was suited to the machine. When I first started to ride the Ensign, the gearbox kept breaking so the factory had some special gears made of very high quality steel which overcame the problem. It had a solid rear frame and riding was not very comfortable compared to the sprung frames used later on. This was found out by experience! – in the Welsh trial, riding fairly quickly down a mountain dirt road, I was confronted by a drainage gully running across the track, the front telescopic forks rode the hazard but the rear end being solid shot in the air. The last thing I remembered was parting company with the bike, the bike then overtaking me in mid air and the handlebars

Vic Brittain (right) takes a break in the 1948 ISDT, held round San Remo, Italy.

Pat Brittain on Kinlochrannoch riding a 150cc Ensign.

striking me across the nose. When I came round, with blood pouring down my face, I remounted but the next few miles were very shaky!

In 1953 Jack Booker, Royal Enfield's competition manager, saw me riding a section in the Welsh Two-Day Trial, and offered me a ride on a special 250cc, which was an identical machine to the 350cc John was riding but had a cast iron Clipper engine installed, which made it heavier than the all-alloy 350 but considerably less powerful. I rode my first 350cc Bullet in the International Six Days Trial which was held in Wales.

In 1955 I graduated on to a full works 350 and joined John and Peter Stirland as the official work's team. The machine was allocated the registration number KAB 543 and although I had many different bikes over the coming years, I kept that same number until changing to a 250cc Crusader in 1965.

As every rider knows, trials vary a great deal. There are different types of events and marks can be lost in different ways. In some trials there are observed sections where you lose marks for stopping or footing, in some events you ride against the clock and sometimes there is a combination of both. The International Six Days Trial is a timed event over rough terrain usually around 1,200 miles long, split roughly into 200 miles runs per day. The major parts of the bike were marked and sealed so couldn't be replaced once the machine was handed in the day before the event started, and once there the bike was kept under lock and key. You were allowed 10 minutes before you started each day for maintenance, like replacing tyres, but any extra time required usually meant going like a bat out of hell on the last stage of the day to make up a few extra minutes before your allotted clocking-in time. If you completed the week without loss of marks you were awarded a Gold medal, the team which lost the least amount of marks won the event outright.

John and I competed in the ISDT a number of times behind the Iron Curtain, the first time was quite a shock. Journeying down on an Austin A40 pick-up loaded with the bikes and spares we left West Germany's wide tarmac dual carriageway and turned down a narrow dirt road with grass in the centre. We couldn't believe this was the main road into Czechoslovakia, it looked as if we were the first ones to use it for years. We went down the road for half a mile before coming to the border post. On both sides was a tall wire fence with look-out posts where armed guards were patrolling on horseback. The road continued to zig-zag through concrete bollards and then go across a barren flood-lit area. We wondered if we would ever get back out again! Every village we passed was in a very poor state of repair. The paint was peeling off the walls and loudspeakers in the streets were booming out what we imagined was eastern propaganda. I remember going out to a dance organized for us by the official of the trial, and a lad about my own age, who turned out to be the band leader, getting me on one side

ISDT 1955. Pat Brittain (350 Bullet) with red scarf and flowers.

and in broken English asking me about wages and prices of goods in the West. He told me there was only one shop that sold each type of goods in each town and a pair a shoes took six months' wages to buy. Things have improved since then.

However, the trial itself was run to perfection, like a military operation, and the army was heavily involved, with soldiers everywhere. Each day a young girl would tie a red scarf round our necks, and at the finish a nurse would bath our eyes. We also received a bouquet of flowers from yet another girl. The British riders stayed in the same hotel, each hotel had a flag flying from it emblazoned with a red star. I remember finding the food not to my taste. Spare parts were so difficult to obtain in Czechoslovakia at that time, we would be offered £10 in their money for one second-hand sparking plug, which was a lot of money to them. Czech money wasn't any use to us as we couldn't exchange it and there was nothing we wanted to buy, but we did give some parts away which were not required. We stayed in interesting places in other ISDT trials. In Garmisch, Partankirchen, the bikes were kept in a *perke-ferme* at the base of the ski jumps, in Poland at Zakopane we were the first people to stay in a hotel which was purpose-built for the winter Olympics.

Most of the major trials were trade-supported, that is, Enfield's signed a contract with Castrol for its oil, Shell for petrol, Dunlop for tyres and so on, they agreed with the manufacturers of those products to use their goods. If we were successful we would be paid a bonus by each of them.

Every third or fourth trade trial, Enfield's would send a lorry to the garage in Walsall to collect our bikes. They would be taken back to Redditch where Charlie Rogers and his team would completely overhaul them. Sometimes they were delivered back to the garage, at other times we would collect them from the time office (next to the main gate) on a Thursday evening. We liked to practice on a Friday for any of the trade-supported events taking place on a Saturday.

In one of the Scott trials (I can't remember the year) it had been raining hard all the day before the event and was also pouring on the day itself. Around 180 competitors started and I think about 21 finished in the time limit. I remember this trial particularly well as we came across a swollen river that had to be negotiated twice. On the first lap, an earlier competitor had tried to cross but his machine had been swept away downstream, I believe it was recovered the next day. A number of riders were debating how to reach the other side when Jeff Smith took a flat-out run from the far side of the field and jumped across, we all followed in turn. Unfortunately, on the second lap the take-off point had got very muddy. I myself landed short of the far side and the rear brake was ripped off by a submerged rock. I completed the rest of the event without a rear brake which proved quite exciting. After that event it was a phone call to Charlie for some repair work.

Halfway round you stopped for fuel and usually had a tot of whisky which seemed to do you a power of good until the effects wore off.

Quite apart from the major events, we rode most weekends in national and local trials. We didn't worry whether or not we were paid by Enfield's, sometimes we were not entered as work's riders but just enjoyed riding and competing. Fortunately we were both employed at the family garage and we could leave work early, depending upon how far away the events were being held. Often they were miles apart and we could, say, be riding in Ripon (Yorkshire) on the Saturday and Hampshire on the Sunday, then the next weekend Northern Ireland on the Saturday and the Cotswolds on the Sunday. Many a time as we drove the pick-up home we would be so tired that whoever was driving would have his head out of the window trying to keep awake! We would be back at work Monday! – washing our bikes down in our lunch hour and staying over in the evening to get the bikes ready for the next weekend.

My two years of National Service began in 1958 and to travel to and from camp at Bordon in Hampshire, I used a 700 Meteor which proved quite a quick road bike. I was allowed leave at the weekends to ride for Enfield's but rode for the army when required.

When I first started riding for Royal Enfield in 1953, Charlie Rogers had a free hand to develop the trials bikes as he wished with the result that the machines used by us were quite different from the standard models. The 350 Bullet had a special all-welded light frame made from Reynold's 531 tubing, the engine was more highly tuned with special light flywheels, the bottom half of the engine plus the gearbox was cast in a material a third lighter than the standard alloy parts, the standard full width hubs in alloy were replaced by a single special casting of the lightweight material, and the petrol tank, originally steel, was made of aluminium. One weak point was the telescopic front forks, they were prone to leaking and losing the damping, Charlie had some special castings made which used the internal parts of the Norton forks (these were far superior) disguised as Royal Enfield which we found much better. Also the oil filter on the bottom of the timing cover casting was prone to damage if caught on rocks and was omitted, again a special casting made for our bikes.

After 1958 the policy of the company changed and we were asked to ride standard bikes. It was felt that this was better marketing strategy if people could buy the same bikes as the ones we were riding.

In the early 1960's Sammy Miller started developing the Bultaco two-stroke machine which was of Spanish manufacture. This being a lighter and easier bike to ride, the

Pat Brittain on the Devil's Staircase, en route to a special first class award.

big four strokes started getting increasingly uncompetitive. Enfield's answer was the smaller 250 Clipper and although I managed to win the Colmore Cup trial, the writing was on the wall. The British motorcycle industry was in a state of decline and had, unfortunately, no answer to the Spanish and later, the Japanese invasion.

Looking back, John and I were very fortunate in that we were able to travel and see places that we would never otherwise have seen.

Some awards won were:

1953	Best 150cc	Manville Cup Trial
	Best 150cc	Welsh Two Day Trial
1954	Best 250cc	Scottish Six Days Trial
1955	Winner	Hoad Trophy Trial
	Best 350cc	John Douglas Trial
	Best 350cc	Mitchell Trial
1956	Winner	Vic Brittain Trial
	Best 350cc	Streatham Trophy Trial
	Best 350cc	Cotswold Cup Trial
1957	Best 350cc	Clayton Trophy Trial
	Missed some events, started National Service	
1958	Runner-up	British Experts Trial
	Fifth	Scottish Six Days
	Best 350cc	Hoad Trophy Trial
	Best 350cc	Clayton Trophy Trial
1960	Best 350cc	Clayton Trophy Trial
	Best 350cc	Welsh Two-Day Trial
1962	Winner	Colmore Cup Trial

Gold and silver medals in International Six Days Trial.
Seven special first class awards, Scott Trial.
Member of winning manufacturer's team prize on many occasions.
Number of top ten finishers in ACU stars.

JOHN BRITTAIN

It's a debatable point how much my father helped us. He never pushed us but we were always messing around on push bikes.

When I was old enough to have my licence, in 1948, there was a deteriorating situation in the Suez Canal and trials were cancelled for that year because of the petrol shortage. To compensate, Wolverhampton Motor Cycle Club arranged for bicycle trials instead. Pat and I entered and thoroughly enjoyed it. That's where we acquired a taste for competition.

I learned to ride on a DMW but I was then approached by the James company who offered to lend me a machine if I rode for them in competitions.

My first big trial on the James was the Clayton Trial near Buxton, held on the August bank holiday of 1949. My father took me there and before the trial began we had a look at the course. There was this one section called Cheeks Hill on the Buxton to Leek Road which was just a little rut on an S-bend. My father dismissed it as being so easy that it wasn't even worth looking at. I made an absolute hash of it. I think I lost every point possible. I found the trial very hard going and was thoroughly disillusioned.

I just kept riding on my James and gradually found myself winning quite a lot of local trials and class awards such as the Midland Centre Trials. Towards the end of 1950 I was approached by Fred Bladon and Major Mountford who asked me to ride for Royal Enfield.

I rode for Enfield for fifteen years. During all that time I never thought that I was riding for myself, I was riding for Royal Enfield against Triumph or BSA or one of the other motorcycle companies.

I thought the 350 Bullet was an excellent bike and was soon winning events such as the 1951 Northern Experts Trial. You could say the bike was bullet-proof! The engine was brilliant. We used to rev and abuse it, when we had to go up a long muddy hill we used to open the throttle absolutely flat but the Bullet went on forever.

My first big win was on a 350 Bullet in the 1952 Scottish Six Days Trial. It was one of those times when the people who are expected to win don't and a young up-and-coming player, with nothing to lose and everything to gain, comes up and wins. It caused quite a stir at the time. I was the youngest rider ever to win the Scottish Six Days.

The Monday and Thursday were based at Edinburgh and the Tuesday, Wednesday and Friday were at Fort William with a circuit of about 200 miles each day. On the Saturday, there were no sections and virtually all that you had to do was to ride back from Fort William to Edinburgh within a certain time. This meant that whoever was winning on the Friday night was likely to win the Trial.

Unknown to me, there was a stop and start test at Blackford Hill, Edinburgh. When I got there, somebody said, 'Your father is up there, on the hill'. I told them they must be mistaken because my father had stopped at home. I didn't know that Jack Booker and Fred Bladon had telephoned him and said, 'We think your son is going to win'. Between them they had arranged for my father to go up on the overnight train and I was very surprised when I saw him.

He went up on the rostrum with me when I was presented with the J R Alexander Trophy. Mr Alexander, who had a big machine business in Edinburgh, presented me the cup, and he put a £5 note in it for us to go and have a party. I was a bit young and naive in those days so Dickie Davies took control of it. He was competition manager at Dunlop's and the heart and soul of any party. We all went out for a meal and Dickie played the piano.

Major Smith gave a party to celebrate at the Green Dragon, Sambourne. All the Enfield team were invited and I was presented with a leather holdall. We were all so pleased, Royal Enfield didn't make all that many motorbikes and it was like a small motorcycle company winning against the giants – BSA or Triumph. Looking back, I can see now that the three of us, Peter Stirland, my brother and myself put Royal Enfield on the map. We were in the motorcycle magazines, winning class awards, team awards and premier awards which must have been first class advertising.

The fact that I had won one big trial gave me confidence and in the same year I went on to win the Cleveland Trial and the Alan Jefferies Trial, both in Yorkshire, the Mitchell Trial in Wales, the Greensmith Memorial trial and the Shropshire and Reliance Trial, both in Shropshire, and the Shropshire Cup. One success which gave me particular pleasure was the winning of the British Experts Trial in the Cotswolds. My father had won the cup in 1936 and had been joint holder in 1939. The press made a lot of the fact that I was only twenty years of age. I have a magazine cutting which says, 'It may well be a long time before another father and son can claim a similar success'.

Among my trophies is a very heavy cast iron statue, about eighteen inches high, of a worker shovelling with a hod. I

An extremely youthful Johnny Brittain with Charlie Rogers, foreman of the competition department. Johnny is mounted on HNP 331, his most successful mount.

won this in 1953 when I was a member of the winning British team in the International Six Days Trial in Czechoslovakia. The team manager was Len Heath and the other riders were Jim Alves, Hugh Viney, Bob Manns and Jack Stocker. The five members of the winning team were given four heavy fluted glasses about two feet tall, and the statue. As I was the junior I was relegated to the cast iron worker. I'm very glad now though that I had it, I've grown to like it and it has lasted all these years. At the end of the

This was the last time Great Britain won the trophy. The winning team was given the opportunity to host the next year's event and so in 1954, the International Six-Days Trial was held in Llandrindod Wells.

I can't begin to count the number of times I was wet through and frozen on these trials! The wettest trial that I have taken part in was one of the Scott Trials in Yorkshire in the early 1950s. Not long after we started we came to a ford in flood. The river was running waist high and the only way we could get through it was to race towards it at speed, take off and land in the shallow waters the other side. Pat and I got over safely but when Bill Nicholson from the BSA came to jump, his handlebar grip came off in mid air and he plunged straight down into the river.

I was probably at the pinnacle of my career in 1957 when I was the ACU's Trial Rider's Star, winning the Alan, Scott and Streatham trials and scoring high points in nineteen other trials.

As for the Royal Enfield factory itself, I didn't really have all that much to do with Enfield people. Sometimes Jack Booker and Charlie Rogers would come and watch and make encouraging remarks. I sent my expenses in to Jack Booker and they were always paid promptly, I never had any problem. The way the bikes were looked after was first class and they were superb to ride. I always found Royal Enfield very efficient. There was only one time when my bike wasn't ready, then the night watchman let me into the competition department and I helped myself and took it back on the Monday morning. Charlie Rogers was furious, but this was the only time that a few harsh words were said.

I was far more terrified by some of the plane trips than by any hazard in the trials. I was flying in a tiny plane over Poland, when I noticed oil spraying out of the engine and spattering on a side window. Then the plane suddenly dropped several hundred feet and the altometer started spinning round. I thought, 'This is it!' and I was quite surprised when the plane recovered and continued its flight.

Our plane made a terrible landing in a blizzard when I went to the 24-hour Swedish Trials in 1956 or 1957. I have

Johnny Brittain winning the Scottish Six Days Trial on his 350 Bullet in 1952, aged 20.

event, after the presentations, we had to stand on the rostrum while our national anthem was played and hold our trophies high in the air. My arms were nearly breaking holding up this heavy statue. I thought our national anthem was never coming to an end. I always wanted a fluted glass after that and I eventually received one in Tatra, in Poland.

Johnny Brittain on a 350 Bullet in the 1955 ISDT, held in Czechoslovakia. He won a Gold medal, no marks lost.

never been so cold. We were riding all day and all night through snow and ice. I went through a stream and the water had turned to ice by the time it hit my face.

I had another hair-raising experience in a plane in 1961 or 1962. I had, in 1960, started my own business and was finding it difficult to get away to the Scottish Six Day Trials at Fort William, so I worked until four in the morning and flew to Scotland. The plane kept circling round and round on take-off and I thought, 'This is strange' then the pilot announced that a technical fault had been discovered and we would have to return to base. I'm glad to say that the fault was corrected and it wasn't even necessary to land.

I branched away from the family firm and opened my own motorcycle shop in Church Street, Bloxwich. Enfield's were good sellers, or perhaps that was because I sold them. The trials were good advertising and I had large pictures of myself all round the shop. By 1963 business was flourishing, I was married with a house to maintain and it was impossible to do everything. I had been riding in trials for fifteen years and was getting fed up with the constant travelling. In 1960 and 1961 the Enfield had had a waiting list for bikes but this had now disappeared and they were beginning to tighten the purse strings. It was therefore mutually agreed that we should part.

There's a postscript to all this. I hadn't ridden for twelve months when I was persuaded to take part in a trial on a little two-stroke Bantam. I was convinced that I could still ride. It got stuck in the first stream and I couldn't restart it. That was the road to nowhere!

JOHN ELY

I was idly browsing through Motor Cycle News adverts in 1979 when I noticed a Royal Enfield 500 twin advertised, registration LWP 424. I lost no time in phoning up and going to have a look at it and there it was, battered and rusty but just about recognisable as the 500 Twin on which John Brittain rode in the International Six Days Trial in Czechoslovakia in 1953, as a member representing Great Britain's victorious Trophy team. Sad to say Great Britain has never won the Trophy since.

Royal Enfield that year also won the Manufacturers' Team Prize at the same event. Riders were John Brittain (Trophy Team), Don Evans (Vase A Team), Jack Stocker (Trophy Team), all mounted on 500 Twins. They also all won Gold Medals. I have not heard of the other two machines, I am sure that mine is the only one left in existence.

I once owned the late Jack Stocker's Twin, LWP 422, which I bought from him. It was on show at his motorcycle business in Reading after the ISDT. I asked if it would be possible to buy it from Royal Enfield as it really appealed to me. I kept it eight years before selling it, an action which I have always regretted.

Jack was an extremely nice man and was a great help when restoring LWP 424 as many of the special parts were made by him originally, many of his old photographs came in very handy. I am proud to say that it is now back to its original condition.

John Brittain's 350cc single, which he rode in one-day trials, HNW 331, is now in the National Motorcycle Museum.

Johnny Brittain gets his time card stamped, 1953 ISDT Czechoslovakia, riding the 500 twin LWP 424.

CHAPTER EIGHT
Testing – Testing

Police Headquarters at Hindlip, Worcestershire. Roger Boss (centre) hands over machines to Chief Inspector Thurston.

ROGER BOSS: from 1950 to 1967

Spending most of my daily working hours on two wheels, it was inevitable that I would be involved in the odd accident, but a stretcher case three times in a month made me realise how hard the road is. Also the remark, 'It won't be you who will need the stretcher next time, it will be your mother' made me a little more sensible with the throttle. The one good thing about my accidents was the necessity to visit the work's nurse whom I eventually married.

Following this series of mishaps it was suggested by one of the senior managers that my services with the company should terminate, but my immediate boss, Tony Wilson-Jones, spoke up for me and a compromise was arranged. I was not allowed on two wheels (except for my bicycle) for a period of two months after which I was told to be more careful.

Tony Wilson-Jones was an exceedingly nice person. He was the technical manager in charge of all the development work, a very large man whom I shall always picture in his long riding coat, green trilby hat and Mk IX goggles, completely enveloping a tiny RE 125 handchange struggling up Beoley Hill. Tony was a very clever man and was so technically-minded that if you asked him the time, he would tell you how the watch worked. He wrote many technical papers, one of which I remember was 'Steering and Stability'. This necessitated many hours spent at the Motor Industries Research Association (MIRA) proving ground with a 350

Bullet rigged up with a variety of special devices and what always intrigued me was that if you rode the machine in a straight line, then pushed the left-handlebar forward, turning the front wheel to the right, the machine steered to the left or vice versa.

The experimental shop was staffed by the foreman, Geoff Hay, two testers and an apprentice. When we were not on the road we would assist Geoff testing an engine on the dynamometer to assess its performance. Modifications would then be made to cam profiles, timing, exhaust systems etc to obtain the best power curve to give maximum performance coupled with a reasonable fuel consumption.

During my early road-testing days I was given the first 125 unit construction machine (gear box and engine in one streamlined unit). This had a prototype foot change as opposed to the previous hand change. I was allocated a circuit in the Hunt End area of Redditch by the old sewage works, through some little-used bumpy lanes and a few faster made-up roads. My instructions were not to vary from this circuit. Although an exciting novelty for a few weeks, it then became very boring. In an attempt to relieve the monotony I arranged for the local road man to time me on each lap which gradually got faster and faster, yes I did!!

We later increased the capacity to 150cc and fitted a very simple rear suspension in the form of a swinging arm with an open chromium plated coil spring. The machine was marketed as the RE Ensign. With further modifications – a more conventional type swinging arm and damper units this was sold as the Prince.

During the early fifties we saw the need for a large capacity twin-engined machine. We therefore redesigned the 500 twin, upgrading the engine to 700cc. I was given the prototype and instructed to keep to the faster main roads and get as many hard miles as possible on the clock. I usually used the road through Stratford-on-Avon to Oxford which has a variety of nice fast bends and a few long stretches. The machine I was allocated had a Watsonian sidecar attached. The reason was that we were in the process of altering the rear end of our normal frames and by cutting through a section of the frame and fitting a pointer to each side of the cut, the rider, when cornering hard, if he looked rearwards at the same time could see how much out of line the frame moved.

Motorcycle combinations were very popular at that time, but the technique of riding one was totally different to solo riding. The main point was when taking left hand turns the sidecar always wanted to lift up over the machine. Tony Wilson-Jones suggested I should place a number of full sandbags in the sidecar to counteract this tendency until I was more familiar with the outfit. After the first morning I become over confident and dispensed with this extra weight. During the afternoon I met one of the BSA testers on a small Bantam machine. A large combination is not the best outfit to chase a hot little Bantam along winding country roads!!

After the accident I was, with the help of the BSA lad, able to get the outfit out of the field and back on the road, but it took most of the afternoon and a variety of heavy implements plus a lot of brute force to get it back into something like its original shape. Because the 700 was a new machine, Reg Steel, the chief tester in the production test shop, always took the outfit home at night and brought it back for me each morning. There were very few men who could outstrip Reg in flowery language and I dreaded handing over the unit that evening. I therefore parked it outside the test shop and hid round the corner. Out came Reg, pulling on his gauntlets. 'I reckon he's turned it over', then walking round a little further, 'I'm sure he's turned it over'. After a full circuit, 'I'm b... sure he's turned it over!' At this point I knew he was very angry and decided my face-to-face with him would best be left until the morning.

There were very few machine faults which Reg failed to note, he had an uncanny ear for the mechanics and would pinpoint any fault in the engine which would have to be rectified to his complete satisfaction before he would put his signature on the final ticket.

He was a tough character in every way, but one thing he was very sensitive about was the lack of hair on his head. No-one had ever seen him without some form of headgear on. He would arrive at work in the morning in his riding attire complete with black beret and would change to a cap for work. To do this, he would stoop down low between motorbikes in the test shop after making sure no-one was looking and then, in one practised movement, surreptitiously slide the beret off and replace it with the cap. This action was reversed when leaving the works. I was unfortunate one day

Testing at MIRA under the watchful eye of the press. From left to right; Alan Baker, Vic Willoughby and Roger Maughling from The Motor Cycle, Enfield's Tony Wilson-Jones and Brian Crow. Roger Boss is on the machine.

to break down in Alcester quite close to Reg's house. He had just come home for lunch and invited me in for a cup of tea. I became quite excited thinking I would now see the 'promised land' but I was disappointed. Reg ate his meal wearing a cap.

On another occasion Reg had a very nasty motorcycle accident at Coughton, fracturing his leg very badly. The ambulance arrived but it was a long time before he could be persuaded to let them put him in the vehicle. After he had been in hospital for a few days a number of the testers decided to visit him. Although our prime reason was to cheer him up and show we really did care, the thought did cross our minds that we might see him without a hat. But we were disappointed, obviously suspecting a visit from some of the lads he had strategically placed a number of pillows all round his head.

Roger Boss relaxing at weekends.

The daily runs soon built up a considerable mileage on the prototype Meteor which suffered few major modifications. There was one, however, which I remember well. Whilst travelling fairly rapidly outside Stratford-on-Avon on my way to Oxford the engine suddenly developed a most horrible noise – clutch in and walk to the nearest telephone box. The works lorry then came out and collected the outfit, the engine of which was then stripped in the experimental shop. No wonder it produced such an awful noise, the crankshaft was broken. It was now necessary to find out if this breakage was a one-off or whether it was a fatigue fracture which would require some modification. The next step was to rebuild the engine with a similar crankshaft to the original and to build up as many miles as possible in the shortest time.

The answer was to use a solo machine and take advantage of the outer circuit at MIRA. This particular circuit was the one used before the present banked circuit was built. The facilities at MIRA, even in the early days, were very useful to vehicle manufacturers with a variety of rough ground surfaces, dust tunnels, hump-backed bridges etc, also a very accurate timing strip. The old outer circuit enabled the rider to maintain a consistently high speed for long periods with some slower bends where frequent use of the gear box could be made. Some time later, after many more miles, the crankshaft broke again. Another engine was built and similarly tested. This again failed, very close to the previous failure mileages, proving without doubt that major modification was required. This was carried out and we did not experience any further problems with the crankshaft breakage. The particular episode illustrates the importance of ensuring that prototype machines were given a hard life. I dread to think what would have happened if this fault had not been discovered and we had gone into quantity production.

The 700cc Meteor was introduced in a very attractive copper beech finish and the initial demand was very encouraging. With further modification and more sporting styling it was marketed as the Constellation. The engine capacity was later increased to 750cc and with further improvements became the Interceptor.

My days as a tester were generally enjoyable although there were times in the middle of winter when it was not at all pleasant and I sometimes wondered if I should change my occupation, particularly when, arriving back at the works after a long day's riding, it would be necessary to call for assistance to get off the bike and struggle to the stove to thaw out. But after the circulation returned one would think about the sunny days in summer, 'wonderful!' particularly as it was not then necessary to encapsulate one's head in a plastic dome.

Many exciting and amusing episodes arose during my testing days, one in particular was on a Friday the thirteenth. The managing director, Major Smith, asked me to call at New Street Station, Birmingham, to collect a fresh salmon which had been sent down from Scotland. The fish was about three feet long and wrapped in some damp sacking cloth strips. I was on a solo machine and had to sit on the tail section with the rest of the salmon forward along the petrol tank and protruding over the handlebars. Arriving back into Redditch I was taking a right turn off the main road, concentrating on balancing the salmon when to my horror, over my front wheel came a bicycle together with a huge policeman complete with black cycle cape. I had steered directly into his path.

Whilst struggling to help the six foot plus officer to his feet I was pleased to hear from an independent witness the words 'You didn't ring your bell, constable'. Although the large upright black cycle was very badly bent, the only damage to the policeman was a bloody nose, and whilst he was trying to stem the flow, his immediate and natural reaction was to produce his notebook. However, he then realised because he was involved in the accident he was unable to take a statement and would have to contact the station for assistance.

In those days there were no personal radios and we had to take over a small room in the local Post Office. In due course, the station sergeant arrived and seeing the constable dabbing his wound and looking forlornly at his mangled cycle he could have been likened to the 'laughing policeman'. I was allowed to make a statement later that evening at the local station when the sergeant, seeing how worried I was, assured me that I should have no fears, as independent witness had already made a statement to the effect that the constable was riding at a 'furious rate' and did not ring his bell. How one can ride at a furious rate on the old upright Raleigh-type cycle with Sturmey-Archer speed I will never know. I think the witness was not a great lover of policemen. Fortunately, no case ever arose and the policeman's bicycle was repaired free of charge in our cycle section.

After my marriage to the work's nurse and the thought of a future family, I decided I would like a less hazardous occupation and enquired if there was a vacancy on the sales side. I was very fortunate in this respect as our sales

The 700cc Meteor.

representative for Wales and the West Country was nearing retirement. After a few weeks in the sales office, I accompanied him around Wales and was introduced to our network of established dealers.

My transport as a sales representative in the mid-fifties was a rather basic Ford Prefect with the old side-valve engine, not very quick but fairly reliable. I did, however, use a motorcycle on many occasions and this was very much appreciated by my customers. It was particularly useful during the Suez crisis when petrol was rationed. I was able to use my car allowance in the bike and therefore cover my territory unrestricted.

Finally I became sales manager, responsible for all UK motorcycle sales, this included arranging annual shows, the main one being Earls Court. We also exhibited at Blackpool and Brighton. The Earls Court Show was the highlight of the year. It was our opportunity to show the public our new range of machines and to try and get some idea of their likes and dislikes for the future. Our office, always stocked with the necessary liquid refreshment, was the venue for our dealers. Many used this opportunity to renew their annual stocking agreements with us and to place their initial orders for the new season. The show was particularly important in this respect as it gave us some indication of future production schedules. There was usually a very pleasant atmosphere during these exhibitions and what impressed me was the general attitude of most of the sales reps who, although always endeavouring to obtain an increasing share of the market for their particular company, were so friendly towards each other. I think this stems from the fact that most genuine motorcyclists have a great sense of comradeship. I can remember how in the evenings, a variety of manufacturer's reps would congregate at a chosen restaurant after the close of the show and the friendly banter which built up would make today's TV comic programmes seem very tame.

When, in the mid-sixties, E & H P Smith *supposedly* merged with Enfield, the staff were assured that it would be to the benefit of the company, this certainly proved to be untrue. Although under the new management, we continued production of motorcycles, it later became obvious that this was not their long-term intention. The situation became very plain to me when, having been negotiating for many months with a large northern police force to purchase a substantial number of machines, and having checked with the managing director that we were definitely continuing production of this particular model, I visited the force headquarters and finalised the firm order. The following day this was processed through the sales office and instructions issued to the works.

One can imagine my surprise and disgust when the managing director informed me that further production of this model would cease. I often wonder what the chief superintendent must have thought of our company when I had to advise him of the situation. For some time I had felt that we were not going in the right direction, it was at this point I realised this was the beginning of the end, which later proved to be so.

The land and buildings, which included a lovely cricket pitch and sports area were sold to the Redditch Development Corporation, the stock of spares and motorcycles disposed of in various ways and the machinery etc, sold by auction. Did E & H P Smith see the potential of the Redditch New Town when they originally took over the company? And who made all the money?

BRIAN CROW: from 1950 to 1967

I joined Royal Enfield when I was eighteen, in 1952. My father took me to see Major Mountford (whom he knew slightly as he had sold a few Enfield cycles in Studley) and Tony Wilson-Jones, who took me on to work in the experimental department under the foreman, Geoff Hay. I did not have too much experience but I was very keen. Two days later I found myself astride a 500 twin heading off with Geoff to the MIRA (Motor Industry Research Association) test track. For the first six months there were just Geoff and myself with the comings and goings of various engineering apprentices and then Roger Boss returned – he had broken his leg, scrambling.

Roger did all the serious testing and I learned as I went along. We were joined by John Eggleton for his apprenticeship period. This was probably the happiest period of my working life. Every Sunday the four of us would take part in local trials. After a time Roger left the department to become a sales representative. From then on I usually did all the serious testing on prototype machines.

The experimental department did all the testing of prototypes and new development bikes. This was quite different to the test shop, where new motorbikes were tried out before sale. I worked on the testing and development of all new bikes from 1952 to 1963. I was under Tony Wilson-Jones, the technical manager, who was also in charge of the apprenticeship schemes. He was extremely clever and a real gentleman, all his conversation was well above our heads. We were always fascinated by the fact that he rode to work on a motorbike wearing a trilby and the trilby never blew off.

Our work in the experimental department was to ride 250 miles each day, summer and winter, to try and wear the engines out. We were not supplied with protective clothing except for a very insubstantial long black riding mac. Helmets were not provided but we would not have worn them anyway, we went for the macho image and wore a black flat cap or beret, goggles, gloves and wellingtons. In later years we were supplied with helmets and, very sparingly, Barbour suits which were not replaced until you had many holes in your old one.

After riding my 250 miles one winter's day, I was frozen to the bike! I rode round the back of my parent's house, fell against a shed and put my fist on the horn until my parents came out. They had to drag me in front of the fire to thaw out! The next day I was back at work. They said I was a bloody fool, but I was motor bike mad. I ate, slept and breathed motorbikes. After riding them all the week, I spent my weekends riding in trials. I enjoyed working at Royal Enfield so much that even if I had not been paid, I would still have tested the bikes. I loved the bikes and the people were so friendly. Everybody knew everybody and many people stayed there for all their working lives. Looking back,

Testing windscreen and panniers at MIRA. Brian Crow (right) and Roger Boss.

it was so much better than the highly pressurised system I had to enter when Royal Enfield closed down.

The track was extremely useful to us and I have spent weeks there. It was at MIRA that I recorded the fastest ever speed on a Royal Enfield bike produced at Redditch, 120.8 mph on a Constellation. When we first developed the sprung frames known as the swinging arm, we made our own suspension units but we found that they did not stand up to rough treatment so we bought the parts in. We had a choice of suppliers so, to decide which was the best, we spent weeks and weeks riding round and round the

Belgium pavé until the swinging arm snapped. How my kidneys stood up to this kind of treatment I do not know. We found that those from Armstrong Patents in Yorkshire were the best and so we used them on standard equipment from then on.

Roger Boss and I were the first two to ride the Crusader. Reg Thomas designed this very complicated machine from absolute scratch. Originally it was designed as an ordinary, low performances going-to-work kind of bike then round about 1955 it developed into the sporting 250cc model.

The main problem we had was that the pump wouldn't clear the oil away and it would throw oil out when it was driven hard. We thought about that problem for days. In the end Gilbert Baker decided to put a drill through the crankcase, which had never been done before. I was the first one to drill that hole. Later on, this was adopted for all other Crusaders, when the crankcase was drilled scientifically.

Later on Geoff Hay was made foreman of the Redditch engine assembly department and I was asked to move up as foreman. I believe I was the youngest-ever foreman at the Redditch factory. This was a difficult time for me. I was still doing all the high speed testing and I was now, in addition, running the shop, mostly with the help of young apprentices. I was only a few years older than they were, and although some apprentices were really enthusiastic, like Mervyn Panting who still races a 250 Crusader in Classic road races and Tony Donachie who had a very good reputation as an amateur boxer, others were a real handful.

In 1957 I was not very popular with the Company because I sued them for damages. I had a bad accident while testing and broke my arm. The accident was not my fault. To save money, the wrong parts had been put in a gear box and it seized up while I was riding at 110 mph. There I was, not able to work with a wife and two small children to support and the company would not pay my wages. The management even had the cheek to come down and ask if I could go back to work because they needed me. I discovered that they did have insurance but just to protect themselves against losing any tester's services.

In about 1959 Berkeley Cars were making a three-wheeler sports car using the Excelsior engine. They wanted to fit an air-cooled engine and after some negotiation, Royal Enfield agreed to supply them with the 700cc engine which was used in the Meteor and the Constellation. However, a condition of supply was that we were given a car for a month to test, to check that the engine performed well when fitted. The car was made into a four-seater to cope with the extra performance and I was given the job of testing it. I was driving round the track with one of the apprentices, Frank Rickards, when I turned the damn thing over. We were not hurt, in fact we just lay there upside down on the bank of the test track laughing. The car was very light and the brakes were hopeless, they turned the car either right or left, you knew you were going one way or the other but you never knew which way.

About the same time the Indian Motor Cycle Company of America went bankrupt so, for twelve to eighteen months, Royal Enfield manufactured bikes for them. The Americans liked really big bikes, so we adapted ours to take big balloon tyres and lengthened the wheel base. These bikes then had the Indian Motorcycle badge slapped on them and off they went to America.

In 1960 the experimental department was merged with the competition department under Charlie Rogers and I became foreman of the service department (repairs) under Cecil Booker, the service manager. Then, in 1963 I was invited to join the sales department and received the prize of a company car. I covered Wales, the West Country and the Midlands.

I remained in sales until the Redditch factory closed down in January 1967. The last few months were very difficult knowing that we were probably closing down. When I attended the 1966 Earls Court show with Doug Bellamy (the only other sales representative retained), we were told not to take any orders but put on a good face to the public. It was rumoured that the Americans were interested in buying the company.

We were all made redundant on 31 January 1967. The service department was kept open for another twelve months, then it was sold to Velocette. Jack Spencer, the service manager, moved to Velocette with the stock. The underground factory at Bradford-on-Avon persuaded Reg Thomas to go and work for them where they continued to make the big twins such as the Interceptor for another two years. Royal Enfield ceased trading in June 1970.

CHARLIE BLUNDELL: from 1946 to 1951

I started at the Royal Enfield in June 1946, working with six others in the test shop, testing bikes. We would take each bike for a couple of laps on the Enfield test track and a minimum of nine miles on the road. We did this for all bikes except the 125cc which were considered to be so reliable they only needed a brief test. We then had to rectify any faults.

If a bike had a fault or needed some adjusting we would add it to the row of bikes in the shop until we could get round to it. When we were busy, there could be a row of a dozen or twenty bikes waiting to be rectified. Sometimes, an export order would be a few bikes short, then Major Smith would come into the test shop and ask what the matter was with the various bikes. He would then go down the line and start them all running, saying, 'This one sounds all right, it can go', and he used to send some of these bikes off for export. The strange thing was, he was very deaf and no way could he hear the bikes running.

This picture, which nearly made the front page of the Redditch Indicator, resulted in new riding suits all round for the testers.

During the war, petrol was rationed but Enfield's used to have a petrol tanker which went down to the garage to be filled for testing the bikes. We were only supposed to put a pint into each bike but we used to fill the engine up to the top, take the bike home and syphon most of the petrol out. That's how Tommy Guise used to get his petrol when he wanted to go fishing so he couldn't say anything to the rest of us, but sometimes he used to come into the test shop and say 'Look lads, according to our records on petrol consumption, we're only doing one mile to the gallon so cut it down, be careful'. Or sometimes there used to be a memo on the notice board saying that the test shop was using too much petrol.

At the end of the war the seven of us in the test shop were asking for new coats but the management (I think Tommy Guise was the main culprit) kept fobbing us off and the new coats never materialised. So we fished out all these torn and ragged coats, tied them round with bits of string and called the *Redditch Indicator* out. They were interested in putting it on the front page. However, when the management got wind of it, they stopped it and we were all sent to Belstaff's in Birmingham to get new coats. (see p 118)

The Bullet with the aluminium engine first came out at the end of the war in 1948 or 1949. It went into production but when it came into the test shop we found that the piston used to seize within a couple of miles, usually within half a mile. The pistons and barrels had to be redesigned, otherwise it was a marvellous machine.

There was always some sort of escapade going on in the test shop. One Christmas, all the testers went for a booze-up at the Neville at Cookhill, among them was Horace Cleveley who was a marvellous biker despite the fact that he had a bad leg. We all had a couple of drinks then we went back into the test shop which was all clean and tidy ready for Christmas including a row of about thirty bikes, each one propped up by a stand at the side. Horace was the last one in and as he swung into the shop, he caught the last bike and over it went, then this caught the next and the next and the next and over they all went like a pack of cards. It did quite a lot of damage, handlebars were bent and tanks were scratched. Horace just fell over helpless with laughter.

One of the testers came back to work late after dinner hour. He said that he had gone to see his girl friend on Mount Pleasant and her husband had unexpectedly arrived home so he had dived into the pantry. He had tried to make an exit through the window and had got stuck, so he had had to stay there until the husband returned to work and the girlfriend could pull him free.

Bikes were my whole life. I spent every weekend either racing or motorbike scrambling, or during the summer, organising events. Almost every weekend there would be an event somewhere, and every club Worcester, Hereford etc. – would enter a team. I rode my own bike for the Enfield from 1947 to about 1954, I had a 350 and a 500 Bullet. I won the Maudsley Rose Bowl, the David Greg Replica and the Worcestershire Team Trophy together with Reuben Hunt and Jack Dyson. I founded the Alcester Motor Bike Club in 1946, was secretary for the first twelve years then became chairman and president. We organised scrambles ourselves and we also organised a lot of grass track or mountain racing. We had courses at Haselor, Aston Cantlow and Bordesley Green.

The short-circuit racing Bullet tested by Charlie Rogers in 1955.

These motorcycle events were very popular, we had between 2,000 and 4,000 people at each event.

After working at Royal Enfield for five years, I left to work on Sunbeams at the BSA, riding BSA bikes, I was then a representative for Corgi motorcycles until these folded up.

I found Royal Enfield a funny old place. The wages were rubbish and yet everybody stayed there.

CURLY ROGERS: from 1948 to 1959

I've been called 'Curly' since my schooldays for obvious reasons. The war had been over for three years when I joined Royal Enfield, in 1948, although national service was still compulsory and so my career at Royal Enfield was interrupted by two years in the RAF from 1951 to 1953.

Despite the fact that I was only sixteen and hadn't yet passed my driving test, I first went into the test shop which took the larger bikes for a nine-mile run and the little RE2s for a couple of miles round the Enfield test track. For a short time I was testing both with trade and L plates. We were gambling on my passing first time, which fortunately, I did.

After a few months I moved to the experimental department where prototype engines were run for four hours on the bench, then put into the machines and taken for testing. There were only three of us working in there, the foreman, Freddy Broach; another apprentice, Pat Weicher; and myself. Freddy was a northerner, a tall, thin, lean bloke who called a spade a spade – he was very down to earth. He was an agreeable chap and I got on well with him.

I remember my first day out in the experimental shop very well. Freddy Broach took me round the course and when he had shown me the route he said, 'All right, now you take me round'. The day was very, very wet, I didn't know the local lanes and was going flat out. A bend zoomed up and I couldn't get round it and I came off in Love Lane. Fred followed me round the corner and found me emerging from a nest of stinging nettles with a badly stung face and a bent bike. He didn't say much although he was annoyed that I had managed to damage a prototype bike on my first day.

I worked for three years in the experimental department during which time I was testing the prototypes of the G2 350 Bullet and the 500 Twin. These were very good bikes, we didn't have many problems with them. However, I also tested the RE2 which was a development of the RE1 (the Flying Flea) and this was horrendous. It was cheap all the way through and not developed properly by a mile, in my opinion. I could break that without leaving the grounds if I wanted.

NIGEL BUCKINGHAM: from 1957 to 1962

I started in the machine shop in 1957 as a member of the 'Black Hand' gang, working with cast iron. After a few months I transferred to the service department where I heard that one of the testers was transferring, leaving a vacancy. I was absolutely fanatical about bikes. They were my whole life. For me it was bikes from the moment I opened my eyes in the morning until I went to bed at night and I wanted that job very badly indeed. So I went to see the works manager and I said, 'I've had a lot of experience of Enfield bikes, I have a 700 Twin myself so you know I'm capable of riding a big bike, and I think you ought to give this vacancy to somebody already on the premises'. With that, I was given the job. Charlie Rogers was in charge of the testing department, next in command came Harry Watton, then there was Mick Bowers, Mac McGowan and me. We were testing experimental bikes, riding them hard and putting mileage on them, to see if they developed any faults.

I lived for my work, I always put on a lot more miles on than was required. I would get home at night, have my tea then I'd be off again with my mate, Ken Wilkinson. We often went to the coast for the evening, somewhere like Weston or Bream. In those days, you could buy eight gallons of petrol for a quid and I was earning £11 or £12 a week. I enjoyed every minute, even when I had to go out in the snow. To some of the older testers, it was just a job. Sometimes when they stopped at a cafe they would fix the throttle and let the bike run to artificially clock up the mileage, but I never did that. The day that Major Smith died in 1962 the whole factory closed and we were given the day off. What did Mac McGowan and I do? We went on our bikes to Chedworth, Weymouth, Weston and Cheddar. We might as well have been at work.

I was mainly testing the new Bullet which was a 350 version of the 250 Crusader, and the 750 Interceptor. The Bullet was very good winding round the country lanes and the Interceptor really went on the motorways but there weren't many built then, the M5 only ran from Kempsey to Ross.

A lot of the testing round about 1961/1962 was on the Super Five. Frames were made in a variety of materials and a leading link fork was fitted instead of a telescopic one. As each new part was fitted I had to test them out by giving the bikes a really good thrashing. Often, we went to MIRA where we put the bike round and round the high speed track to see if we could blow it up, then we would take it on the pave (rough road) at 28 mph to try and shake the bike to pieces.

Round about the same time, I was on a 750 Interceptor with 400 miles to be put on the clock. I went to Ross-on-Wye but on the way back, a hole developed in one of the pistons. Anyway, I limped back the last forty miles, locked the bike in the workshop and went home. The next morning, the bike had gone. All that was left was a pool of oil. It turned out that Tony Wilson-Jones had returned late to the office, decided to go home on one of the works machines and had chosen the Interceptor. He didn't even notice that there was something wrong with it. I had to go over to his house at Kings Norton and rescue it.

The testers had a marvellous time, life was full of fun and we played all kinds of games. The little two-stroke smoked and we would try to get round the Enfield test track quickly enough to catch up with our own trail of smoke.

When we went home, we were not allowed out through the factory gates until the hooter went so there would be a line of motorcyclists, about six of us, all revved up and just within the main gates, so that as soon as we heard the hooter we would all make a mad dash and compete to be the first to get out through the gates (where the road narrowed) then off we'd go, roaring up Bates Hill.

The social life, too, at Royal Enfield was really great. There were dances on a Saturday night and sometimes special dances, such as the Christmas dance at Warwick or the Foxlydiate. The highlight of the year was the apprentices and office girls' trip to Blackpool. We were all just kids late teens and early twenties – and it was an introduction to living. We had a good booze-up and went round the fair. The hotel doors were locked at midnight but I got separated from the others and didn't arrive back until two in the morning. I thought, 'Help, I'm locked out!', then I noticed a grating leading to a basement room with some of our party in it so I banged on the grating until they let me in.

In one way, I was very sorry when I was caught speeding and the resulting publicity ended my employment with Royal Enfield. I offered to return to the service department but this was turned down. In another way, it did me a good turn because I went to Chloride Alcad and doubled my salary.

JOHN HOUGHTON: from 1953 to 1955

During my competition years I won over a hundred cups, trophies and medals. The most exciting competition was the 350 Class of the Cotswold Cup in 1954/55 which I won on a Bullet. I was called up for my two years national service in 1951 and I continued riding an Enfield. I would have liked to have ridden the Bullet in the 1953 Scottish Six Days Trial but the army gave me a BSA Gold Star 500. When I came out of the army I was offered a job at Royal Enfield. I was supposed to go into the competition department but I went instead into the test shop and the management kept asking me to do just another fortnight there. I kept saying, 'When am I going to move?' but their reply was always, We're very busy and we can't spare you from the test shop. I stayed in the test shop for some two years.

The big twins had to have 50 miles put on the clock, the Bullet model J, nine miles, and the little RE2's just two laps. The test track was about 200-300 yards across with banked sides. We used to take the bikes right up the bank to see how far we could go without turning over. In the centre of the test track were several buildings including the steel stores. Harry Watton used to wheel the swarf out in an old barrow and if you timed it right, you could just miss him when he got halfway across the track, giving him the fright of his life.

One of the testers was fascinated by the big diggers and he used to leave his bike ticking over to clock up mileage while he watched roadworks. When it snowed, Percy Holder and I did this, too, we stopped in a layby near Rollswood, put our bikes on the stand in top gear and let them run while we had a rest. At that time, Eddie Young was on repairs and he said to us, 'Don't leave your bikes to run on a stand again'. We asked him how he knew. He told us that the nuts on top of the rocker covers became red hot.

In 1954 I was helping to test the biggest order the Enfield ever had – the 800 Bullets ordered by the Madras Motor Company for the Indian Government for use in the war against Pakistan. That's how the connection with India started. We were testing from seven in the morning until seven at night seven days a week – we had to produce our normal quantity of bikes as well as these Bullets.

By 1955 I had been riding a Bullet for about four years and it occurred to me that I would like a change. I fancied a James, and someone told me that Peter Stirland was bringing his James back and was going to ride Enfield's instead. I went to collect the bike from a van at Drapers Farm – it arrived minus the handlebars. I fitted a pair of handlebars on it and took off to the Draper Trial. When the results came out I was second in the Trial and I had won the prize for the best 250. A short time later, I also won the Cotswolds Trial. After that, I stuck to the James.

The results of the Trials were published in the *Daily Herald* and various motorcycling magazines. Major Smith noticed my name and said, 'Doesn't that bloke work for us, why isn't he riding our bikes? Get him back on our bikes!' Oliver Wythes and Gilbert Baker asked me over and over again to ride an Enfield. Oliver Wythes would pop in and say, 'Come on, our kid'. However, the management were still messing me about, giving excuses to keep me out of the competition department. So when, in the end, Major Smith said that if I didn't ride an Enfield bike I would have to leave, I left and went to work at Matthews, motorcycle agents in Stratford and Evesham.

John Houghton competing in a Cotswold scramble.

CHAPTER NINE
Learning for a living

Charlie Rogers (right) with the 500 Twin used in the ISDT selection test, and Alan Rogers.

Mac McGowan: 1947 to 1967

My first job at Enfield was in the gauge room under Brian Giles. The job was mainly that of booking gauges in and out with a certain amount of inspection. On my first day, I had to get pencil and paper and start on a long row of cubby holes, called 'cubs', cleaning the contents, looking up the serial numbers and making a note of them. The cubs contained all kinds of jigs and tools to cover not only Royal Enfield's requirements but a supply of hubs and brakes for other manufacturers such as Scotts, New Imperials and Phelan & Moore who made the Panther Motor Cycles. All my notes were then thrown away as it was just a character-forming exercise.

However, apprentices were not, as a general rule, treated as navvies, they usually had just as much prestige as anyone else in the factory. If a problem needed sorting then Major Smith, Jack Booker, Tony Wilson-Jones and an apprentice or two would all stand round, chucking in ideas and an apprentice's ideas were considered to be just as good as anybody else's.

Neither did apprentices get all the basic, dirty jobs, for example, lighting the cast iron stove was done by whoever arrived first in the morning. You would take the departmental wheelbarrow to the building department and fill it with off-cuts which you shoved in the stove. You would then pour half-a-pint of petrol over them, select a long off-cut which you lit from the geyser and, standing well to one side, you would apply this to the contents of the stove. It was very important to first remove the ashes, otherwise they blew all over the workshop. I have never known any accident occur from this method of lighting fires.

There was a story told by Percy Holder, the test shop foreman, that two workers had a bit of an argument and so worker A went and got worker B's sandwiches and put them on the fire, worker B then got worker A's hat and shoved it in the stove. Worker A then got worker B's jacket and burned that. By the time they had finished the whole lot had been burned, sandwiches, jackets, coats and wellies.

At some time during my apprenticeship I found myself in the competition shop. I was then totally ignorant about motorcycles and more interested in gun-making. However, I found myself engaged in preparing bikes for the International Six-Day Trial of 1958, for Peter Stirland, Johnny Brittain, John Fletcher, Terry Cheshire and the like. A few months later, the Enfield were also racing at Thruxton and Charlie Rogers said to Tony Wilson-Jones, 'You can't expect us to prepare another set of bikes in such a short time without extra help, Mac's becoming quite useful so can we keep him for another six months?' It is thus Charlie Rogers whom I have to blame for my career in industrial engineering.

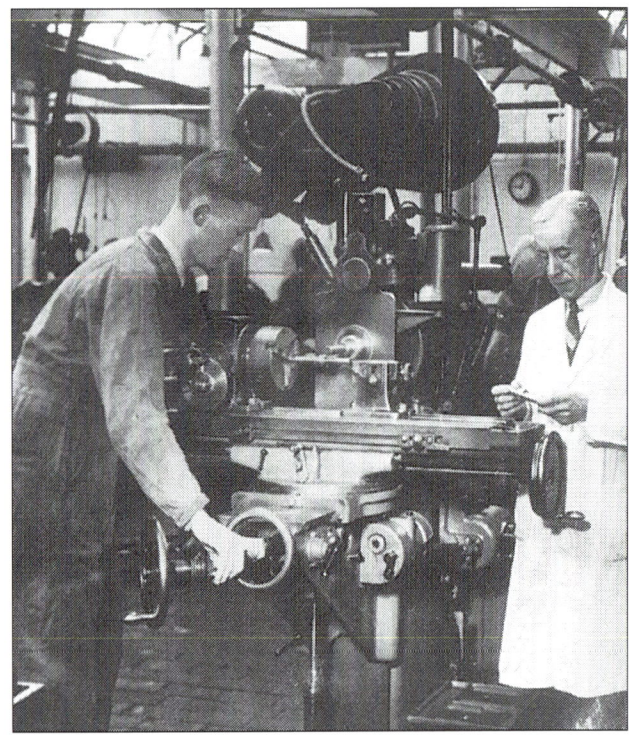

An apprentice learns his trade, under the watchful eye of toolroom foreman Les Purser, 1948.

As I had become a very useful character I was moved next door to the experimental shop, responsible for the development of prototype machines. Eighty or ninety percent of a new bike could be made up from bits and pieces which were already in the factory, but the other ten or twenty per cent had to be specially made, which was where I came in.

At that time, Brian Crow should have been the foreman but he was off sick as he had had an accident at MIRA. Some poor punter had bought a Constellation and the gear box had seized up on it and he had been killed. Brian Crow was sent to MIRA to drive a Constellation hard to try and recreate the accident. He was successful in one way, in that he did manage to get the gear box to seize, but unsuccessful in that he did not manage to stay on the bike. He did what he later described as a handstand in the air and came down on his hands, driving the bones of his forearm up through the bones of his upper arm.

The experimental shop later merged with the competition shop so I was again working under Charlie Rogers and more or less became a fixture in the competition department.

At the time we had a large order from Edgar and Rathbone Pashley, of Stratford, for motor rickshaws with a 350cc engine, the front end was a motor bike and the back end was rather like a handcart. The engine assembly shop was already producing Crusaders as fast as they could, so the factory was scavenged for people who were able to build engines so that they could set up a second engine line from there. I got myself adopted by Sid Normandale of the engine shop, building 150cc 2-stroke engines for the Prince motorcycle, until the man who did the rectification on the engines ran off with somebody's missus so that the post was vacant and I moved there. After rectification I returned to the competition shop and remained there until I was lured to Hymatic by higher wages.

Reading a bike magazine one day I noticed that E & H P Smith were buying up a number of firms associated with motorbikes, such as Alpha Bearings, Hi-Ton of Selly Oak (who owned Albion Gear Boxes) and Royal Enfield. I saw that they had engaged Hermann Meier who was an expert on the development of the two-stroke racing engine, and Geoff Duke, the international TT rider. I thought 'Aha, they're building a base to produce motorbikes in a bigger

Enfield Apprentices Association Dinner, 1948.

way', so I let it be known that I would like to go and work at Enfield's again. I spent my last three years there working on the development of a 250cc two-stroke racing engine which was called by Leo Davenport, who had a romantic streak, the 'Grand Prix'. I was got rid of in the first major batch of redundancies in 1961.

JOHN HILL: from 1961

One of the most hilarious weeks of my life was spent in the tool room of Royal Enfield back in 1961, when I was working there as an apprentice. The tool room was the hub of the factory, about thirty people worked there and we made all the tools and gauges needed in the works.

Early one morning, a deputation from the drawing office arrived with these impressive-looking papers and drawings. The tool room foreman and one or two others inspected the plan. It turned out that it was a design for a rolling road, which was to recreate the wear and tear of the open road on the motorbike. The testing of these machines was an expensive, time-consuming and at times dangerous exercise and, should the drawing office be able to test bikes artificially, this would be of great benefit.

This rolling road turned out to be nothing more than a second-hand electric motor turning what looked like a miniature wooden water wheel about the size of an oil drum and fitted with wooden blocks about two inches deep. As the drum turned round, the blocks bumped against the bike wheels and it was hoped that this would simulate an uneven road surface. A brand new bike, fresh from the assembly line, was suspended above the drum. The contraption was switched on for the proving test with the result that the bike leaped about three feet into the air. Much discussion took place and it was decided that the bike needed a weight on it to hold it steady. Everyone stood there saying, 'Not me!' and, 'You're not getting me on that!'. The only person brave enough to have a go was the foreman and he didn't last more than a second or two.

Major Smith having a go on a cycle road roller.

Further discussions took place. The foreman and the drawing office thought that perhaps the wheel needed to go more slowly. Then they decided that the blocks should not be as deep as two inches. Despite all their efforts the contraption did nothing but shake the bike to bits. However, entertainment-wise it was better than a bucking bronco.

They spent a week tinkering about with it before they finally gave up.

After a year at Royal Enfield, I transferred to the Austin Motor Company (now Austin Rover) which had a much better apprenticeship scheme. I subsequently founded the John Hills Ltd MGB/Triumph Centre in Lakeside, less then a mile from the old Royal Enfield factory.

DAVID WILSON: 1954 to 1965

There was no better firm than Royal Enfield for training apprentices. The different departments covered every aspect of engineering, welding, machining, plating, paint spraying, grinding, milling – it even had a chromium plating department. There were about 70 apprentices in employment at any one time and we were paid about £2 a week. The management laid on special events for us such as the apprentice's Christmas dinner and the Blackpool outing for apprentices and office girls. I had a girlfriend who enjoyed dancing so I went to the Saturday night dances in the Canteen but I couldn't afford the five shillings entrance fee so I joined the dance committee and was able to get in free.

I thoroughly enjoyed my apprenticeship. An apprentice was supposed to move to a different area every six months but I liked my first department, the diesel shop under Bill Kings, so much that I stayed there for twelve months, then I went to the toolroom and enjoyed it so much that I stayed there for the remainder of my apprenticeship.

We had a great deal of fun in the toolroom, for example, while someone was kneeling down, seeing to a machine, we would paint the heels of their shoes silver or white. Most of us had motorbikes and sometimes we would nip out and screw somebody's brakes on, then when the rider went to go home, the engine would keep stalling. The department was heated by a coach stove in the centre of the floor and someone would always stop the chimney up with rags during the summer so that when the cold weather arrived and fire was lit, the shop would be filled with smoke.

A lot of the tricks would be considered very dangerous now and had they been discovered in those days we would have been sacked on the spot. This made them even more amusing and exciting. There's no point to a prank if there's not an element of danger. Believe it or not, we used to make gunpowder and put it in odds and ends to make it explode, this was a speciality of Les Bachelor. It was quite accepted that when bonfire night was near, fireworks were brought into the factory and let off indoors. We used to put bangers around and let them off. One year, I let off a Roman Candle and one of the explosives from it shot down the tool room and went off in Jack Powell's waistcoat!

In the toolroom it was traditional to wear a smock, which buttoned down the front and had two pockets. The workers wore a brown one and the foreman a

Many police forces were supplied with 350 Bullets, this is part of the Leicestershire constabulary's mounted force.

127

white with a small green and gold Royal Enfield badge saying *Stuff*. When a fellow finished a fag he would drop the nub end in your smock pocket. Once, I was halfway along a road which ran between buildings when I smelt burning, and I looked down and there was a hole in my smock the size of a bucket and the edges were smouldering.

One of the odd things about Royal Enfield was the various strange characters who wandered round the site, particularly some of the labourers who earned a couple of pounds each week doing odd jobs and collecting litter. There was the man who walked round all day saying, 'Cuckoo', another wore a bowler hat and blew a trumpet.

I worked there for eleven years, from 1954 to 1965. When we were sold to E & H P Smith, it was obvious that the factory was being run down. They formed a company to sell off the machinery. We used to arrive at work and find a chalk mark on a machine and we used to say, that's going to go next, and sure enough, within a few days it would be gone. I therefore applied for a job at High Duty Alloys and more than doubled my wages. I was twenty-three years old when I left, at Royal Enfield I was earning £10 a week, at HDA I was earning £22.

LENNIE RUDGE from 1957 to 1960

In 1957, when I was fifteen and fresh from Bridley Moor Comprehensive, my father took me for an interview at Royal Enfield to see about an apprenticeship. The only question which I was asked was, 'Do you want to be an engineer or a draughtsman?'

I was never any good at drawing so I chose engineering and the papers for a four-year apprenticeship were signed. I soon discovered that, as an apprentice in the factory, you had absolutely no prestige at all and you were the absolute pits. I spent the first three months putting the tips on mudguards which nearly drove me insane. Looking back, I wonder what this was supposed to teach an apprentice. I didn't learn anything much except self-discipline.

It seemed to me that the Royal Enfield apprenticeship was not so much for engineering as an apprenticeship for living. I don't know how they decided to allocate apprentices to the different departments, it seemed to be just a matter of luck. You were supposed to spend six months in each shop but if you got on well with the people in there you stayed longer. I stayed for twelve months in the competition shop.

However, I must say that the apprenticeship seemed to work and by the time you left there, you could turn your hand to anything, electrics, carpentry, vehicle maintenance – anything. Perhaps this was because the factory made everything itself and didn't buy anything in so we were given a fantastic grounding in every skill. In 1992 we had a reunion and I met a number of people who had worked at Royal Enfield and they had all done well, many of them were self-employed. They were running coalyards, garages, pubs, motorcycle shops and engineering works. I myself have a cycle shop.

I don't know how the workers survived on their wages in those days. One woman told me that she saved all her wages and it was enough to take her family to Blackpool for two weeks every year. Just imagine, she worked the whole year so that her family could have two weeks' holiday. A lot of the workers had allotments and grew their own vegetables. Any excess was brought into the firm and sold, there was always someone with cabbages for sale. Yet most people seemed quite content with their lot. I think that perhaps they didn't know any other life, they were caught in a time warp.

When I was sixteen, the foreman said to me, 'Have you passed your motorbike test yet?' and I replied, 'No, I'm taking it tomorrow.' The foreman came back with, 'Well you're in the competition shop tomorrow'.

There were a lot of people there who did a normal, mundane job. In the experimental and competition departments it was different. We were at the forefront of the motorbike world. We were working on experimental and competition bikes and it was my job to clock up the mileage to see what faults, if any, developed. I was bike crazy. I rode all day for the competition department then rode my own bike each evening. Motor bikes were my whole life, I would have done the job just for the sheer fun of the ride even if they hadn't paid me. I didn't think of it as a job, to me it was an opportunity to ride motor bikes.

Looking back, I was given tremendous responsibility. I was given a bike and told to clock up, say, 300 or 500 miles, then the bike went back to the department to be stripped down. If I had returned to the department and had not clocked up the mileage, then I would have been in trouble. They would have wanted to know if I had been to a café or fishing or something. Once I returned with a piece of fishing line wrapped round the sprocket. I really got told off over that, they said I had gone fishing but I hadn't, I don't know how it got there.

I was often in trouble but there was no malevolence in my scrapes, they were just the result of high spirits and the management was wise enough to treat them as such. There was one time when we were experimenting with a cheaper version of the Bullet, instead of using a steel barrel they used an alloy which they hand-painted black and we had to race each one two or three times round the test track – as it was a cheap bike it didn't have a long test. The engine got very hot and gave off this thick, black smoke and if you were not careful, when you returned the bike to its stand in the test shop you smoked the place out and you were not very popular.

One day, the two other apprentices and I returned from a ride and stuck our bikes on the stand without letting them cool down first and the department was full of these dense black fumes. You could hardly see a yard in front of you. Then who should walk in but Percy Holder, the senior tester, with Major Smith and two colleagues. We thought we were going to get killed. We just scampered and returned ten minutes later when Major Smith had gone. Percy was a little man in a white coat. When he saw us he said, 'Hey, I want a word with your lot!' and did we get told off! However, a few days later, Percy said to us, 'Shall I tell you what Major Smith really said about that smoke? He turned to his colleagues and said, "Do you remember when we used to do that?"'

The factory was closed for two weeks annual leave during the summer but I used to go in and do stock-taking, not so much for the money but for the fun my friends and I had in the empty factory. There were several great heavy electric trucks, steered by two levers, in the stores. My friend and I were having a race in them when he turned a corner and didn't control his truck properly and smashed straight through the wall of the Stores!

On the door of the competition department was a large notice saying, 'No Admittance' but anybody of any importance used to wander in. Charlie Rogers used to go spare. Works' riders like John Brittain, Pat Stirland and Terry Cheshire used to call in. Terry came from some way away and he always brought along his mechanic, his wife, his granny, the dog and a budgie in a cage. There was nowhere for them to sit and they just used to wander round all day.

The following year, which would be about 1958, I worked in the cycle assembly shop. The management decided to look into the possibility of producing a lightweight 150cc sporty, 'cafe racer' type of bike, rather like today's BMX but a motorbike, and as they wanted it to appeal to my age range I was involved in its development. It was not designed from scratch but was built using many of the components that we already had in stock. I was allowed to use it and my friends loved it. Whenever I parked it outside the fish and chip shop everybody crowded round, wanting to know how much it would cost and when it was going to be produced. It was standing in the cycle assembly shop, all beautiful and gleaming when Major Smith came to look at it. He stood there, looking at it for a few minutes then he slowly shook his head, and that was it! We never produced it. Six months development work up the spout.

Nearly all the young men at the factory were full of enthusiasm for scrambling and racing. We won many of these local and county events which did a great deal to promote Royal Enfield bikes. We were allowed a discount on our spare parts, but a discount was no use as we had no money at all. The older men used to find us the bits and pieces that we needed, then we had the hair-raising job of smuggling them out.

In the three years that I rode motor bikes, I only came off once but then I had a nasty accident at the Astwood Bank crossroads. A car was coming the other way and it turned in front of me and there was nothing I could do to avoid it. I ended up 72 feet away and my shoe was 60 feet in another direction. I was in hospital for a long time, when I returned to work they gave me a nice, easy factory job but I couldn't stick it and I left. I didn't even finish my apprenticeship which had another year to run. It was eight years before I got on the back of a motor bike again.

PETER NORMANDALE: from 1953 to 1968

Royal Enfield cycles were some of the best ever made. If you had an Enfield bike and you looked after it, it would last you a lifetime.

Working at Enfield was home from home. It was just like a family. My dad worked in the paint spraying department, my wife's uncle was Clarry Mills who was on bike assembly in the 1940s and another uncle, Sid, was the gaffer of the cycle finishing shop. If your dad worked there, then you worked there. Everybody knew everybody else.

My dad and Harry Knight put the gold lines on the cycles and bikes with a mustard tin. I don't know who thought of the idea, but they had an axle with a wheel in and they filled a Colman's mustard tin up with paint and fitted it on the axle. There was a hole in the bottom of the mustard tin and as they ran it up the mudguard the paint ran out and made a line. The lines round the petrol tanks and across the top and bottom of the lines were done by hand. Later on they used transfers.

I began an apprenticeship with the Royal Enfield on 28th December 1953 and went there straight from school. If you wanted a design apprenticeship or some kind of technical apprenticeship such as jigs and fixtures then you needed a qualification of some kind but for an engineering apprenticeship no entrance qualifications were needed. However, you had to go to College one day a week and two evenings.

Two things surprised me about the factory. The first was the number of oldish men working there. I would say that a quarter of the workforce was over fifty. The second was how spotlessly clean the factory was. Everyone said that Royal Enfield was one of the cleanest places to work. It was noted for it.

I started work under my uncle in the cycle finishing shop. I was then struck down with pneumonia and it was twelve months before I put in an appearance again!

A piece work system was in use where you were given a price for a job and you had to work out how much money you had earned and fill it in on this docket. Every Wednesday, the girls from the progress department came down to collect up all the paperwork for the jobs. Half an hour later they would be down to say, 'You're wrong, I don't get it to that, the price given is such-and-such'. If you fancied one of girls you used to give a ridiculous price so that she would have to keep coming down.

In the machine shop I saw something which I hope never to see again. Opposite the line of women on inspection was Les Hughes' office and next door to this was a drilling machine. One young apprentice was working on the driller when his tie got caught in the machine. This young man was fully dressed, he was wearing vest, shirt and trousers with overalls over the top of all that but the machine picked him up off the ground and whirled him round between the drill and the machine and he was left wearing nothing but his boots. He was unharmed except that he was shaking like a jelly. One of the women lent him her smock to cover himself up with.

My third and final move was to the inspection department, and there I stayed for the next five years, as I gave up my apprenticeship. In those days, there were very few text books and most of the work from College was by dictation. Although I'm very quick at maths, I'm a very slow writer and I just couldn't keep up. I struggled on for eighteen months but I finally had to give up. This was a blessing in disguise as I became assistant chief inspector in the department.

I was called into the design department several times to measure motorcycle parts for them. The management would buy a competitor's bike and strip it down with a view to copying it.

Almost all the women working at Royal Enfield were extremely nice. They usually worked on the lighter jobs such as packing and inspection. The machine operators were also on the whole, very decent, but there were one or two capstan operators who were very coarse. They were really doing a man's job and had to stick up for themselves, competing against the men and occasionally it made them very tough and very basic. Elsie was one of these women, all that she did was put the threads on nuts but she was brilliant at it, she was the only one who could do the job and she was a law unto herself. She came in whenever she felt like it – nine or ten o'clock – and worked whatever hours she felt like. She wore a long dress over which she put a sack with a hole cut for her head and arms and tied round the middle with string. She worked with machine oil which was a thick, black grease, and at regular intervals she wiped her hands on the front of her sacking in order to take a large quantity of snuff. If any young man came near she would try and grab him and even chase him. If you were a naive young apprentice the blokes used to find reasons to send you in her direction just for a laugh. One of the local managing directors sent his son to do an apprenticeship at Royal Enfield, this young man used to fly past Elsie and out through the emergency exit. One day, someone noticed him coming into the department and locked the exit door. He found himself stuck there with Elsie advancing on him and he was so terrified that he fainted.

I was in the Fire Service at Royal Enfield and there's a story attached to this. My house is only a short way from the original Royal Enfield factory at Hunt End and so in 1968, when the factory went up in smoke, I went to have a look. Dunlop's were using it as a tyre storage depot and the fire had really taken hold, it could be seen for miles around. There was a great commotion and it was totally chaotic. No-one was allowed into Enfield Road but some of the Firemen recognised me and said, 'You go home and get your clobber on then come and join us and give us a hand'. So I helped to put out the fire at Givry Works.

I finished at Royal Enfield in 1960 and went to work at HDA. My father was already working there and he told me that there was a job going on Inspection. I was doing virtually the same job for more money and less hours.

MERVYN PANTING: from 1955 to 1962

When I left school in 1955 I wanted to go into the RAF as a radio or radar operator but my dad refused to sign the papers. Instead, I found myself being interviewed by Tony Wilson-Jones with a view to an apprenticeship at Royal Enfield.

There I was, a young boy of sixteen, brought up in the country all my life, never having seen the inside of a factory and I found myself working in one. It was overwhelming. I went home with a headache day after day for the first few months – and assembly was a quiet department. It was the continual hum.

The atmosphere was marvellous. I can't describe it except to say that it was like a family. The wages were secondary, which was a good job, because when I started I was only earning £2 0s 6d (£2.02) and that included 6s 8d (33p) a week travelling allowance. I tried not to spend my travelling allowance and rode my push-bike from home to Redditch

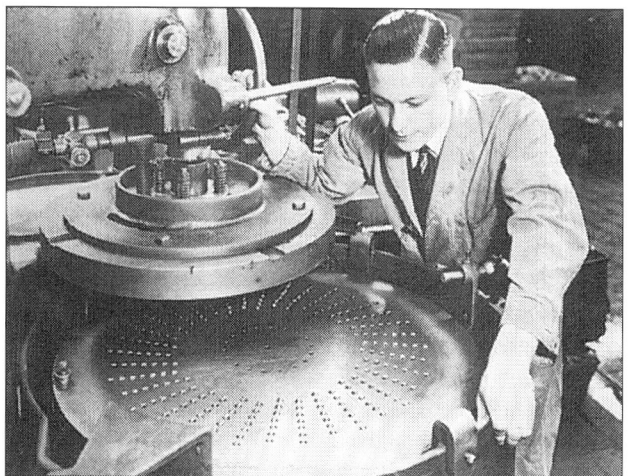

Grinding mainshaft bearings, circa 1937.

each day, a round trip of 26 miles. On my night-school night, or if the weather was bad, I stayed with my brother in Redditch. I did that for eighteen months until I bought my first motor bike, a little RE2. It cost £45, so I paid £30 and arranged to have £1 a week stopped out of my wages but sometimes, after the various stoppages, I hadn't earned as much as £1 so they couldn't deduct the repayments!

Everyone used to try and smuggle motorcycle bits out of the factory (although we weren't as bad as the Austin who lost a car a day through petty pilfering). The works police used to stand on the gate, watching everybody as they went past. We were up to all sorts of tricks. If you strapped an exhaust to your bike alongside the cylinder it looked like a twin cylinder and the works police would let it pass. When the Crusader first went into production, one of the workers wanted to get hold of a cylinder barrel, so he stuck it in a flower pot and put a great big bloom on top. The works policeman said, 'What's that?' and he called out, 'Wedding anniversary!'. I later bought an old 1936 Morris 8 which soaked up the oil so I took a Tizer bottle into work and got my supply of oil that way.

I spent six months in assembly and was then transferred to the tool stores under Sid Hearne. I catalogued and stocked drills, all machine tools and other bits and pieces; and I had to cut up material for the tool room to make jigs and fixtures.

After a few months working on a capstan in the diesel department under Bill Kings, I went into one of the most unpopular departments – plating. Enfield's did their own chromium plating in acids supplied by W Canning held in six huge vats, each about twenty feet long by seven feet wide. The fumes were terrible, we had fans in the roof but no breathing equipment. Rows of long copper tubes were stretched across the vats and everything to be chromium plated had a wire attached so that it could be hung in the acid. The acids dropped everywhere and although I wore a big rubber apron, rubber gloves past my elbows and wellingtons, my trousers usually fell to pieces after a couple of weeks. The foreman was Harry Anderson.

One incident which amused us was when the labourer at the department bought a ring that he said was solid gold. He had paid an arm and a leg for it. We said to him, 'That's never gold, give it to us and we'll test it for you'. So we fastened it to a piece of wire and hung it in the acid. The next morning, just the shell of the ring was left. It had only been gold-plated.

Then I found myself in rectification, where bikes were corrected after testing, under Percy Holder, a short, stiff man with a ruddy face and a bit of hair pushed back. For some months we were up at MIIRA nearly every day of the week. MIRA was a long, oval, banked track, about three miles in circumference. Inside that was a timing straight with a stop and start light, a stretch of cobbled road known as the 'pave', and the 'washboards'. There was also a dust tunnel and a water splash. Brian Crow was doing a lot of testing on a 700cc engine that had been put into a Berkeley four-wheeler. I was spending some of my time on a 150 Prince.

I also helped to build the prototypes and often took them to MIRA for testing. At one time we were working on a five-speed gear box which was a terrible thing, there was a neutral between each gear and when you tried to engage a gear, it wasn't positive enough. The bike was to be called the Super Five but I said to Charlie Rogers, 'Don't put this gearbox into production!' It died a super death because Roger Boss suggested building a GT racer for teenagers which came out just after I left.

There was a cafe at Meriden where you could get a mug of tea and a piece of toast for a shilling, and all the testers used to meet there together, from Triumph, BSA, and Ariel, there would be about a dozen of us. Then we would all clear off to MIRA together. I had my first bump at MIRA. I was putting mileage on a 700 Constellation and going at 70 mph when the twist grip simply came off the handlebar. I went up in the air and came down in a heap but fortunately I was only bruised.

From 1958 to 1959 I served on the apprentices committee. Although Tony Wilson-Jones and Bob Sandilands were in charge of the thirty or so apprentices, about half-a-dozen of us were selected to form a committee to look after apprentices' rights and also to help to coordinate, and sometimes organise, various events such as dinners and outings. We had some clout, one of our campaigns resulted in apprentices not having to work short-time. We felt that this was fair as apprentices were only working a four-day week anyway, one day a week being spent at College.

Several outings were arranged for us each year. We went to Triplex Metals to see how castings were made, and we had a look round the Austin factory. We also went to see the underground factory at Westwood, I always remember that particular visit because one of the apprentices was meddling with a machine and he turned a handle and did several thousand pounds' worth of damage.

I had a disagreement with the management just before one Christmas, I think it was 1961. A large order for Princes came in for the Christmas market and I had to go and help on the Prince line, where Mr Beckingham was the foreman. A message came up requesting that I went to MIRA with Bonky Bowers but I refused. It was damn cold outside. I said that as I didn't work in that department I didn't see why I should have to go out in the cold. I was never asked to go back in the development department again.

I finished my apprenticeship soon after I refused to go to MIRA and the only job that was offered me was frame filing, where you put the frame together then welded and filed it. I went to see Gilbert Baker and said, 'I've been an apprentice and I'm worth more than a frame filer's job'. We had an argument and he sacked me. On the way to his office to get my cards he stopped and said, 'Well, where would you like to work?' He rang round to see if there was a job anywhere else but he could only find one on a capstan so I said I'd take that. However, the machine turned out to be a milling machine, not a capstan. When Gilbert Baker came through afterwards, I asked him how long he had been at the firm and what his position was. Then I said 'You need to get your facts straight, this is a milling machine, not a capstan!' Gilbert's comment was that I was a cheeky young sod.

Afterwards, Brian Crow saw me on the milling machine and asked Gilbert Baker if I could transfer to his department. Gilbert said, 'If he wants the job, he's got to come and ask me for it!' So I poked my head round his door and said, 'I've come to tell you I'm going to work for Crowy on Monday!'

I left in 1962 when Enfield's started to go downhill but once you get Royal Enfield into your blood you can't get rid of it. Although it's over thirty years since I worked there, I still spend all my spare time maintaining Enfield bikes and taking part in Vintage racing events.

HILARY PANTING: from 1947 to 1961

My memories of Royal Enfield are very happy ones – especially the trips to see Blackpool illuminations which were organised by the girls in the office. In fact, that's where I first met my husband! I started in 1956 in the post room under Mrs Hemming, who happened to find out that my sister was a hairdresser so she asked me to cut her hair for her. I would do a quick trim in the department's walk-in safe in the dinner time. From there I picked up the comptometer very quickly and as I was advised that comptometer operators were very much in demand, I went into the wages department under George Fairgreave.

Our wages were better than most because, whenever High Duty Alloys had a pay rise, we got to know about it and kept going on at George Fairgreave until he gave in. I know that some people on the factory floor were only earning 2½d (1p) per thousand or something ridiculous like that. They used to have to work during their holiday times to get some extra money.

Our offices were often re-arranged and this was when Vic Bott used to come along. He was marvellous. He would say 'We're going to move this there and put such-and-such here and it will look like this' and he'd do a quick sketch and when it was finished, to our amazement, it would look exactly like his sketch.

I left in 1961 when I was pregnant and although I was looking forward to my new life as a mother, I was really sorry to leave Royal Enfield.

CHAPTER TEN
Enfield India

Sundaram inspects the Bullet engines with Oliver Wythes, works manager (left).

DEREK NEWMAN: from 1950 to 1960

During the early or mid 1950s there was in India a policy that they themselves would try to manufacture anything which was then being imported, to save currency. The Madras Motor Company (which was a selling company) was the main agent for Enfield bikes throughout the whole of India, and it was decided that they would start trying to manufacture the 350cc Bullet with overhead valve.

Various engineers came over to Enfield to learn about the motorcycles. First was Sankirim, one of the eight sons of the owner of the Madras Motor Company who did an apprenticeship over here. He was followed by a younger brother, Sundaram, and then an older man, Harry Sandford, amongst others.

The Madras Motor Company started off by receiving the Bullet in kits and simply assembling them. Then they began to make the frames, mastering the art of sheet metal work so that they could make the mudguards etc. After this Enfield's began sending the engine in parts for the engine to be assembled in India. Eventually, they were also manufacturing the engines which meant that they were then making the complete bike.

Most of the manufacturing in India was done on the basis of a joint venture with a British company but in the case of the Bullet, India kept the controlling interest, that is to say, they owned the company rather than having a 51/49% partnership. If something was manufactured in India, then the government would put a tax on any imports of similar items, which meant that the Madras Motor Company had few, if any, rival bikes or competitors.

For the next thirty years the design of their bike remained unchanged, then in about 1984, they began exporting them back to Europe and the UK. They shipped a sample bike back to Enfield's and asked them to redesign it to make it more suitable for the UK market. A couple of years later Lacksmann, the managing director, came over to negotiate the manufacture of the 500 Bullet.

Most of Sundaram's brothers worked in the Madras Motor Company, which also makes the Enfield stationary engine. About twelve or fifteen years ago another plant was set up at Runipet and they started making Zundapp motorcycles under licence, under a similar arrangement to that made with the Enfield Cycle Company Limited.

EILEEN NEWMAN: from 1953 to 1962

Sundaram was only in his late teens when he came over from Madras to start work in the jig and tool drawing office under Bob Sandilands. There he was, pursuing a new career in a strange country, not knowing anyone. He was literally thrown in at the deep end. My husband was also working in there and was roughly the same age and so he was asked to look after Sundaram.

Derek and I were going out together, I was about eighteen years of age and I worked in the production department next door. We took Sundaram with us wherever we went, he was very good company and it was no trouble to make up a threesome.

Sundaram, from the Madras Motor Company, inspects a Bullet with Oliver Wythes (works manager) 1958.

When Sundaram went back to Madras he asked Derek if he could go and run his company out in Madras for three years. We had all the papers arranged and everything but just before we were due to leave my father-in-law fell ill and we felt that we shouldn't leave him. But we kept in touch and we invited Sundaram to come to our wedding in 1959.

Then Sundaram got married and five of us from the Enfield were invited. It was the most memorable experience of my life. The wedding built up over days, on each day there was a different ceremony and something new would happen to the very beautiful bride. One day, she had her hands and forearms painted so that she looked as if she were wearing lace gloves. On the day of the wedding we were received by boys and girls wearing garlands and entertained with music and videos. The actual ceremony took place on a raised dais. There were 4,000 guests at the wedding and we were the only Europeans so we stuck out like a sore thumb!

After the ceremony, we were taken on a tour of Southern India. We were there for six weeks in all, entirely at Sundaram's expense. We still write to each other and they have sent me photographs of their children, they now have two sons.

Incidentally, one day, Gilbert Baker, the works manager, came into my office and said, 'Eileen, we want to show one of the motor bikes off' and he asked me to sit on a little Ensign 125 while it was photographed. I only did this twice, the girl who was usually featured in the advertisements was Patricia Mason, a very striking girl, tall and slender with dark hair.

VIC BOTT: a memory of Madras

For over a year I worked with the head of the team, Harry Sandford, on the planning preliminaries such as floor space, bench dimensions and so on. He was Anglo-Indian, a nice, popular bloke, who had begun his career as a representative of the Ford Company in India. He was a brilliant engineer and he needed to be, there was very little in India in the way of raw materials or technical expertise for him to work with. One example of his initiative was that he made a power press from the legs of a crashed Dakota aircraft.

EDDIE WRIGHT:

The four main people involved in the Madras side of Enfield India were the two young Indian brothers, Sankirim and Sundaram, an Anglo-Indian by the name of Harry Sandford, and Gannish. Both the brothers came over at intervals during the year, usually staying two, three or four weeks.

Sankirim was very definitely the boss. He was a tall man, rather aloof, nevertheless he was very business-like. There was no doubt that he had been very well-educated and he spoke in a grand manner.

However, Sankirim had one peculiarity. He would say he was coming to the works at a certain time and he wouldn't arrive. Time would pass and we would get a series of strange cables saying that he had a lot of officials still to consult and so on. Sometimes he would be six to eight weeks late. It would turn out, in the end, that his astrologers had advised him not to come. This seemed so alien to his nature, you would not think that he could be affected by anything like that. This put tremendous pressure on us because he would come with a large order and if we had, say, four months to complete it, the loss of six or eight weeks was a serious matter, and everyone had to work overtime to get the work completed.

Sundaram, the younger brother, was also a very accomplished man, well educated and a lover of classical music and ballet. He was in his early twenties, tall like his brother and although he was quiet he was very likeable and friendly. He was very much under the influence of Sankirim and at every decision he said, 'I must ask my older brother.' He often popped in to visit us after work in the evening. We had a radiogram and he used to say, 'Do you mind if I bring some records along and see if they are what I think they are?' He dropped in to visit other workers as well, Oliver Wythes often invited him to dinner. Sometimes Gilbert Baker, the works manager, would pick us up and we would all go for a meal at the Swan at Alcester.

I thought that the Anglo-Indian, Harry Sandford, was the most able and practical of them all. He had a good engineering background and spent several weeks here. He was quick to pick up all the manufacturing, assembling and testing methods. He bought a number of Enfield machines – millers, lathes, capstan lathes etc and he also attended machinery sales around the country, buying many machines which came to Enfield to be packed and despatched. He must have been a big asset to Enfield India. The last letter I received from him said that he had left the company and had, I think, gone to work for an oil company.

Mr Gannish was much more egotistical and self-assured. He was in his mid-twenties, of medium height and he said that his father was the President of India Airways. He stayed with us for longer periods, probably two to three months at a stretch. He was particularly interested in the fibreglass department and spent a lot of time in there.

The management team involved with the Enfield India project. Left to right: Harry Sandford, Oliver Wythes, Sundaram, Major Smith and Vic Mountford. Photo: Jim Freeman.

We also had visits from the factory workers who would stay two or three months at a time, picking up bits of knowledge here and there.

ROGER BOSS:

One of the most popular and successful machines we ever built was the 350cc Bullet which was marketed as a sporty road machine and in a variety of specifications for the competition rider. It proved particularly successful as a trials machine and in the hands of ace trials rider, Johnny Brittain, won many prestigious awards. Because the machine was reliable and easy to maintain, we received a very large order from the Indian army.

The specification was almost standard and they were finished in a matt sand colour. These bikes were urgently required by the army for use in their war with Pakistan and one of the major stipulations was that they should be seize-proof. This meant that when they were removed from the wooden crates, they could be used to their full potential immediately without the necessity for 'running in'. Each machine was given a good road test with strong use of the throttle and those which suffered a tightening of the piston were returned to the assembly line, where barrels and pistons were interchanged to rectify the problem. I can remember being seconded to the main test shop to assist in getting this order completed on time, we worked seven days a week for a number of weeks. There is no doubt it was this order which started our connection with 'Madras Motors' and I can remember our then Sales Director, Major Mountford, going out to India and successfully completing a contract for the supply of Royal Enfield machines.

The company, now Enfield India Ltd, are marketing the 350cc Bullet in quite large quantities in many parts of the world and it seems ironic that we are now importing a motorcycle which helped to keep the name Royal Enfield amongst the successful post-war manufacturers.

CHAPTER ELEVEN
The lull before the storm: American Indian, an early scooter and the Britax Hurricane

The US-spec. 350 "Hounds Arrow".

JIM FREEMAN: from 1948 to 1966

I left school in late 1939 and, after taking a written IQ and maths test, started work at the Enfield, aged 14. My first job was in the time office under Frank Clarke. We were the only two working in that office, Frank was Chief Commissionaire, he had been a Sergeant Major in the first world war, he had a loud voice and used to stand outside the factory urging the latecomers to hurry in.

The time office was a tiny building on the right-hand side of the drive as you went in at the main gate. The workers' clocking-in shed was about fifty feet long with a glass roof and in there were about ten or eleven huge clocking-in machines. When a worker clocked in, the time was printed on a band of paper running round the edge of each clock face. Once a week I had to collect up the paper bands and calculate how many hours each of the thousand or so employees had worked.

Another of my jobs was that of sorting out the wages tins. Everybody was paid in a tin about half the size of a cocoa tin with their clock number on it, then they threw the tin into a large box. I had to sort out the tins and put them in order, from 1 to 1,200, or whatever.

Then I moved from the time office to the progress department, where Frank Lewis was in charge, making out tally cards for motor bikes and push bikes. This was a large card, about A4 size, divided up by perforations so that you could tear off a piece at a time. Each operation was listed on a part of this sheet, for example, fit handlebars would be on one section and fit gearbox would be on another. The bike would go round the works with its tally card and when each operation had been completed, the worker would tear off his portion of the tally card. These were collected together and handed in. The wages department used these tallies to pay the wages of the day workers, and it provided the progress department with a record of how much of the work had been completed.

I used to prepare the tallies for about 300 to 350 motor bikes and between 900 and 1,200 push bikes each week. The average for push bikes was about 1,100. Over a year we used to manufacture about 50,000 or 60,000 push bikes.

My time in the progress department came to an end in May 1943 when I volunteered for Air Crew and joined the RAF for four years. I returned in June 1947 and went into the drawing office.

One of the advantages of Royal Enfield was that everything was done on site – crankcases, pistons and rods were machined there and most items were made on site. We had a polishing shop, a plating shop and a press shop and a number of machine shops which were laid out with capstans, drilling machines and grinders and all kinds of machines. We even had a cast iron section for cylinder heads and barrels. We were therefore rarely hit by shortages of parts because we did everything ourselves and didn't have to rely on outside suppliers.

In the late 1950's I worked on the drawings of the initial designs for the Indian Motor Company. The first person to come over from the USA was Bob Finn, who stayed in Redditch for two or three months. He went through the specifications and photographs with me of the various bits and pieces which needed to be specially made, such as the American Indian crest and a special carrier on the rear of the bike. Royal Enfield eventually produced a whole range of bikes for the American market, from the 250 to the Trailblazer, Woodsman and Tomahawk. They were fitted with upswept exhaust systems, 'Jiffy' stands and larger tyres.

I remember Reg Thomas' first designs for the Airflow enclosures. I helped Ron Pearson with the pattern making, he built up the shape out of balsa wood, then it went to George Neale who looked after the fibreglass moulding on the experimental side. George had three or four women on the experimental side layering it up for him.

Not long before we closed down, in about 1965, I was drawing the Lucas part of a headlamp encased in a fibreglass moulding and matched with the petrol tank, rear mudguard and seat assembly. This was for a new design of 148cc bike which was supposed to be our next big project. Three of four of them were actually built but the production costs were found to be too high so it was abandoned.

Another abandoned design was a scooter designed by Ted Pardoe in about 1950, long before the Italians brought theirs out, which used a 98cc stationary engine. After building a couple of prototypes, that was put on one side. Reg Thomas also designed an electric mower and Major Smith took it to try it out on the lawns in front of the Enfield offices. Major Smith was only a small chap and the lawnmower virtually ran away with him. He said that the gears were wrong and nobody liked to tell him that the fault lay with him and his short legs. The mower was pushed under my desk and forgotten, so when the Enfield closed I gave a fiver for it. It's still in my garage but it doesn't work.

We also produced a large range of cycle accessories, the most unusual of which was, I think, the low gravity carrier, an enormous metal basket which was carried on the front of the bike and which almost reached the ground from the handlebars. It was designed for use by tradesmen. I found one very useful at the beginning of the war, when I was in the progress department. I had to fetch small parts from Allcocks in Redditch so I used to cycle round with my low gravity carrier and fetch them in that.

I married a girl from the diesel drawing office in 1952. The company owned several houses, and George Smith, Major Smith's brother who was Company Secretary, offered one to me to rent. I said that I wasn't interested in renting but I would like to purchase so we negotiated a price and I bought it. That was in 1957 and we are still living there.

PAUL SAVAGE: from 1954 to 1956

My heart dropped when I saw my first job. I remember it very well. I went to Royal Enfield because I was very keen on motorcycles and there I was assembling a girder fork that was being made under contract for Britax. Basically, it was the fork off the Flying Flea that was being used for the little Britax Hurricane with the tiny Ducati engine. I didn't do an awful lot of those and my next job was putting the stays on mudguards. This was a terribly boring job, even to a sixteen year old who was being paid for doing it. I supplied the mudguards for an assembly track where the men were on piece work and I was often in trouble for not doing this quickly enough and holding the men up.

After about six months I went onto cycle frame assembly. It seemed to me that I had to do an awful lot. I said to an old-timer who worked in the department, 'I don't think the piecework prices are very good on this job'. He said, 'I'm not surprised, the rate fixer hasn't had a look at it since before the war'. I pointed out that 1939 was a long time ago and he replied, 'No lad, not the last war, the 1914-18 war'. I must say that it wasn't as bad as all that, the workers had been given various cost-of-living allowances and other additions to their basic wages so that their wages had been increased, but not all that much.

I spent six months on frame assembly, then moved into the machine shop. One day I was walking past one of the capstans when I caught my ankle on all the swarf spilling out from the machine and cut it to the bone, I walked calmly to the surgery, leaving a trail of blood, but then I passed out. I was taken to Smallwood Hospital where I had to have five stitches and my leg was in plaster for six weeks.

Being a stroppy youngster I said that I was going to sue for compensation. This frightened my father. He worked at

Enfield motorised mower, 1947.

another large Redditch firm, Terry Springs, and he said that if I sued for compensation Enfield's managers would be on to Charlie Terry and he would be out of a job.

I then worked on crankcases for a few weeks under Harry Hay. I worked my way through piece work to the princely sum of £3 15s (£3.75) per week. Then the rate fixers came and said that they had to re-time the job, it had to be made up of smaller material. This cut my earnings to £2 10s per week. I couldn't live on that amount – my weekly contribution to my mother was that much.

So I protested with my feet and walked out in June 1956. I wasn't the only one who complained about the Enfield. I had two cousins who worked there just before the last war and my aunt complained to my mother because my one cousin was only fourteen and he used to be sent to the bank each week to collect the entire wages for all the workers in the factory.

Anyway, everything worked out for the best and I'm very happy now with my own small business supplying motorcycle parts for obsolete motorcycles.

RAYMOND JONES: from 1951 to 1966

Oliver Wythes was the works manager when I worked at Royal Enfield and I was always known as his nephew. I did call him Uncle Oliver but he was actually my second cousin. To me, however, he was more of a father. There are two words which describe him exactly, rumbustious and old-fashioned. He had plump, ruddy cheeks, flaming red hair and a personality to match. He always wore an expensively-cut suit with a fob watch. Not only did he provide me with a home but in 1951, when I was fifteen, he found me a job at the Enfield factory doing paintwork. I was not very successful at that, my interests lay in engines. I was therefore transferred to engine assembly. I had to prepare crankcases, putting in the bearings and cam spindle, folding the cases up to match and selecting the correct flywheels which went up in one tenths of a thou. From here I moved to diesel engines which I didn't like and I ended up in the service department, repairing two-stroke 125's such as the Ensign and later, the Prince.

Thanks to Uncle Oliver, I became a proficient mechanic and even suggested some improvements to the bikes. The clutch on the Prince was fixed on to the crankshaft, which looked neat but really clonked when you changed gear. One day I got hold of a Prince and fitted it with a cushdrive on a primary gear without a puller. The design department came down, looked at it and copied it, then began fitting it as standard. I never had any recognition for that. My final job was fitting a modified crankshaft to the Constellation, I did 114 and never had one back for repair.

My foreman was Fred Simmons and one day he discovered that we were trimming the bearings and tightening up the head races on the Bullet G frame. He said, 'If I catch anybody doing that, I'll sack them!' This shouldn't have been done because it made the steering less flexible. We showed him the problem and explained that this was the only way that we could tighten up the head races. Freddy Simmons had a go and in the end he started doing it himself.

After the traumas of my early years I really appreciated the fun that we had in those days. We were always teasing the apprentices. There was one called Roger who was a first class academic but you couldn't trust him to put a nut and bolt together. He came from Alvechurch and his father bought him a Lambretta but each time he had to turn a corner he would get off and walk. We sent him off to Tony Wilson-Jones, the technical manager, to ask for some advice on driving. I would have loved to have been a fly on the wall.

We had to wheel the motor bikes up ramps on to a stand about three feet off the floor in order to work on them. I said to one of the apprentices. 'To save us pushing the bike up the stand, you ride it up and we'll stand each side and catch you once you're up there'. So he rode it up and there was nobody there to catch him. We were hiding close at hand, though, we couldn't have let him fall, there would have been terrible trouble.

A young apprentice, Colin, came to help me on the two-strokes. I said to him, 'Do you know anything about big ends?' He said that he didn't. 'Well', said I, 'You have to make sure they are really round and to do this you have to kneel down and roll them all over the floor with your hand'. After he had been doing this for a few minutes Freddy Simmons came in and said, 'What the b... hell are you doing Colin?' When Colin told him Freddy looked at my mate, Reg Brambleby, and me and said, 'You're a right pair of devils, you two are!'

I would have liked to have stayed at Royal Enfield but I could see the way that things were going – the Bullet was off to India, the Constellation and the Crusader were going to Westwood – it was obvious that the place was going to close down so I answered an advertisement for a mechanic to work on Post Office vehicles and moved to the GPO.

ROD HILL: from 1950 to 1951

I went to the Enfield in 1950. My father knew Jack Lyes who arranged for me to have an interview in the service department. I was only a kid so I had all the dirtiest jobs. I had to take the engines out of the bikes, strip them down and wash them off, ready for 'Baggy' Parsons to rebuild them. 'Baggy' would often show me how to do this.

I heard this story from a friend of mine, Harry Farley. During the war, Major Smith was worried that his night workers were not getting a proper breakfast, so he decided to keep pigs. I don't know exactly where he kept them, probably on the Enfield allotments. All went well until the time came to kill the pigs, then Major Smith asked around to find someone who could do the deed. He heard that little Fred Gateley could kill pigs and asked Harry to bring him into work on the back of his motor bike. Fred didn't take too long to kill the pigs and went off to entertain himself for the day at Redditch until it was time to go home. When he turned up for his lift home, he was as drunk as a lord and he could hardly stand up. Harry wondered how he was going to get him home. Anyway Harry put him on the back of his bike and he swayed this way and that exactly in time with corners, although Harry never knew whether it was by design or accident. Two days later, Harry had to take Fred back to the Enfield to cut the pigs up and exactly the same happened again, Fred rolled up at the end of the day hardly able to stand up.

I thoroughly enjoyed myself at the Enfield, I had a really good time and was sorry when I had to leave in 1951 to do my national service.

JEAN WORMINGTON: 1947 to 1958

I went to Royal Enfield straight from school when I was only 14 and I was working there for over eleven years, from 1947 to 1958. I started in the post room and worked my way up to the service department of the English sales office.

In 1951 I was elected Redditch's deputy carnival queen. I was delighted to find myself in the Enfield magazine, *Revs*. There was no parade of bathing beauties in those days, what happened was that we had a carnival dance, we were in evening dress, and from the dance floor we were chosen to stand in a line-up to be inspected by the judges. There were no prizes, you just did it for the honour.

Jean Wormington (extreme left) runner-up to Carnival Queen, 1951.

The other highlights of my life were things like the day that I had a new typewriter. And I can remember the first biro that came into the office. They were great big fat things and Vic Mountford had the first one. We were all very jealous.

REG BUGGINS: from 1940s to 1950s
by his two daughters, Beryl and Sylvia

Our father was Reg Buggins one of Enfield's commissionaires. They were members of a national organisation known as the Royal Corps of Commissionaires which was the post-war equivalent of today's security firms and supplied staff to large factories, hotels etc. It was primarily composed of ex-regular NCOs and warrant officers. The Enfield employed a number of commissionaires, they also employed approximately the same number of works police but they wore a different uniform and were recruited direct by Royal Enfield from the general public. Among the commissionaires and works policemen were Major Riddings (Head Commissionaire) Tommy Kings, Tommy Fox and Dick Bolton. Tommy Fox lived in a flat above the canteen. We were surprised to learn that he had the French VC.

The commissionaires worked shifts which were 6 am to 2 pm, 2 pm to 10 pm or 10 pm to 6 am. Quite often, a commissionaire or a works policeman failed to turn up for

Reg Buggins and Major Riddings, two commissionaires.

work, perhaps off sick, then my father would work another shift. Many a time he cycled home the eight miles to Cookhill for a meal and a brief rest, then he would have to turn round and cycle in again.

SYLVIA BUGGINS: from 1948 to 1951

I suppose Royal Enfield was wonderful for the men, they had their motor bikes, but to Beryl and I it didn't hold quite the same appeal.

I had been brought up in the little country village of Cookhill all my life, even going to school there, then suddenly I was removed from a quiet rural life to work at this enormous factory. I was petrified. I had to take the post round and I got lost every day! The men used to whistle every time you went into a shop, I used to slink in and hope nobody had seen me.

I hated the journey. Each day I had to cycle the three miles from Cookhill to Astwood Bank to catch the work's bus. I paid 2d a day to leave my bike round the back of a house by the chip shop on the main road (which has now been demolished). There were dozens of bikes there, all piled up, when you wanted to retrieve your bike to go home, you had to lift all these other bikes off it. In winter the journey was terrible, in snow or bad weather we had to walk the three miles to Cookhill. I was so cold!

I went to the service office between 1948 and 1951 and used to type the invoices. I also unofficially typed the fixture lists for Colin Poole who ran the football club. The team did so well that the results were usually in the *Redditch Indicator*.

I left for a better job, but I didn't leave the Enfield behind, my sister and my husband worked there as well as my father.

BERYL BUGGINS: from 1951 to 1956

I went to work in the production control department in 1951. I had to print the clocking in cards and job slips and do the payroll for the whole factory. On top of this, every time the Enfield won a trial I had to notify all our agents. There were hundreds and hundreds of them. Their names and addresses were embossed on little metal plates about four inches by an inch-and-a-half, and there were shelves and shelves of them. I had to slot the plate into a machine and print the address on an envelope. It took me several hours to print them all.

Our foreman, Mr Lewis, was very strict. He didn't like to see you talking and laughing together, if he noticed us collecting in a group he used to come up and give us all jobs to do. Nevertheless, we had a lot of fun in our office, everyone thought we were quite mad.

HENRY COLLINS: from 1951 to 1961

On my very first day working in the Despatch department at Royal Enfield, someone dented the van. I was delivering to a factory in the centre of Birmingham and when I came out of the works, I was told that a lorry had just backed into my van. The lorry drove off but I chased him and he stopped between Moore Street and Carrs Lane and admitted it. Sid Parsons was very nice about it. He said 'These things do happen and anyway, you have the name and address of the man who did it.' Sid Parsons was good to work for, he was in his fifties, tall and blonde and a good counties bowling man. Four of us worked in the despatch department, we had a navy-blue uniform and cap which we had to wear at all times. If Major Smith passed us on the road and we were not wearing a jacket or cap, we would be called into his office on our return to explain why.

One of the perks of the job was that my family were insured so that if I had a light load, I could take them with me. My two boys were just toddlers at that time and their favourite trip was to Dunlop's in Liverpool, where I had to collect seats for motor bikes, as this meant a ride through the Mersey tunnel.

The trip to Lapland

In July 1951, three cycling friends in Leicester decided to embark on a most unusual holiday – to cycle to Lapland and back. They chose Royal Enfield Bullet 3 bicycles with unitized frames and forks for the eight-week journey. They crossed the North Sea to Esbjerg in Denmark, cycling via Copenhagen to Stockholm, travelled north through Lapland and beyond the Arctic Circle to Narvik in northern Norway. The roads gradually deteriorated, until in the far north the surfaces consisted of loose dirt with awkward ruts. They had hoped to reach the North Cape, but 300 miles from their destination they encountered continuous blizzards of up to 60 miles an hour, which upset their schedule. The food was provided by the nomadic Lapps so their diet comprised frozen fish, salt pork and poor quality bread, with goat's milk to drink. This was the land of the midday sun, and daylight lasted 23 hours out of the 24.

They rode south through Finland to Helsinki, crossed the Baltic Sea to Stockholm and returned to England via Denmark, Germany and Belgium. They returned to Leicester where they were greeted by the Lord Mayor.

There is no record of any problem with the bikes, nor of how many hot baths they needed on their return.

CHAPTER TWELVE
The end in sight

Probably the last racers to be entered by the Enfield. From left: Richard Stevens on Series II No. 2 production racer, mechanic (unknown), Chris Ludgate on Series I No. 10, Reg Thomas and Roger Shuttleworth. Richard and Chris worked in the development shop. Photo Wiltshire Times and News.

REG BRAMBLEBY: from 1963 to closure

When I first joined the Company in 1960, it was one of the last of the best years for the sales of motor bikes and the factory was going full tilt. During the summer months we would start work at 7 am (which was one hour's overtime as normal starting time was 8 am) and go on until 5.30. I was working on motor bike repairs, I had to do what I thought was necessary then take the bike out on the test track for a test. The bike then went to the testing department where it was put through its paces again on the road.

One of the great advantages of the Enfield bikes was that they were quick and easy to service and repair. I remember when Bob Currie, then editor of Motor Cycle, brought his bike in for a new engine and when he returned some thirty minutes later, the job had been done. He couldn't believe it. He quoted this sometime later in one of his articles, but it was done by about four of us all having a go for the hell of it.

Although we were busy, the pace was quite leisurely, there was no-one with a big stick standing over us. People used to say that the repair section was a law unto itself, they didn't realise that it would take a day or two for the bike to reach us by train and we first had to obtain the spare parts from the service department stores – an exercise in itself as all had to be fetched and recorded on the job card by the storeman, a very time-consuming and pedantic exercise. We then we had to fit the parts, test the bike and return it by train. I must admit that we did work at our own pace and I didn't know what pressure was until many years later when I went to work for a coal merchant. There, if someone ran out of fuel they wanted it the same day and were not prepared to wait an extra day or two until we got around to it.

I had a lot of help from various people in the factory. If parts were in short supply, the men in the new motorcycle assembly shop were always helpful. The foreman was Geoff Hay, who later went to India for a month to assist in the setting up and refining of their production line which still produces bikes today. 'Kipper' Gibbs was also helpful and so was Ken Sherwood, the wheels expert.

I also occasionally visited the competition department for advice. We used to call it the 'Enfield secret society' because security was very strict and unauthorised workers were not allowed in. This was run by Charlie Rogers, a rider who had represented Britain at the International Six Days Trial.

Reg Brambleby (and employee) on a Continental GT.

Because of the involvement in the sporting side many top line riders visited the factory, such as John Hartle, Mike Duff and, of course, Geoff Duke. Johnny Brittain was the Enfield works trials ace with many successes. As well as being well-known within the motorcycle fraternity they were household names, as they appeared regularly on TV at weekends in scrambles and trials.

Another of my occasional duties was that of taking army bikes to the military establishment at Cobham in Surrey to be tested. I would take one bike there and bring back another on the works' 'hack', a big twin and box sidecar, built to carry a bike. I also helped out at the motorcycle show and local open days and displays, such as the display at Ragley Hall when young lads were allowed to ride Enfield and other makes of bikes round the field. Many of them had not ridden before so it was a rather risky exercise and in some ways more entertaining to watch than organised racing.

To me, and to many of the other men who worked there, Royal Enfield was play, not work. We were all motorcycle fanatics. I can't tell you how fanatical about motorbikes everyone, including the general public, was in those days. There used to be crowds of over 30,000 at the Hawkstone Park scrambles in Shropshire. The kind of events where Royal Enfield did well were trials, these were often international events and British bikes could be seen to be winning them! There was something patriotic in the tremendous public fanaticism.

We were all totally dedicated and would do anything that involved a motorbike, health and safety was the last thing on anyone's mind. I remember in the middle of one winter (I think it was 1962) Enfield's were having problems with over-oiling, so Norman Thomas and I were given two brand new 250s and told to ride them around for a week to test the oil consumption. The roads were sheets of ice and it was so cold that the River Avon had frozen over. Norman and I stopped in Stratford and went for a walk under Clopton Bridge on the frozen river.

I remember one incident where we had a bike which had come back from a customer through the dealer. The customer said it was making a funny rattle and the dealer asked us to have a look at it. The dealer rode the bike up to the Enfield factory, then Brian Crow gave it a turn or two couldn't hear much wrong and asked me to take it up and down the motorway (the M5). I took it for a good run a 70mph, returned to the factory and said to Brian that it did rattle a bit. When we pulled the side casing and gear cover off we discovered that the gearbox had never had a drop of oil in it. The gears had turned black and blue where the material had disintegrated. By rights, that gearbox should have seized and thrown me off, why it didn't I shall never know. Although I didn't think this was funny, it did give rise to some amusement in the department.

We had a lot of laughs in the factory. One incident that brought tears to our eyes was when a very well-to-do young lady arrived in a sports car with daddy's Enfield lawnmower in the boot for repair. We told her to take it to the lawnmower shop, a small building in the centre of the test track. She parked her car outside the Shop, opened the door and was met by a barrage of bad language which included 'And you can p... off for a start!' The foreman thought it was a factory worker opening the door and had given her a standard factory greeting.

Sometimes the jokes went a bit too far. Once, one lad went to roar away on his motor bike and he found that someone had used a rope to attach his bike to the nearest lamp-post. He went flying over the handlebars. There was a terrible fuss about that but no-one ever found out who had done it.

Quite a lot of petty pilfering went on. I used to travel to work in a motor bike and side-car which I left parked in the Enfield car park. At the end of the day, everybody would have to go out through the main gate where the commissioner, one of the old Sergeant-Major school, kept his eye open for unauthorised bits and pieces going out of the factory. One evening, not long after I had got home, there was a knock on my door and a neighbour of my mine, who also worked at Enfield's said, 'Can I have my engine?' 'What engine?' asked I. He answered, 'The engine that I put in your side-car today!'

I was walking through the service department workshop one morning in about 1966 when Roger Boss grabbed hold of me and asked me what I thought of the two-stroke Enfield. I said, 'Not much!' and listed all the rectifications needed to correct some basic faults. Roger asked me to repeat this to 'the Boss' as he was thinking of updating it, and he pushed me into this room where the whole Board were gathered which included Geoff Duke, who was a hero of mine. He was a first class motorcyclist, World Motor Cycling Champion six times and Sportsman of the Year in 1951. I now stood there and, in a bit of a dither in such company, I can't even remember what I said. I noticed later that it had been dropped from the range.

The Enfield factory was still busy when I transferred to the offices of the sales and service department in 1964. I was in charge of the guarantee claims, writing letters to customers and telephoning them to sort out mechanical problems. Most of them could be dealt with by one of our standard letters which said, for example, 'Thank you for your letter, we are sorry that you are having problems, this is a most unusual occurrence'!! and so on. About 45 people were employed in the sales and service department overall, with approximately five women and four men in the offices. One of the men handled bicycle sales, another, Charlie Blundell, dealt with export sales, a very tricky subject at that time. Sometimes parts were sent as a free gift to a country to pass

Sheffield's Wilf Green – one of Enfield's most supportive dealers for a great many years.

149

on to another country with payment coming in by the back door. Very often the cost of air freight to the States would be twice or three times the cost of the item and the paperwork involved was extraordinary. It was a wonder we ever exported anything. As the factory declined the personnel left and were not replaced until, by the time of the closure, the sales and service department comprised just four of us in the office, four in packing and four mechanics.

At Christmas 1967 a large notice, more than A4 size, went up on the notice board saying 'Have no fears for your future employment – your future is assured. All members of staff will receive a £10 bonus for Christmas'. Six months later, despite all efforts by the Board, riders and workers, the company closed down.

You could say that we were forced off the road by the car, particularly by the Mini which was cheaper than one of the better bikes. Another reason for the decline in sales was the wave of prosperity of the 1960s, people found that they were able to afford a car.

It was very sad day when the auctioneer and the bidders arrived. The auctioneer was standing over elaborate machines which had cost thousands of pounds asking for a few pounds to get it off his hands.

For the seven years that I worked there I received £90 redundancy money which I used for the deposit on a Morris Minor. There was a lot of unemployment about and I was quite relieved when I was asked to continue with my same job at Velocette, who had bought the rights to sell Enfield spares.

The general manager of the Enfield spares and service division was Jack Spencer, an extremely helpful character who was known to us as The Councillor, as he had done so much charitable work that he had been elected a local councillor and was, at one stage, Chairman of Redditch Council. He was also moving to Velocette from Enfield and so he oversaw the whole process. Most of the spares had already been sold before the final closure to the two main dealers, Gander and Gray of London and Wilf Green in Yorkshire. The remainder were put into crates, loaded on to lorries and taken over to Velocette. The new department was called 'Enfield Spares and Service Division (Velocette) Limited'.

Velocette Limited was a family business producing motor bikes which had been founded in 1904. When I went to the factory in Hall Green two things really surprised me. The first was how old-fashioned the place was. The machine shop couldn't have changed since the 1920s and the manufacturing machines were still driven by belts and pulleys! The second was how very small the place was – about the size of a village school. Yet they produced such magnificent motorcycles! At Velocette I continued with similar work, selling spares and making out invoices, mostly proforma invoices except for the main agents who had accounts. About ten of us had transferred from Enfield's including mechanics and invoice typists and we were provided with a small office, stores and workshop.

I worked there for a few years but the wages were so low that it became uneconomic for me to travel over to Hall Green every day and I was very sorry when I had to find work nearer home. When I joined Enfield's way back in 1960, a motorcycle was your passport to personal independence. Now this has been replaced by the car, and general-purpose motorcycling as a means of transport has joined the steam age as a relic of the past.

VIC BOTT: and the Revelation

I was due for retirement when E & H P Smith took over but we were offered an increase in salary and so I decided to continue to work. A couple of years later, Leo Davenport sent for me. He said that he wanted to put a cycle on the market with a twenty inch wheel and asked me if I could design it. He wanted to know how soon I could have a prototype ready. Jokingly, I said 'Two weeks!' and he jumped at that. I knew I had landed myself with a problem. It usually took years to develop a new bicycle. It was clear that I couldn't go through the customary design channels so what I did, was that I laid an enormous piece of paper on the floor, drew a profile of the bike to size and gave it to the design department to build. Within a week a girl was trying out the cycle by riding it to Stratford. After that, of course, all kinds of tests had to be made to make sure that the bike was safe but within twelve months it was on sale in the shops. The bicycle was called 'The Revelation'.

REX WEARING: from 1965 to closure

In October 1965 I moved jobs just across the road from High Duty Alloys to 'The Enfield'. I wasn't particularly pleased to be still working in Redditch as I had applied for a job nearer my home in Harborne, with Hi-Ton in Selly Oak, a part of the E & H P Smith group. In the event they hired two new management accountants and I was taken on for group strength but sent to Enfield. I was working directly to Bob Cassey whom I always respected as a 'gentleman boss'.

High Duty Alloys was part of Hawker-Siddley, manufacturing jet engine blades and aircraft forgings. Local people warned me I would find a sharp contrast at Enfield and they were right. E & H P Smith were originally in the electrical business but had expanded into a quoted company of about twenty/thirty small subsidiaries being mainly small Midland engineering or factoring firms. They had recently acquired another group centred in the south called Amalgamated Industrials. Having paid two million cash for that acquisition they were consequently short of capital. I was told they had a cash price set against every company at which they were prepared to negotiate a sale. The MD of one of the subsidiaries told me 'These Brummagem business men would sell the paint off the walls if they could scrape it off!'

Smith's chairman was E C Roberts who mainly looked after the London half leaving Robert Cassey, the managing director, to run the Midlands. Leo Davenport was MD of the Enfield Cycle Company with Oliver Wythes, a director who had been Enfield's works manager. J D Shepherd was Smith's company secretary, visiting frequently, while Barry Smith was Enfield's company secretary.

My job was to analyse the profitability of the company. It had been bought by Smith's for, I believe, about £800,000. It was, in fact, a larger company than Smith's. Due presumably to shrinking business and lack of new product investment it had over £300,000 in building society accounts. This fact, together with the run-down look of the place, looked ominous for the future. When I inquired as to what the capital expenditure authorisation procedure was, I was told, 'There ain't any!' I said, 'No procedure?' 'No ... no capital expenditure.' This sounded like a death knell to me.

Smith had formed a separate company to sell off surplus machine tools from Enfield. Apart from that there were product sales of motorcycles from a small single assembly line, the spares department, bicycles, diesel engines and some small business introduced by Smith in hydraulics and overhead lines. The latter was a warehousing job, buying in parts for electric pylon construction. It employed four or five poor Asian labourers who were supervised by a West Indian foreman who was the only one who could communicate with them! Neither this nor the hydraulics lasted long at Enfield.

As to profitability there was still a small motor bike competition section, which could do little but keep the name alive. Spares were the only truly profitable area, the pricing formula being: cost + 20% x 3 but this was obviously on a

The Vic Bott designed Revelation cycle.

dwindling base due to diminishing sales. The volumes of the main products were clearly insufficient for the size of the place, which echoed with emptiness in places. Decisions to buy out more and more components had only, in my view, hastened the decline.

To be fair it seems that after the take-over there may have been an intention to 'make a go' of Enfield. They had appointed Leo Davenport, a Lightweight TT winner, as the new MD and produced a new small-wheel bicycle. However, the size of the task, plus the state of the industry and the shortage of capital, all pointed to it being a lot easier to sell up. A revitalisation of Enfield on the original site would have been a major technical and financial operation.

I felt sorry for the loyal older employees who had stuck by their lifelong jobs. The younger staff had mostly left for better prospects. Wages were about half those paid across the road at HDA, where the unions were showing their muscles by striking for the first time ever.

Enfield had, I was told, been an old-fashioned paternalistic set-up under the autocratic regimes of the previous owners. I saw no sign of any union activity.

The pension scheme provided for contributions from the employees only until the age of forty when the company would start to chip in. So the final pension would often depend on company top-ups based on the director's wishes.

As the factory wound down the staff faced the choice of waiting for redundancy, paid at the statutory minimum in most cases, or seeking another job. Some chose to go and thereby sacrificed the lump sum due after many years' service.

Rumours about what was going on during the run-down ran through the place. In the office we found that the shop floor usually knew what was happening better than we did. Years afterwards I found out how they knew. Cassey had a very large table in his office on which were kept piles of correspondence, one pile for each company. The night-watchmen could read them at their leisure.

I discovered that the board were using reports I wrote to help hawk the various businesses around prospective buyers.

Although there was a slump in the bicycle trade, the manager of the cycle department used to say 'Everybody will come back to two wheels eventually.' Not soon enough for Enfield. I valued the bicycle business as a going concern. No buyers were found on this basis, and I was surprised when it went at scrap value.

Having worked hard at establishing the motor bike costs, the next important decision from the Board seemed to me (and I was not privy to their meetings) to get out of the motor bike business. They proposed a big price increase to their main customers, who were American dealers, expecting to kill the trade. Surprised by the acceptance of the increase and the need to continue production, the assembly line of the Interceptor was transferred to the Westwood factory near Bradford-on-Avon, utilising the canteen building.

After the sales of product lines and machine tools, the remainder of the contents were auctioned off. Cassey sent his secretary round after the auctioneer to note down how much each major item realised. A lot of the expensive specialised plant went for scrap prices. Blokes were coming in, stripping down the plant to take out the copper and any other valuable items, then scooting off, leaving the rest on the floor.

The Enfield Cycle Company was eventually sold, really just a shell with a name and spares business, to Norton Villiers, which was a part of the Manganese Bronze group. Only one employee remained on the books, he went to Norton with his job of supplying Enfield India with CKD kits (Completely Knocked Down motor bikes) but soon he too was redundant.

After the disposal of the main product there remained only the site and the diesel engine business. A technical paper by the Enfield designer, Tony Wilson-Jones, had been read by John Goulandris. He was one of three brothers operating the London part of the Goulandris shipping line. The family operated from Greece, New York and London. They said that they owned in total a bigger fleet of ships than the Soviet Union. John was the one who dabbled in other ventures. He had a hobby farm (with prize bulls) and he told me that he wanted to produce a tractor (for Greek farmers), an electric car, a speed boat and a hovercraft for shipping cattle out of Australia without using dock facilities.

He read my diesel engine report and came to see the place, bringing a retinue of staff, including a personal trainer and chef, to stay at the Chateau Impney.

I valued the stock early in 1967 and eventually he bought the business for £80,000. He did not seem bothered about lack of orders, which meant some of the stocks would take years to shift. I was offered a job with him but declined.

E & H P Smith staff moved out to Kenilworth offices, and I was sent out to various companies in the group. Cassey was moving towards retirement and it was decided to consolidate the group headquarters in London. Meanwhile Goulandris came back for me as his company secretary had left. So I went back to Redditch again as financial director of the little Enfield Industrial Engines Ltd.

In 1968, Goulandris had plans for the diesel business. An old London taxi was fitted with an Enfield engine and we drove it round an old airstrip at Honeybourne to prove that it could be used for a tractor. Meanwhile, four draughtsmen had been employed as designers in a Leamington office under Nossiter, paid for by our little business. Two big power boat engines arrived and a new Japanese boring machine was acquired (these separately financed by Goulandris). Then came the old story. We didn't have enough work. New engine orders were thin, we were producing in only twos and threes. We pushed the spares orders through but with a diminishing turnover of only about £8/12,000 a month, we were going to need support. Machining work which Goulandris said could be obtained from VW never materialised.

The Enfield factory, occupying a large prime site near the centre of Redditch, was sold by Smith's to the new government-financed Redditch Development Corporation for £900,000. We were its first tenants in the new industrial estate being formed round our ears. Walls were rebuilt around us, causing the long-suffering machinists to work in overcoats for a period.

Goulandris had bought Diva Cars, an old sports car outfit in London and put in a Baronet, Sir Jon Samuels, to design an electric car. Some components were purchased from major car companies, including Ford, who had abandoned their similar projects. A contract had been obtained from the CEGB to supply about fifty prototypes for evaluation. Goulandris hoped to produce a car for sale at about £500. He used me to do an investigation. My report advised him to complete his contract then give up. He was not pleased. Further friction arose between us when I said we could not be expected to carry on self-financing a complex product in ones and twos. He said it could be done in a small shed if necessary. Not long afterwards he sent me a personal letter explaining the need for economies and would I like to take time off to look for another job! We agreed compensation and thus ended my interesting, if not career-enhancing, connection with the Enfield story.

Postscript

After I left in the spring of 1969, the diesel business was moved to the Isle of Wight, where Goulandris had other interests, taking a very small band of employees. And there it died. In 1993 I was on holiday on the island and found the site where a notice said 'Enfield Industrial Engines' on a workshop, but nothing else. Could some of those stocks still be called for? Certainly, the engines were capable of lasting for many years, Made like a gun indeed.

Goulandris called his power boat 'Miss Enfield' and won a race round the Isle of Wight with it. He eventually produced an Enfield electric car which I saw on television being air-freighted to America. Sir John is still in the electric car business, recently seen on television with another prototype (not Enfield this time!).

EDDIE WRIGHT: The close down

E & H P Smith paid £800,000 for the Enfield factory, plus the factory at Westwood, plus the goodwill, plus all the money in the bank. In actual fact, no money changed hands but there was an exchange of shares. The Enfield concern was easily worth a couple of million. Cassey told me that the Board members of E & H P Smith had considered buying Royal Enfield when it was first put on the market but they decided that it was too big for them to handle. Then a representative of the Board had paid them a visit and begged them to take it over. They had thought about it and decided to have a go.

Bob Cassey was the managing director of E & H P Smith and he had very little interest in running the Enfield company. He was a finance person and for a good part of the day he sat in the Boardroom reading the Financial Times and other papers, trying to determine what was going to do well in the future and what he should buy next. They had 88 factories, if there was money in it, they would buy it providing it was freehold.

Nevertheless, he was an extremely pleasant and thoughtful person. I had to visit the Black Country with him one day just as a cold spell set in. He said to me, 'You look perished, where's your coat?' I said that I had not got it with me. He said, 'Let's go and buy you one!' I said that I couldn't afford one at the moment and he said, 'We'll put it on my expense account' and that's what he did. He bought me a really smashing coat.

Leo Davenport was a most unusual character. He was very friendly and always fooling around, doing things like making signs behind people's backs which, after the dignity and presence of Major Smith, completely took you by surprise. He used to call me into his office and say, 'How are you my old sparking plug?' (a term which I didn't like – I used to say to him 'You throw sparking plugs away when you've finished with them'). Sometimes he used to insist that you sat in his chair.

When the management of E & H P Smith first arrived, they asked all the senior staff to go for interviews and some were dispensed with. Later, Cassey brought his son in to manage a new department which was supplying overhead fittings, then he sold this part of the company to Morgan Crucible.

During the last few years they were having a go at anything. They had architect's quotes for turning the canteen into a candlepin bowling alley, they were making pneumatic cylinders and they even turned out a few unicycles but they were just clutching at straws. One of the problems was that none of them had had the experience of running a company as large as Royal Enfield.

When, in 1966, the news leaked out that we were closing down, Cassey asked me to transfer with E & H P Smith to their Solihull office. However, they could only give me a three-year contract and so when I was offered a job with the Redditch Development Corporation who had been set up to develop Redditch New Town, I accepted it. I transferred to the RDC twelve months before the Enfield closed down, but because the RDC were buying the Enfield site for £900,000, I got heavily involved with the transaction.

Lined up in the yard outside the building was a row of specialist manufacturers' setting tables, six feet by three feet, made from cast steel and costing hundreds of pounds each. We warned E & H P Smith several times that the demolition contractors were moving in and that they needed to get the tables out of the way by the eighth week after the Corporation had taken possession, but nothing happened. The demolition firm arrived from Birmingham and, of course, the first thing they did with their ball and crane was to go 'bong, bong, bong' in the centre of every table. Smith's were outraged and they wanted to sue us but fortunately, one of the warnings had been by letter and was down in black and white.

Just before E & H P Smith sold the Enfield site to the Redditch Development Corporation in about 1969 or 1970, the northern end of the factory was let to an upholstery firm who were making three-piece suites. They had a lot of foam in stock and one night it all went up in flames. The maintenance department and office were next to this part of the factory and were burned down. I had carefully collected together all the Enfield photographs and plans and stored them in there and the whole lot went up in smoke.

JACK CLEMENTS: The closedown

During the early 1960s the management called a series of meetings in the different shops and told so many of the workforce at a time that E & H P Smith were acting as a Holding Company and coming in as partners to Royal Enfield. In future there would be two managing directors, Vic Mountford from Royal Enfield and Leo Davenport from E & H P Smith.

Smith's owned half-a-dozen small companies, such as Alpha Bearings and Stevens Brothers from Wolverhampton, and it was hoped that they would bring a lot of work to Royal Enfield. We all had an increase in salary and we were on cloud nine. Initially, the merger seemed to be a success, we were never on short time. The factory was kept busy with increased orders and our range of products extended to such items as overhead line components (for example, insulators and lightning conductors). We also did some work for High Duty Alloys. Then gradually things began to go downhill. I could see that from the quantities that were ordered in the batches. The first orders for, say, crankcases would come in 250 batches but as the orders dropped so the batches got smaller.

The closedown occurred quite quickly. First of all the polishing and plating shop closed and everyone who worked there was made redundant, then about every four months, another shop would close down with the relevant redundancies.

We knew about eight months beforehand that the factory was going to have to close. It was all very sad. In the early 60s there were about 30 working in the toolroom but then a few at a time began getting their notices and in the end there were just four left and me. When the factory closed, I was the only one there.

It was another two years before I became redundant, because I was transferred to the diesel engine side which was bought by a Greek millionaire shipbuilder by the name of John Goulandris. The air-cooled diesel engine was one of Royal Enfield's past triumphs. During the 1939-1945 war a small team from Royal Enfield had been asked to go to the Falklands to advise the army stationed there on its use.

RITA NATI: from 1951 to closure

For three months in 1969, from the beginning of October to the end of December, the front room of my little terraced house became the registered offices of Royal Enfield. The post arrived at my front door and the wages were put up on my best dining table. As I left the house each day to work elsewhere, Joyce Clarke would arrive to spend the day seeing to the post, managing the accounts and generally running the company with a little help from me out of working hours.

It happened this way. The Greek shipping owner, Goulandris, had bought the Industrial Engine Department of Royal Enfield. He wanted to stay where he was and continue to rent the small building on the old Enfield site, but the new owners of the site, the Redditch Development Corporation, told him that he must buy the building if he wanted to stay there. Goulandris eventually gave up negotiating and decided to move to the Isle of Wight. He took with him twenty-one of his Redditch staff: twenty men and one woman – I was the woman. My job was to do the accounts and the wages. I couldn't make up my mind whether or not to move so Goulandris suggested that I should stay in temporary accommodation in the Isle of Wight and try it out for a while

In the October of that year, the Redditch site was vacated and we all moved to the Isle of Wight. I discovered that the factory there hadn't been completed and so I came back together with my ledgers and the accounting machines, and set up office in my front room. I found a temporary job leaving Joyce to handle the office work. My neighbour, Mr Bellamy, was commuting at weekends so he took the wages and any post with him when he went back on a Monday morning.

By the December, the premises had been completed and I went out again, taking my seven-year old daughter with me. The factory was very attractive, it was a 1950s building, all glass, which had been divided into different departments. A short walk away, in the harbour, was the boat house, Goulandris had made a good job of that, too.

He provided me with a very nice bungalow right in the middle of a wood, and I would have liked to stay, but the problem was that it was so isolated that my daughter had to walk over a mile to catch a bus for school and the weather was cold and wet. We therefore decided not to stay so I accepted my bit of redundancy pay and came home again.

I was amused by the fact that I had been made redundant three times while sitting at the same desk. The first redundancy came when Royal Enfield closed, the second when E & H P Smith moved out, and the third from Goulandris.

I had started at Enfields in 1951 and like all the other new young office girls, I had begun in the post room under Mrs Hemming. About eleven of us had started within a few months of each other, we went round in a gang together and have remained friends all through the years, in fact we had a reunion dinner only last year. Mrs Hemming was a real schoolmistress and kept you in order. You weren't allowed to talk and if you were longer than five minutes on the loo she would be banging on the door, telling you that your time was up. On the other hand, she mothered us all, particularly me because I had only recently arrived in England from Italy and my English was not all that good. We had to attend College one day a week and she used to ring the College up to see how we were getting on and arrange for extra tuition if this was necessary. She gave us little tests like pieces of shorthand to see how we coped, then we were placed in the most appropriate department for our skills.

I had to make out invoices for all kinds of weird and wonderful things. Even then, not everything the design department produced was marketed. George Neal told me that he invented the scooter before the Italians. He used to pull my leg about it, saying, 'I beat your country to it!' He said that he had designed a little scooter in the 1940s with the same kind of styling as the Lambretta and the Vespa. He was so upset that he had invented it but had never received any recognition for it.

If Royal Enfield came back now to Redditch I would go and work for them without any wages. The firm was great.

SALLY HAWTHORNE: from 1963 to 1966

I was only sixteen when I went to work at Royal Enfield in 1963 and quite naive. There were various signs which should have told me that the writing was on the wall but I didn't recognise them. I was interviewed by George Fairgreave who told me that I would be going to college to learn how to use the comptometer. In the end, I just went to a private house in Cedar Road for a few afternoons, I think my tutor was an ex-employee. That was a real cost-cutting exercise.

George Fairgreave was the manager of the wages office which was where I settled after a few months in the post room. Mr Fairgreave was a slim, smallish man in his fifties, always very busy, he zoomed around the office. We had to fill in, by hand, the clocking on number, the name, the national insurance and income tax (using a handbook) and the total, net and gross. When the wages were handed out the recipient had to sign his name on the tear-off portion at the bottom of the card and I had to collect those in on a Monday morning. From the middle to the end of the week we were putting all this information on the payroll by means of Burroughs Accounting machine. Then we had to go through the whole lot and work out how many £1 notes we needed, how many ten shilling notes and how many coins, ready to be collected from the bank. I didn't put the wages up but ever Friday morning I had to lay the wage packets out.

Mr Fairgreave didn't seem to pay a lot of attention to me. I always felt that I never really knew him, but he was very kind. When we were made redundant in 1966 he found jobs for us. I came back one dinner time and he said, right out of the blue, 'I've got an interview for you at the West Midlands Trustee Savings Bank'. What a mouthful! I wondered what on earth it was.

I thought at the time that I had to work at a pace but it was nothing compared to today's standards. Occasionally, we had to rush to get the work finished so that we could go home on time and that was all. We were always able to stop for our breaks which is more than can be said these days when office workers usually have to work right through. The factory workers seemed to have to work hard for a pittance, but I earned £3 a week when I first started.

I was very sorry when the factory closed because I think that was the happiest three years of my life. Everyone was so kind. Mind you, our office didn't seem to have half as much fun as the accounts department next door, every time you went in they were having a laugh, our office was quite strict, accounts seemed more relaxed.

I've never been as happy in other jobs as I was at the Enfield. I don't know whether that was because it was my first job or what. If the firm reopened and the same job was vacant, I would have no hesitation in leaving my present job and taking it.

LEO DAVENPORT

The reason I was in the motorcycle industry was because my father was works director of the famous AJS company. When I was at school he allowed me work in the fitting and machine shops during holidays and weekends. At the same time I started motorcycle racing in speed trials, hill climbs, sand racing, etc. Of course, I had a lot of help in having the best in motorcycles, I was probably the youngest rider to win the IOM TT race.

I always wanted to be a doctor, but it was not to be. I did take up medicine and became a physiotherapist and masseur. I had my own practice at Wolverhampton, treating people for rheumatic complaints, and I was sent patients from local doctors, together with many miners who were sent each month from Wales to Droitwich. I worked with a wonderful orthopaedic surgeon, Dr Milles, he taught me a great deal.

This is how I became Managing Director of Royal Enfield. I had bought Stevens Bros of Wolverhampton which became very successful under my management. A public company, E & H P Smith Ltd were looking for successful companies to purchase, I sold Stevens Bros to them but I had to agree to stay on for three years. They asked me to let them know of any other successful company that might be for sale. I was successful in finding several excellent ones for them, they were very pleased and rewarded me well.

One day, to my surprise and delight, they invited me to become a director of the main board of E & H P Smith Ltd. I had always hoped that one day I would become a director of a public company.

At a later date we had an opportunity to purchase Royal Enfield (The Enfield Cycle Co Ltd). Before finally deciding to buy Royal Enfield they asked me if I would manage it and become managing director, as I was the only director on the main board who had had experience in the motorcycle manufacturing industry. I was made very welcome by the Royal Enfield directors and senior officials. Gilbert Baker, the works manager, was excellent. I made him a director of Royal Enfield. He was thrilled. Major Smith's son Barry was helpful to me. Others who helped me were Reg Thomas, head of the drawing office, a superb draughtsman; Tony Wilson-Jones; Jack Booker; my secretary, Miss Hadley, and many others.

Royal Enfield required more work so I started new departments – a company for selling machine tools (machinery), a company for manufacturing and supplying huge supplies of overhead power line fittings to the CEGB, and I obtained subcontract work from firms such as Jaguar. I closed down non-profit-making departments and was able to employ everyone to other departments. No jobs were lost.

I was responsible for producing the small wheel cycle with a lot of help from Reg Thomas. I named it the 'Revelation', each one was marked with my initials, LHD/MK 1. It became a best seller. I also produced a new motorcycle, the Turbo Twin, which sold very well.

I decided to invite all main agents to Royal Enfield for them to tell us anything that we could do to improve our motorcycles for they were much more in touch with enthusiasts than we were. It was most successful. They came up with excellent ideas for improving the look of the motorcycles and sales increased. Later I decided on a new look. I had all tanks painted red and the name Royal Enfield put on the tanks in large white letters.

I went to the USA to meet our agents there. I had checked before I went and found we were losing money on the big twin. The increase in price had to be substantial but they accepted it and with the new look, sales increased.

We had a factory at Bradford-on-Avon making components for the RAF and the navy, there was spare factory space there, so I transferred the manufacture of the big twin to Bradford-on-Avon. All turned out to be well, no jobs were lost at Redditch. I was congratulated by my co-directors on the main board of E & H P Smith Ltd.

In spite of my opposition, the main board decided to close down Royal Enfield and sell the factory contents and the industrial land. They decided to sell off other companies in the group so I resigned from the parent company and repurchased Stevens Bros at Wolverhampton.

I am certain that, had I been able to persuade my colleagues at E & H P Smith not to sell Royal Enfield, I would have continued to make the company successful by introducing new business and ideas, I had computers in mind.

Leo Davenport, pictured after his winning ride in the 1932 Lightweight TT on a New Imperial.

CHAPTER THIRTEEN
Requiem

Vic Mountford on a small-tank, high handle-barred export model.

As a senior manager, I attended Major Smith's Forward Planning meetings, and at one of these in the 1950s he said, 'I've sent Vic Mountford out to Melbourne to find out what they say about the Japanese motorcycles to see if they are much of a threat. The report is too complicated to read out but our agent, Clarkson, says that they are no threat at all as the engines are too complicated. Brittain and others agree with him'.

My comment was that we had heard the same remarks about the Italian scooters such as Lambretta which had wiped out the smaller end of the market. I said that I was very suspicious.

Eddie Wright

My father, George, worked at Royal Enfield and in the late 1950s he was the first person to arrive at work on a little Honda. This caused an uproar. Everyone wanted to know what a Royal Enfield employee was doing riding a Honda and during the morning he was sent for by Major Smith, who asked him why he had bought it. My father replied that everything which is standard on a Honda, you had to pay extra for if you wanted it on a Royal Enfield.

Major Smith asked if he could borrow the bike for a couple of days and in return George would be loaned an Enfield. When the Honda was returned, dad asked Major Smith what he thought of it. Major Smith said, 'It's alright but if people want quality they'll buy one of ours!'

Colin Wheeler

ROGER BOSS: from 1950 to 1967

Over the years many people have asked me why the British Motorcycle Industry collapsed. There is no doubt that the Japanese invasion was not taken seriously enough when it mattered. When Honda introduced their machines they were very attractive to the younger buyers. Sensibly priced, relatively trouble-free, they were backed by strong publicity, particularly when they began to dominate the racing world. There is, however, in my opinion, a sound reason for the Japanese success. They were able to start with a completely clean sheet and with the necessary finance behind them were able to assess and design what engine capacities, styling and prices the world wanted. They spent a great deal of money and time developing their prototype machines until they were completely satisfied they were of the highest standard. Then, with the benefit of new production techniques, made them in huge quantities enabling them to retail at highly competitive prices.

DEAN MURRAH (Kansas, USA)

The view from the USA

I have never actually owned a Royal Enfield motorcycle but was parts manager for Cooper Motors of Los Angeles from early October 1961 through to the end of August, 1965. However, I did work on many different models in my earlier Kansas retail shop days. Most of them were Indian-badged machines, which dated from 1955. So I was more or less familiar with many of the 1950-on models when I joined Frank H Cooper and his struggling importing and distribution business. Frank had been an AJS and Matchless importer and distributor since about 1947 through the time Associated Motorcycles Ltd slipped the rug out from under him by buying the almost-dead Indian Company from Brockhouse Ltd, who then dropped the Enfield models and overnight were in the Matchless (but not AJS!) business in the USA!

When I joined Cooper Motors that first Monday in October 1961, there wasn't a whole lot going on. I knew most of the RE dealers in the Los Angeles area as some of then also sold AMC bikes. The ex-AMC parts people at Cooper's never warmed up to the Enfields and I soon was made aware by our few dealers what the problems were – scanty spares coverage for the Indian-badged RE models. I addressed this problem as soon as I could, and once a fair stock of pre-1960 spares were at hand, cash flow started to improve. We knew the 736cc Interceptor was coming but we were stuck with a large stock of '60 model 700cc competition twins without lights. Frank appealed to the factory and they got Lucas to supply the parts at a rock-bottom price. Enfield, I thought, were always very good at working with their distributors or agents, and this large effort on the lighting equipment was a case in point. We had to move these bikes, and we got it done in time.

Major Mountford was indeed a very fine gentleman, and did his best to get us what we wanted and needed in the way of suitable bikes for this market. But Enfield was one of the smaller companies and it was always tough for them to go head-to-head with the likes of the BSA Group, AMC Ltd, etc in this market. The 736cc Interceptor was a pretty decent bike, very smooth for a vertical twin. But the early ones in '63 did suffer from holed pistons occasionally. I airmailed these pistons to the late Tony Wilson-Jones, Enfield's service manager, so many times that he finally wrote me to stop, they were aware of the problem! As I recall, the problem was due to a 'wandering spark' from the K2F magneto, or the firing tip of the KLG plugs was too close to the USA-market extra-high compression pistons. I've long felt many of the engine problems of all the British vertical twins stemmed from the Americans demanding more and more power from what were essentially 500cc designs already long in the tooth!

We had this perceived notion that the American rider had to have a bike that would jump 50 feet when the lights turned green! And beat everybody to the next light! So we had to have more power, larger engines etc. However on a long-distance trip in this country, chances are these hot dogs would sooner or later melt down. I am sure we over here are at least partly responsible for the eventual demise of the British motorcycle.

I recall one summer, Major Mountford was over in the midst of Elliott Schult's incredible dirt-track winning streak on Shell Thuet's 'big head' 500 Enfield single. Something like 16 heat race wins, trophy dash wins and expert main event wins in a row! Naturally, we took the Major out to the Friday night half-mile races at Ascot Park, now torn down and but a memory. Luck was with us and Elliott won it all again that night! And never before had any of us seen an Englishman get so excited when Elliott pipped a Gold Star rider at the finish! He was shouting, and jumping up and down in the stands! I doubt if the Major had ever seen one of his products go like that one!

Shell was our dealer in Lynwood, another LA suburb, and when Enfield closed up he sold out and joined Yamaha's race department. And in time was the brains behind the Yamaha 650cc dirt-track vertical twin effort and the rise of one Kenny Roberts in US and later, European GP racing. Shell, a long-time Indian dealer, had been racing Indian-badged Enfield's from the start, and eventually 'got it right' so he could beat the BSA Gold Star singles with what everyone perceived to be an inferior design.

Sad to say, the few excursions Shell and Elliott made outside their home Ascot track with their 500 single were seldom successful. Over the years, this one engine had been developed for Ascot, and it was a winner there. But on other tracks it wouldn't last. So it was essentially a sprint engine. Do one Friday night race meet at Scot, then go into it before the next race to get back the 44hp at the back wheel on Shell's home-made dyno! If 44 came up on the dyno, Shell knew Elliott had a good chance! Any less, and it would be tough!

Over the years, Royal Enfield's, as everyone knows, had a reputation for oiling system problems at high speeds. I forget now how the 'bloody Yanks' in the guise of Shell Thuet, Mel Dinesen, Sammy Pierce and maybe some others, overcame this problem with relatively minor mods made to the crankcases and timing covers. At one time I knew this (from Shell) but by now the details have escaped me, it was a fairly easy job, taking off the timing cover and altering the breather system. Shell (and I think other dealers) did this on new bikes right out of the crate, thus avoiding future customer unhappiness as the engines now were for all practical purposes, oil tight!

One Southern California 'tweak' the factory did go along with us on, was the waisted-type con-rod Allen bolts, made by the same supplier in LA that made the rod bolts for the then all-conquering 'Offenhauser' Indy race car engine. After we had some early 736cc twin rod bolts break, Mr Wilson-Jones agreed to go with the American 'Offy' type bolt. So production was started early on and I freighted over by air many, many boxes of these rod bolts. I never heard of one breaking in my time once these super tough but 'stretchy' bolts got into engine assembly.

I recall the LA company making these bolts was 'Unbrako', a British company that would not make this kind of bolt for Enfield! Yet their Los Angeles plant would make them! Another LA-sourced part that became standard in the big twins was cast-iron valve guides. OEM guides were bronze and the lousy rocker geometry (even Wilson-Jones admitted that to me!) literally ate them up in short order. They got to be quite a problem, so Frank went to work on it and wasn't afraid to move mountains to arrive at a solution. Exhaust valves were another weak spot.

This too was solved by Frank looking into it – and in the end he got Oldsmobile F-85 V8 engine two-piece valves (the aluminium GM V8 now in the Rover 3.5 litre car) turned down and shortened to suit all the RE twins. This two-piece exhaust valve had the 'good stuff' at the head end, and the 'cheap stuff' for the stem! Somehow fused together, but I never heard of one coming apart! I shipped these valves and guides in many batches to Redditch. I believe it was Mountford who commented one time on the exhaust valves that they could have got by with Stellite on the stem ends, but Stellite was too expensive for them to use in production. Expensive in England, maybe, but a common, everyday item used in this country for hardening steel bits and pieces in severe use.

Sometime in the early summer of '65, Cooper's leased building was sold and we knew it was to be torn down to make way for a gas station. We were in what was the northwest corner of the 'Watts' area, and in mid-August *THE* riot erupted! I had already given notice I was returning to Kansas, and Frank was on the prowl for a suitable building near his home in Glendale (he found one in Burbank) so everything sort of came together at once. My last week with Cooper was helping with the move from south Los Angeles to Burbank in the San Fernando Valley. And trying to break in my replacement! I suppose it was a good time to leave California and get on the Honda bandwagon, which was really starting to get big in this country.

Enfield's were a good company to deal with, I was sorry to see them go to the wall. If they had only listened to us and fixed that breather problem, which allowed the complicated oil pump system to work properly, the story might have been different.

JOHN JONES: from 1946 to 1956

I remember my mother taking me to the Enfield factory in 1946 when I was just fourteen. We walked through the main entrance and came to the security office. The security officer, Mr Riddings, came out and asked what we wanted and we told him that we wanted to know if there was a vacancy in the service department. He then phoned the factory and a foreman in a white coat, Louis Hadley, came out to see us. All he asked me was, did I know the difference between a left hand and a right-hand thread, to which I replied, 'Yes'. I started on the following Monday. I arrived with my new boiler suit and a tea can and they put me with a man named Jack Banks who overhauled girder forks. Sometimes I did that and sometimes I put new corks in clutch plates. Between those two jobs I swept up and made the tea.

One of my jobs was to blow up the tyres on the little handcarts, no bigger than a wheelbarrow, that were pushed around the department. The tyres were always picking up swarf and other odds and ends and getting punctured. Once, one of the men took one of these little tyres, which couldn't have been more than about six inches in diameter, and pumped it up until it came up to about six foot! Then someone threw a dart at it and it exploded.

I joined up for National Service but worked for Royal Enfield again when I was demobbed. I was the first apprentice to be taken on by the main service department after the war and I was very pleased to be assigned to the repair and overhaul of the Flying Flea, which was a development of the German DKW engine.

I spent ten years of happy working days at Royal Enfield, before I moved to Sheffield and became assistant to a Royal Enfield dealer, Wilf Green. There I saw the other side of the coin.

The 350 Bullet and the Crusader were the two best Enfield sellers, we sold about ten a week of these. The two stroke Prince and 125's also sold quite well but we had a lot of trouble with them, they were very 'iffey'. The crankshafts broke and there was no spark – they were difficult to start. I didn't find that Enfield's topped the best buy list of bikes. The BSA, Triumph and Ariel were better sellers and better bikes. The Enfield bikes leaked oil everywhere and all kinds of silly little things went wrong with them. The designers and the management didn't seem to move forward together. For example, the mudguard stays repeatedly broke and you would have thought they would have fitted a stronger stay but no, they went on fitting the old ones and expecting everyone to replace them. Once a bike was designed, that was it, they then just seemed to sit back on their laurels.

BOB HUMPHRIES: from 1950 to 1964

Since leaving Royal Enfield in 1964 where I served a technical apprenticeship, followed by some years in Produce design engineering, I have been involved with most of the major automotive companies both in the UK and abroad. This experience includes design work for Dr Steffan Bauer, BSA-Triumph's Engineering Director at Umberslade research centre, similarly for Alec Issigonis in the power unit design office at British Motor Corporation, Longbridge. I have also been technical representative to the automotive industry for Lucas Industries involving the diverse interests of fourteen manufacturing plants etc.

The ability to compete in these high profile areas was partly the result of my grounding at Royal Enfield. The capability of Royal Enfield has not been recognised either in motorcycle or wider industrial circles. I would like to correct this.

Although my involvement began in 1950 with an interview with the daunting Tony Wilson-Jones, there is so much history to Royal Enfield. I will not detail this, it would fill many pages, but in the 1950s, the company was still a serious manufacturer. The main plant at Redditch covered 35 acres with good buildings. The machinery was gradually modernised and the workforce was capable, loyal, hard-working and not militant. There were other satellite factories at Bradford-on-Avon, Westwood in Wiltshire and Feckenham, although the Scottish shadow factory had closed.

My background gives me the authority to state that in many ways, Enfield was well to the fore in standards and capability in the UK automotive industry at this time. By comparison, Norton, Velocette, James were tiny with little capability. Our quality and standards were better than BSA and competitive with Triumph.

We had a wide range of products. I always thought this too wide, with typically 125 and 150 two-stroke, two different designs of 250cc OHV, the model S, SF and Crusader 350 and 500cc, Bullet, the 500 twin, 700cc twin and eventually the 735cc Interceptor, and many variants including the whole range sold as Indian but based on Enfield.

Our traditional cycle manufacture was still active into the 60s with a large range and volume. Again, we were not just assemblers but were designing and producing most of the component parts and also supplying components to TI groups, Phillips and Raleigh factories.

Enfield Industrial Engines designed and produced a range of diesel engines comprising the 100 mm and 85 mm single and twins vertical and horizontal and a 350cc vertical, both marine and industrial versions, together with transmissions with diverse applications. Reliability was proven by applications such as the Antarctic expedition with Enfield's Ray Watton accompanying the expedition to supervise continuous operation throughout an arctic winter. This was a serious business in its own right. There was no competitor. This part of the business could and should have been developed to be a substantial industry. An Italian tractor manufacturer was, I understand, ready to place large contracts but we were not prepared to invest in this and Major Smith's stance was 'we are a motorcycle company'.

The Enfield engines were also used by other manufacturers. The Berkeley 3-wheel sports car used the 692cc Constellation engine to power this plastic-bodied vehicle and a number were made. Other applications include hovercraft.

The Bradford-on-Avon factory shared an old mill by the river (a few yards from the famous jail on the bridge) with the Spencer-Moulton rubber company. Alex Moulton was the inventor of the Hydra-lastic suspension, first used on the BMC Mini by Issigonis. Royal Enfield and Spencer-Moulton co-operated on a suspension for a prototype scooter. The Moulton cycle with rubber suspension was produced but Enfield (and Raleigh) went their own way. At Enfield Vic Bott designed the Revelation.

So we had product capability, we had the plant, the workforce, the capability, even the markets.

What went wrong?

Well, I suppose everyone has to accept responsibility. We lacked professional drive, maybe we didn't want to expand, the management would not or could not plan for high volume, the workforce were afraid of over-production. I wasn't very popular once when I calculated that the existing assembly line could produce 600 machines per week. They didn't produce any for hours!

It was obvious to me that we should have produced to capacity by planned production at a time when we produced only to order to diverse specification. We should have manufactured in volume. Then the sales team should have gone out and got the business and not the other way round. We were market-led and not product-led. The Japanese and Italians are product-led. On two occasions, to my knowledge, Royal Enfield had to supply a large quantity of machines and they managed to complete both orders successfully. There was the time that China invaded India and India ordered hundreds of 350 Bullets. Then there was another time when someone slipped up and didn't cancel a schedule and we produced hundreds of olive green Clippers. The sales force managed to sell them all, so it could be done. It would have been easy for them to do this with, say, the Crusader which was ahead of anything anyone else made. In my opinion, the export market could have been expanded considerably. They had good agents but you needed more than this. The Japanese, for example, thought that British bikes were wonderful and now collect them!

Another shortcoming was that Enfield's would rarely invest. At that time, a pressure die-casting for a crankcase for a new design of bike would have cost a thousand or two to tool. They did spend some money but it was not enough. They had no confidence in their ability to make and sell. They wouldn't ask for raw material to be supplied until they had an order in their hand to cover its use. The management said that they must never speculate. At least we were not ruled by accountants – although the Bank (which closed BSA-Triumph) may have had a hand.

Major Smith, the Managing Director, ruled. He was an experienced engineer and experience counts. He was respected and addressed as 'Sir'. Nevertheless, I remember him helping me up a ramp with the 700cc Meteor prototype when I was an 18-year old apprentice in Geoff Hay's experimental department. But he was authoritarian. I remember Geoff Bromley (late lamented Geoff) designing a diesel engine and he had spent some time calculating that the cylinder head should be held down by studs of a certain diameter. Major Smith came along and without any calculations doubled them – just like that!

I have described only some of the product range. We did virtually everything in-house – design, develop, tool, plan, manufacture. The design office, together with the tooling office, were central to the running of the plant and very integrated with it (according to the latest so-called 'Japanese' principles). But our staffing levels? – typically four designers and two lady tracers! By comparison BSA-Triumph had 200 in 1970 and Honda, I am told, has 3,000 in one office.

Success is largely dependent on people and how they are used or abused. Enfield has been fortunate to have had some excellent, innovative people who produced a terrific workload (without computers). In many ways the features which became industrial standards were pioneered by

Enfield. I did a four-valve pent-roof cylinder head in 1961. Eat your heart out, Honda!

Above all, I think that chief designer Reg Thomas should be fully recognised. His 250cc Crusader. His 175cc OHC. His streamlined machine (now in a Japanese museum). Reg is too modest. We were first in enclosed valve gear, in our cush drive system, in hydraulic suspension and with quickly detachable full-width hubs. First in all welded frames and so much detail design. The dry sump lubrication system was unique and the neutral selector was always an Enfield feature.

But we were also very wary of being first in production of innovative features. We knew that to hold our position as the world's major motorcycle manufacturing nation we had to move fast, but it was difficult to get commitment. We therefore failed to get our new designs which were designed for high volume into production. I well remember Vic Mountford saying 'Can we make fifty and see if they sell?' Even Reg lost his temper at that!

Reg designed an incredible assortment of machines. He was called upon to produce the drawings for an outboard motor, a lawn mower, a large road-sweeper, not forgetting a machine to climb up the big steel cables of a gold mine in South Africa to clean them!

There were other talented members of the design team. Among them, Reg Sealey who had an enormous black beard and never wore a collar or tie. He was a very clever man but it was clear that Major Smith disliked him because of his appearance. He also annoyed Major Smith by decorating reports and other paperwork with little cartoons, I remember him calling a pillion seat a posterior pad with appropriate sketches. He was never promoted or rewarded and in the end he went to Hymatic Engineering, who lapped him up.

All the old bikes and prototypes were stored in one room at Enfield's which was known as the museum. It was used mainly for visiting children who were taken in and given a ride on the penny-farthing. I had the very sad task, in 1964, of pulling the museum apart. Anything of value was sold or given to museums, the rest was broken up and sold for scrap. At that time very few people had any interest in antiques.

One of the engines which I was told to destroy was the original DKW copied by Enfield and developed into the Flying Flea, used with such effect in Operation Overlord.

I can't resist telling a little tale about the dry sump system. The leakage of oil was partly a machining problem, the engines had a split crankcase, each part of which 'mated' against the other so that the system depended upon both surfaces being completely flat and smooth. To facilitate this, we bought an expensive machine which worked at 30,000 revs. One day, I happened to be walking through the inspection department and there was this Inspector going over the surfaces with a file, on a surface table which was by no means flat! The machine was producing these things and he was mucking them up!

The problem with a family firm like Enfield's is that very often, there is no-one in the wings waiting to take over when the Manager retires or passes away. When E & H P Smith took over Enfield's, they started off with the wrong attitude, sending the work outside the factory. What happened was, they looked at the manufacture of, say, crankpins, and found that they could produce them slightly more cheaply at Alpha Bearings so they stopped producing them at Enfield's. Then the remaining overheads increased. The accountants only took into consideration that one item and not the manufacture of the machine within the factory as a whole.

E & H P Smith bought the Enfield company for a very small sum. They were an insignificant company without any idea how to run an enterprise of the size and calibre of Royal Enfield. What's worse, they were asset-strippers. This soon became obvious as assets went out of the door. They acquired a sizeable integrated plant with every facility, broke it up and sold it off!

Industrial sabotage!

The Royal Enfield Owners Club

The original Club, founded during the 1950s by a group of employees and their friends, ceased to exist sometime after the Redditch factory closed. The current Club was (RE)started by a small group of enthusiasts who met in Bristol during 1976, and now has a world-wide membership of circa 2100 at the time of writing (April 2015).

The R.E.O.C. can be a great help to all enthusiasts as it provides:

- THE GUN magazine, published bi-monthly.
- Machine dating service from the original factory ledgers.
- Machine specialists.
- Extensive library and archives.
- Exclusive badges and Club Regalia.
- Branch meetings and weekend events.
- Assistance with the recovery of registration numbers.
- Assistance with obtaining an age-related registration number.
- The Club provides a calendar of weekend and one day events for the whole family.

The R.E.O.C. is a friendly organisation where your interests in the marque will find fellow enthusiasts, and you will be warmly welcomed.

See our website for more information, or to download an application form to join. Please visit *www.royalenfield.org.uk*.

A Royal Enfield Owners Club meeting at Redditch in the 1950s.

Conclusion

In the heart of Redditch is a large eight-acre public cemetery and there, on the crest of a small rise, are the modest graves of the two great members of the Smith family, R W Smith and Major Smith. They lie buried as they lived, unpretentiously, among the ordinary people of Redditch.

There have been several criticisms of Major Smith, of his autocratic regime and his lack of sound judgement. He is not here to answer those criticisms, no doubt one of his replies would be that it is easy to be wise after the event. The fact remains that he and his father helped to create, and then sustained for seventy years, a factory which provided continuous employment for over a thousand people and whose fame spread across the world.

There are not many men of their calibre and with their passing away the great factory slid into rapid decline and soon vanished forever.

But the last word must surely go to Vic Bott.

I am proud to have played a part in Royal Enfield for all of those years. It had a happy, loyal workforce under good management, turning out a reliable product. The decline of the British motorcycle company, with its multiplicity of bikes sold all over the world, seems to me to be extremely tragic.

During the glory days of the Enfield. A meeting of the Redditch Motor Cycle Club in 1912.